Figural Reading
and the Old Testament

Figural Reading

and the Old Testament

■ ■ Theology and Practice ■ ■

DON C. COLLETT

B
Baker Academic
a division of Baker Publishing Group
Grand Rapids, Michigan

Published by Baker Academic
a division of Baker Publishing Group
PO Box 6287, Grand Rapids, MI 49516-6287
www.bakeracademic.com

Printed in the United States of America

Library of Congress Cataloging-in-Publication Data
Names: Collett, Don C., 1963– author.
Title: Figural reading and the Old Testament : theology and practice / Don C. Collett.
Description: Grand Rapids, Michigan : Baker Academic, a division of Baker Publishing Group, [2020] | Includes bibliographical references and index.
Identifiers: LCCN 2019031837 | ISBN 9781540960764 (paperback)
Subjects: LCSH: Bible. Old Testament—Hermeneutics. | Bible. Old Testament—Criticism, interpretation, etc.
Classification: LCC BS476 .C576 2020 | DDC 221.601—dc23
LC record available at https://lccn.loc.gov/2019031837

ISBN 9781540962768 (casebound)

20 21 22 23 24 25 26   7 6 5 4 3 2 1

To the Rt. Rev. Dr. Mouneer Hanna Anis
and the faculty of Alexandria School of Theology,
in the hope that figural reading will blossom
anew in the land of Origen.

Contents

Abbreviations

General

bk.	book	LXX	Septuagint
ca.	circa/about	p(p).	page(s)
chap(s).	chapter(s)	sec.	section
esp.	especially	vol.	volume
ET	English Translation	v(v).	verse(s)

Old Testament Apocrypha

Bar.	Baruch	Sir.	Sirach

Secondary Sources

AARCRS	American Academy of Religion Classics in Religious Studies
BCOTWP	Baker Commentary on the Old Testament Wisdom and Psalms
BIS	Biblical Interpretation Series
BTC	Brazos Theological Commentary on the Bible
BZAW	Beihefte zur Zeitschrift für die alttestamentliche Wissenschaft
CBQ	*Catholic Biblical Quarterly*
CD	*Church Dogmatics*
FAT	Forschungen zum Alten Testament
IBC	Interpretation: A Bible Commentary for Teaching and Preaching
IJST	*International Journal of Systematic Theology*
Int	*Interpretation*
JAAR	*Journal of the American Academy of Religion*
JBL	*Journal of Biblical Literature*

JECS	Journal of Early Christian Studies
JHS	Journal of Hebrew Scriptures
JLT	Journal of Literature and Theology
JPS	Jewish Publication Society Tanakh
JQR	Jewish Quarterly Review
JR	Journal of Religion
JTS	Journal of Theological Studies
LQ	Lutheran Quarterly
MT	Modern Theology
NICOT	New International Commentary on the Old Testament
NPNF²	Nicene and Post-Nicene Fathers, Series 2
OTL	Old Testament Library
ProEccl	Pro Ecclesia
PRSt	Perspectives in Religious Studies
PTMS	Princeton Theological Monograph Series
PTS	Patristische Texte und Studien
SJOT	Scandinavian Journal of the Old Testament
SJT	Scottish Journal of Theology
TNK	Tanakh
TS	Theological Studies
TynBul	Tyndale Bulletin
VT	Vetus Testamentum
WBC	Word Biblical Commentary
WTJ	Westminster Theological Journal
ZAW	Zeitschrift für die alttestamentliche Wissenschaft
ZTK	Zeitschrift für Theologie und Kirche

Introduction

A World Well Lost

The Eclipse of Old Testament Consciousness

In the classes I teach on Old Testament for first-year students, I often like to point out that "the Old Testament got there first." Understood as a chronological claim about the Old Testament's temporal priority in relation to the New Testament, this statement is little more than a truism. Yet it is a truism that typically underwrites approaches to the Old Testament—approaches this book intends to challenge. No shortage of introductions to the Old Testament view it as a historical introduction or prolegomena to the New Testament. In this approach, the New Testament is typically construed in terms of a theological witness that provides the exegetical underpinning for crucial doctrines in the Christian tradition, while the Old Testament serves as a sort of *preparatio evangelica* that never quite addresses these doctrines, let alone authorizes them in any unique or foundational sense.

More provocative and controversial is the claim that the Old Testament "got there first," not merely in the chronological or historical sense I've just described but also in a theological sense. The Old Testament provides the basic theological grammar for the church's confession on creation, providence, figuration, the nature of biblical inspiration, authorship, Trinity, Christology, soteriology, and ecclesiology. The Old Testament's unique contribution to these doctrines does not simply anticipate or duplicate the New Testament's own witness to the same. Rather, the Old Testament renders its witness to these teachings in its own language and on its own terms. These Old Testament terms shape the New Testament's exegetical grammar and theological outlook, rather than themselves being derived either from the New Testament in the first instance or from an external imposition and "hard reading" of the

New Testament's historical experiences, theological concepts, and semantics back into the Old Testament.[1]

The operative premise of this book is that the loss of an Old Testament consciousness with respect to the theological issues just mentioned lies at the heart of many of the Christian church's problems in our day, in both its mainline and evangelical expressions, especially the culture of Bible reading that is deeply embedded within these groups. With a few notable exceptions, the interpretive implications of the character and identity of God, creation, providence, and figural logic in the Old Testament have been eclipsed in the name of a so-called biblical theology of the two testaments that is little more than New Testament theology.[2] The irony involved in this top-heavy view of the New Testament is all too evident when one considers the fact that the New Testament simply assumes the Old Testament's doctrine of God, creation, and providence, rather than reinventing the wheel on these issues.

Of particular interest is the relation between figural reading and the Old Testament's literal sense, or *sensus literalis*. *Figure* is the term chosen in this book to express Scripture's ongoing theological significance through the changing contexts of history, though allegory might also have been chosen. Contrary to the popular stereotypes of modernity, figural reading is not a non-historical strategy for reading Scripture but a species of historical reading rooted in the Scripture's literal sense.[3] Although the church has not always been consistent in practice, in principle it is fair to say that Scripture's literal sense has been the privileged context for hearing Scripture's theological voice.[4] At the same time, the church has also recognized that in all dimensions—authorial, grammatical, and figural—the literal sense did not deliver its meaning in isolation from but in connection with God's ordering of

1. Although the term *allegory* has often been used to describe this hermeneutic of imposition, this definition hardly exhausts its meaning, nor should it be allowed to foreclose whether allegory has any contribution to make to exegesis. See Christopher R. Seitz, *The Elder Testament: Canon, Theology, Trinity* (Waco: Baylor University Press, 2018), 38–48, esp. 43; cf. also Brevard S. Childs, "Allegory and Typology within Biblical Interpretation," in *The Bible as Christian Scripture: The Work of Brevard S. Childs*, ed. Christopher R. Seitz and Robert C. Kashow (Atlanta: Society of Biblical Literature, 2013), 299–310.

2. See the discussion in Christopher R. Seitz, *The Character of Christian Scripture: The Significance of a Two-Testament Bible* (Grand Rapids: Baker Academic, 2011), 52–62, 137–56.

3. Andrew Louth, *Discerning the Mystery: An Essay on the Nature of Theology* (Oxford: Clarendon, 2003), 96–131, esp. 117–20. The meaning of *figure* is elaborated more fully in chap. 2 of this book, along with its relation to other terms such as *allegory*, *type*, and *metaphor*.

4. Brevard S. Childs, "The *Sensus Literalis* of Scripture: An Ancient and Modern Problem," in *Beiträge zur alttestamentlichen Theologie: Festschrift für Walther Zimmerli Zum 70. Geburtstag*, ed. Herbert Donner, Robert Hanhart, and Rudolf Smend (Göttingen: Vandenhoeck & Ruprecht, 1977), 80–93.

things in creation and providence, as witnessed to in the scriptures of Israel we now call the Old Testament. Isolating the literal sense from the interpretive framework provided by the Old Testament's witness to creation and providence directly undercuts its ability to speak figurally to Israel and the church regarding its christo-trinitarian subject matter. One main aim of this book will be to argue that Scripture's literal sense is not merely an authorial or historical sense but fully embedded within a creational and providential "rule" for reading Scripture's canonical, final, or "full" form.[5] For this reason Aquinas and others in the premodern church did not conceive of the literal sense as a brute fact—and still less as raw historical source material to be reconstructed for critical "truth-telling" purposes—but as a "meditation" on God's providence situated within Scripture's witness to creation.[6] It is here that the loss of Old Testament consciousness makes itself felt in the largely Christ-less Old Testament of modernity, in both its evangelical and mainline denominational forms.

The Old Testament's figural witness to Christ depends on the doctrine of providence inherent to its self-witness. As the Author of time who also orders time, God establishes the end from the beginning and the "latter things" in terms of "former things" (Isa. 41:22; 42:9; 43:9, 18; 46:9; 48:3, 6). The Lord's providential ordering of history is the authorizing context in which Old Testament prophecy speaks a word to the future generations, as well as to the people of its own day. Its christological efficacy depends not on human cognition but on the providential and figural links the Lord establishes between the Word of Old Testament promise and the Word made flesh in time.[7] Compared with the Old Testament, the New Testament offers a rather compressed space, temporally speaking, for learning about life lived under God's providence. As George Adam Smith once observed, in the Old Testament the providence of God is illustrated "to an extent for which the brief space of the New Testament leaves no room."[8] This brief space is due not so much to the temporal

5. Christopher R. Seitz, "Isaiah 1–66: Making Sense of the Whole," in *Reading and Preaching the Book of Isaiah*, ed. Christopher R. Seitz (Eugene, OR: Wipf & Stock, 2002), 124n2.

6. See Eugene Rogers Jr., "How the Virtues of the Interpreter Presuppose and Perfect Hermeneutics: The Case of Thomas Aquinas," *JR* 76 (1996): 64–81.

7. This book follows the convention of most English versions by glossing the tetragrammaton as Lord. Whatever else its problems, this may be said to have a certain precedent in the Hebrew practice of vocalizing the tetragrammaton as *Adonai* and in the LXX practice of translating the tetragrammaton as *Kyrios*. Cf. the discussion in Christopher R. Seitz, "Handing Over the Name: Christian Reflections on the Divine Name YHWH," in *Figured Out: Typology and Providence in Christian Scripture* (Louisville: Westminster John Knox, 2001), 131–44.

8. George Adam Smith, *Modern Criticism and the Preaching of the Old Testament: Eight Lectures on the Lyman Beecher Foundation, Yale University* (New York: Armstrong & Son, 1911), 20.

compression of the New Testament's witness in comparison with the Old's but to the fact that the New Testament simply presupposes the Old Testament's account of history as a providentially constructed reality, just as it presupposes the Old Testament's doctrines of creation and God's character.

One reason the late modern church does not recognize the significance of creation and providence for the Old Testament's figural ordering of history is because its approach to biblical theology virtually equates biblical theology and New Testament theology. If biblical theology is essentially New Testament theology, then we can see why the Old Testament's providential model for understanding history has no exegetical impact on the way we assess the New Testament's christological reading of Israel's scriptures. Given its comparatively shorter historical compass, the New Testament has little room to illustrate the workings of providence or, for that matter, the inner relations between creation, providence, and prophecy on display in the Old Testament. Instead, models for understanding these things are drawn from sources other than the Old Testament, resulting in considerable distortion of their theological significance and role for constructing the New Testament's witness. Such a model for doing biblical theology also naturally fails to recognize the ongoing theological significance and character Israel's history has for the New Testament church.[9] The erasure of the theological significance of Old Testament Israel's history for an understanding of New Testament ecclesiology might therefore be called "ecclesiotelism," because it forms the natural counterpart to a kind of christotelic reading of the Old Testament that effectively evacuates its original voice of any christological significance.[10]

What can be done, and what should be done to address these issues? Authors with different backgrounds no doubt assess these problems from different frames of reference. That said, surely no one can deny that the Old Testament's status as Christian Scripture remains a crucial issue for late modern Christianity. The decisions we make regarding the Old Testament's character tend to shape many other decisions, whether theological, ecclesial, or ethical. For these reasons it is worth considering whether the resources for overcoming

9. See George Lindbeck, "The Story-Shaped Church: Critical Exegesis and Theological Interpretation," in *Scriptural Authority and Narrative Interpretation*, ed. Garrett Green (Philadelphia: Fortress, 1987), 161–78; George Lindbeck, "The Church," in *The Church in a Postliberal Age*, ed. James J. Buckley (Grand Rapids: Eerdmans, 2003), 145–65; cf. Ephraim Radner, *The End of the Church: A Pneumatology of Christian Division in the West* (Grand Rapids: Eerdmans, 1998), 35–39.

10. On christotelism, see further the discussion in chap. 4. See also Don Collett, "Reading Forward: The Old Testament and Retrospective Stance," *ProEccl* 24, no. 3 (2015): 178–96; Don Collett, "The Defenestration of Prague and the Hermeneutics of 'Story': A Response to Peter Leithart," *Reformed Faith & Practice* 3, no. 2 (2018): 32–38.

the loss of Old Testament consciousness in our day may be found in the Old Testament itself. Here I have in mind the character of the Old Testament as a charter narrative that grounds figural reading in its witness to creation, providence, and prophecy. In the chapter that follows, therefore, I intend to explore the Old Testament moorings of the logic of figural reading in the creation narratives of Genesis 1–2, especially the relation of word (*verbum*) and thing (*res*) in creation and the providential character of the link between them. Following that I will turn in chapter 2 to a discussion of the literal sense in the church's tradition, especially its relation to Scripture's figural, metaphorical, and allegorical senses, as well as to the rule of faith. In this context it will be necessary to question whether the Reformation falls prey to a nominalist account of Scripture's literal sense that reduces "things" to "words," thereby opening the door to the anti-metaphysical attitudes driving most Protestant exegesis in our time. Other questions also arise: Was the Reformation's view of the literal sense an inner development of the theological instincts expressed by the medieval *Quadriga*, or was it a radical departure that laid the foundations for modern reductions of Scripture's *sensus literalis* to the *sensus historicus*?

Chapter 3 engages earlier attempts to reform the literal sense, focusing on thirteenth-century attempts to sharply distinguish metaphor from theological allegory as a test case for assessing the theological significance of metaphor and figure in the Old Testament. I will present a series of exegetical excurses on Job 28, Proverbs 8, and Hosea's prologue to illustrate the figural and exegetical significance of architectural metaphors and figures for Old Testament Wisdom and Prophecy. Chapter 4 will assess the fortunes of figural reading under the auspices of modernity. What impact have interpretive concepts such as *sensus plenior*, christotelism, and *Wirkungsgeschichte* (reception history) had on the Old Testament's christological witness?

Thus the threefold structure of this book moves from a discussion of Old Testament *frameworks* for situating figural reading to *exegesis* of Old Testament figures for Wisdom and Prophecy. The book then engages in a critical *assessment* of interpretive models for Old Testament reading that offer alternative frameworks or "rules" for reading its literal sense. I close with the modest suggestion that the figural instincts at work in the early church's reading of the Old Testament offer a needed corrective to scientific exegetical models derived from the eighteenth century. By this I do not mean that modern historical methods have no place in figural exegesis. When properly utilized as servants rather than masters, historical tools of various kinds are helpful for illuminating the figural shape of Scripture. The point to be stressed is that such tools find their proper function and purpose within a figural imagination shaped by the Old Testament's witness to creation and providence, rather than outside that witness.

This book has proved to be far more difficult to write than I originally conceived. Without the support of friends, it would have been impossible. Jim Allard, Bryan Estelle, Josh Van Ee, and Nate Devlin read through earlier versions of chapters 2 and 4 and provided helpful feedback, as well as encouragement along the way. Kathryn Greene-McCreight also offered much needed encouragement at various times during the writing of this book. Jim Kinney of Baker Publishing graciously allowed me the time and space to rethink the original scope of this book, for which I remain thankful. Special thanks are also due to my editor, R. David Nelson, who gave exhortation at critical junctures and patiently waited for this book to be completed. I would also like to thank the editors of the following academic journals for permission to reprint portions of "Reading Forward: The Old Testament and Retrospective Stance," *Pro Ecclesia* 24, no. 3 (2015): 178–96; "A Place to Stand: Proverbs 8 and the Construction of Ecclesial Space," *Scottish Journal of Theology* 70, no. 2 (2017): 166–83; "The Christomorphic Shaping of Time in Radner's *Time and the Word*," *Pro Ecclesia* 27, no. 3 (2018): 276–88; and "The Defenestration of Prague and the Hermeneutics of 'Story': A Response to Peter Leithart," *Reformed Faith & Practice* 3, no. 2 (2018): 32–38. Finally, I would like to express my gratitude to the Conant Grant Fund of the Episcopal Church, which generously awarded me a grant that allowed me to pursue research at the University of Toronto during the summer of 2018 and bring this book to its long-awaited conclusion.

Attentive readers will note the influence of Christopher Seitz at many junctures. Without his constant encouragement to finish this book, it is highly doubtful I would have. His insights on the Old Testament, creation, and prophecy remain foundational for my own understanding of figural reading, insights I have tried to build upon and extend in various ways in this book. I would like to thank him for the many years of stimulating conversations we have engaged in concerning Old Testament exegesis while at the same time relieve him of any of the shortcomings of this book.

▪▪ Part 1 ▪▪
Frameworks

1

Biblical Models for Figural Reading

To recover the Old Testament's foundational significance for figural reading, it is helpful to begin by revisiting the early church's approach to the inner relations between creation, providence, and figural reading. In this chapter I will explore interpretive models the Old Testament provides for illuminating the inner logic of figural reading, beginning with the creation narratives of Genesis 1–2. Of special interest will be the integrated character of the two creation accounts (1:1–2:3 and 2:4–25) and the providential character of history set forth in the second account (2:5–7). Along with the affiliative character of providence at work in the second account, the first creation account sets up an ordering of time that is fundamental for the construction of figural relationships between disparate temporal contexts in Scripture. Failure to reckon with the figural ordering of time inherent in the creation narratives forms the basis for the modern charge that figural reading ignores the importance of historical context for biblical interpretation. I argue that such an objection typically presupposes a particular understanding of biblical history as linear movement, a presupposition out of sync with Scripture's own presentation of the character of history. Over against this, the figural and liturgical ordering of time in the two creation accounts discloses a "rule" for reading the relation of word (*verbum*) and thing (*res*) in creation, providence, and prophecy that is foundational for the way Scripture delivers its theological sense.

Creation and Providence

The patristic tradition differentiated the account of "scriptural days" in Genesis 1:1–2:3 from the "human days" of 2:4–25. This reading suggests that the first creation account (scriptural days) focuses on the days of creation as created archetypes that illumine and govern the original order of creation. The first toledot, or generational formula, in 2:4 introduces the second creation account (human days), focusing on the creation of Adamkind in the context of God's providential ordering of creation—that is, the construction of human history as a providentially ordered reality.[1] The early church's approach to the human days of Genesis 2:4–25 is confirmed by the function of its toledot, which also structures the larger Mosaic Torah.[2] The use of the toledot formula in Genesis 2:4 reflects an instance of what might be called "canonical intentionality"— that is, a hermeneutical guideline that has been intentionally placed at the beginning of the series of toledot formulae in Genesis to help future readers understand its theological function within the larger framework of Israel's Torah. According to Dennis Olson, the generalized character of Genesis 2:4 "makes it clear that the meaning of 'toledot' is not restricted to actual physical offspring. It has been generalized to designate the carriers of the promise and blessing of God into succeeding generations. Thus the inclusion of Moses in the toledot formula in Numbers 3:1 is meaningful and appropriate, even if perhaps secondary and redactional."[3] Viewed from this perspective, the use of the generational formula in Genesis not only is intended to constrain our reading of the book of Genesis but also serves as a hermeneutical guideline for reading Israel's Torah and the history of Adamkind as a whole.

But just how does the generational formula accomplish this function? While a proper answer has multiple dimensions,[4] one aspect that has not received much discussion is the toledot's focus on the providential character of human history. This focus underscores the foundational theological significance of providence and "providential affiliation" for the figural ordering of time in creation and redemption.[5] In order to grasp this function, it is helpful to re-

---

1. For discussions of patristic readings of the creation narratives, see Ephraim Radner, *Time and the Word: Figural Reading of the Christian Scriptures* (Grand Rapids: Eerdmans, 2016), 44–82; cf. Paul Blowers, *The Drama of the Divine Economy: Creator and Creation in Early Christian Theology and Piety* (Oxford: Oxford University Press, 2012), 101–87.

2. See Dennis T. Olson, *The Death of the Old and the Birth of the New: The Framework of the Book of Numbers and the Pentateuch* (Chico, CA: Scholars Press, 1985), 97–118, 186–91.

3. Olson, *Death of the Old*, 106.

4. My discussion complements and extends Seitz's discussion of the work of Sarah Schwartz on the toledot formula in Genesis in Seitz's *The Elder Testament*, specifically with a view toward the significance of Gen. 2:4 for the figural-providential ordering of time and history in Scripture (Christopher R. Seitz, *The Elder Testament: Canon, Theology, Trinity* [Waco: Baylor University Press, 2018], 238–39). It was Seitz who first alerted me to Sarah Schwartz's work on the toledot formula in Genesis, though the argument that follows was originally worked out prior to the publication of *The Elder Testament*.

5. On the affiliative character of the tradition-building process that produced the witness of the prophets and canonical Scripture, see Christopher R. Seitz, *Prophecy and Hermeneutics: Toward a New Introduction to the Prophets* (Grand Rapids: Baker Academic, 2007);

flect on the function of the first toledot in Genesis 2:4. In both Genesis and the larger Mosaic Torah, the toledot introduces not merely the genealogy of physical offspring that follows it but also the entire literary section that extends up to the beginning of the next toledot marker.[6] Thus, for example, the toledot of Terah begins in Genesis 11:27 and does not end with the report of his death in Genesis 11:32 but with the toledot of Ishmael in Genesis 25:12. A study of the toledot formula in Genesis also reveals that its use may be categorized into one of two types: the opening of a *genealogical* list of the father it mentions (5:1; 10:1; 11:10; 25:12; 36:1; 36:9) or the opening of a *narrative* passage (2:4; 6:9; 11:27; 25:19; 37:2).[7]

Sarah Schwartz helpfully observes that "when the *toledot* formula is followed by a genealogical list, there is full compatibility between the phrase's literal meaning and its function. This is because the basic meaning of the word *toledot* is 'children' so its natural function is to introduce a list of the father's descendants. However, when the formula is followed by a story rather than a genealogical list, the word *toledot* cannot be easily interpreted as 'descendants.'"[8] In addition to highlighting the semantic range and adaptability of the toledot formulae in Genesis, this also helps explain the unique hermeneutical function of the first toledot marker. In the toledot "the heavens and the earth" of Genesis 2:4, the name of an ancestor is not followed by either a genealogy of actual physical offspring (cf. 5:1; 10:1; 11:10; 25:12; 36:1; 36:9) or a narrative about the sons of the ancestor (cf. 6:9; 11:27; 25:19; 37:2).[9] In other words, while the toledot in Genesis 2:4 broadly resembles

---

Christopher R. Seitz, *The Goodly Fellowship of the Prophets: The Achievement of Association in Canon Formation* (Grand Rapids: Baker Academic, 2009).

6. Olson, *Death of the Old*, 98–114. While some have interpreted the toledot in Gen. 2:4 as a conclusion (colophon) that closes a literary unit spanning Gen. 1:1–2:4, given its consistent usage elsewhere in Genesis as an introduction to that which follows, such a reading is unlikely. See C. John Collins, "Discourse Analysis and the Interpretation of Genesis 2:4–7," *WTJ* 61, no. 2 (1999): 272.

7. See Brevard S. Childs, *Introduction to the Old Testament as Scripture* (Philadelphia: Fortress, 1979), 145.

8. Sarah Schwartz, "Narrative *Toledot* Formulae in Genesis: The Case of Heaven and Earth, Noah, and Isaac," *JHS* 16, no. 8 (2016): 2–3; cf. also Terence E. Fretheim, *The Pentateuch* (Nashville: Abingdon, 1989), 68. See also the insightful interaction with Schwartz's work in Seitz, *Elder Testament*, 238–39.

9. Schwartz helpfully describes the difference as follows:

The *toledot* formula in 2:4 refers to the heavens and earth, which are not human entities capable of reproduction, and the text that follows focuses chiefly on the creation of man. Many therefore interpret this phrase in a metaphorical sense, explaining the works of creation as the "children" of the cosmos. This understanding is certainly possible, and is even supported by the description of man being formed from dust of the earth (2:7). However, this approach lends a certain creative power to heaven and earth in a sense that contradicts the theological message that God is the sole creator; and the concept

what might be called the "narrative" rather than the "genealogical" class of toledot formulae, its anomalous form sets it apart from these two broad classes. This suggests that the first toledot's unique theological function is to open up a window on the story of Adamkind.[10] The distinctive focus on the creation of humanity in the second creation account is also evident from the fact that the Hebrew term for Adam or Adamkind (אדם) occurs only twice in Genesis 1:1–2:3, though it occurs over twenty times from Genesis 2:4 onward.[11] Schwartz rightly observes that "the *toledot* formula of heaven and earth's focus on their own creation hints at the main subject of the narrative to follow: the creation of the world, *which places humankind and what befalls it at its center.*"[12]

The theological function of Genesis 2:5–7 within the first toledot of Genesis is also instructive. Genesis 1:2 and 2:5 both follow an ancient literary convention; they describe the effects of God's ordering of things in creation (1:2) and providence (2:5) in contrast to conditions that had prevailed previously. Genesis 1:2 provides a description of the world, not before it was *created* but before it was *formed*, in contrast to the formed state of things whose description follows.[13] In seeing the contrast between creation in its unformed (1:2) and formed (1:3–31) state, readers comprehend the effect of divine speech

---

that heaven and earth are the "parents" of the other works of creation is unprecedented in the Bible. According to this biblical paradigm, it makes sense to assume that in this case, the formula does not serve to introduce a narrative about the children of the father it features. (Schwartz, "Narrative *Toledot* Formulae in Genesis," 4–5)

10. For a description of the first toledot as "anomalous" in form, see Schwartz, "Narrative *Toledot* Formulae in Genesis," 15; cf. 29–33. According to Schwartz, the toledot formulae that bear the closest resemblance to it are the narrative toledot formulae of Noah in 6:9 and of Isaac in 25:19.

11. Schwartz, "Narrative *Toledot* Formulae in Genesis," 32–33: "The first account focuses on God's creation of nature with humankind presented as part of nature, while the second account focuses on the creation of humanity, with the rest of nature serving as its backdrop. . . . In the first creation story, humankind is created last (1:26–27), while the second account mentions man's creation first (2:7). The word 'man' appears only twice in the first account, as opposed to twenty four times in the second."

12. Schwartz, "Narrative *Toledot* Formulae in Genesis," 35, emphasis added; cf. also Gerhard von Rad, *Genesis: A Commentary*, OTL (Philadelphia: Westminster, 1972), 42: "Must we not say that the two creation stories are in many respects open to each other? In the exposition it will be pointed out that the Yahwist has an intimate world constructed around man (the garden, the trees, the animals, the wife), while P paces the cosmos in all dimensions before he treats the creation of man. Genesis, chap. 2, complements chap. 1 by its witness to God's providential, almost fatherly, act toward man, etc."

13. Brevard S. Childs, *Biblical Theology of the Old and New Testaments: Theological Reflection on the Christian Bible* (Minneapolis: Fortress, 1992), 107, 112. For a helpful summary of the reasons for interpreting Gen. 1:1 as a main clause rather than a dependent or temporal clause, see Claus Westermann, *Genesis 1–11*, trans. John J. Scullion, S.J., Continental Commentaries (Minneapolis: Augsburg, 1984), 93–98; cf. also Walther Eichrodt, "In the Beginning:

in forming the unformed world better than if the finished state had simply been presented without this contrast. In Genesis 2:5, the twofold absence of rain and Adamkind points to the absence of a providential link between wild growth and rain, on the one hand, and cultivated growth and Adamkind, on the other hand. Genesis 2:6–7 then address this twofold deficit by the twofold provision of rain and the creation of Adamkind to till the earth: "Now no wild shrub of the field had yet appeared in the earth, and no cultivated plant of the field had yet sprouted, for the LORD God had not caused it to rain upon the earth, and there was no man to work the ground. But a rain cloud began to come up from the earth and began to water the whole surface of the ground. And the LORD God formed man of dust from the ground and breathed into his nostrils the breath of life; and the man became a living soul."[14] By having a description of what the state of the earth was like before the LORD (YHWH) sent rain or created humankind, we are in a better position to understand the importance of providence for the history of creation.[15]

The canonical effect of placing Genesis 2:5–7 at the outset of the first toledot is to teach us that the constancy of the created order testified to in Genesis 1:1–2:3 is sustained through time by the divine establishment of providential links or "affiliations" between rain and wild growth and between human life and cultivated growth. Human agricultural life and existence are made possible by the *constancy* of this divinely established order (cf. 8:22). Unlike the Priestly account,[16] the second creation account does not focus on the ordering of creation by divine speech but on the significance of this affiliative ordering for the flourishing or fruitfulness of human life and existence (cf. 1:28).[17] Thus at the outset of the Old Testament's account of creation, Genesis 2:5–7 underscores

A Contribution to the Interpretation of the First Word of the Bible," in *Creation in the Old Testament*, ed. Bernhard Anderson (Philadelphia: Fortress, 1985), 65–73.

14. For a discussion of the translational issues involved in distinguishing wild plants from cultivated plants in Gen. 2:5–6, as well as a defense of the inceptive sense for עלה and the rendering of אד as "rain cloud," see Mark D. Futato, "Because It Had Rained: A Study of Gen 2:5–7 with Implications for Gen 2:4–25 and Gen 1:1–2:3," *WTJ* 60 (1998): 1–21.

15. Cf., for example, Meredith G. Kline, "Because It Had Not Rained," *WTJ* 20, no. 2 (1958): 146–57.

16. Genesis 1:1–2:3 is typically referred to as the Priestly account because it uses the name Elohim to speak of God rather than the tetragrammaton YHWH (LORD) found in the Yahwist account.

17. Rolf Knierim rightly notes that "agrarian existence is fundamental, and not tangential, to human existence. It cannot be considered as the residue of a primitive, pretechnological civilization (see Gen. 3:18–19; Pss. 65; 104; Prov. 12:11; 28:19; 24:27, 30–34; Isa. 5:1; etc.). This factor transcends national and historical boundaries. It is true for all humanity. It is neither confined to Israel's land nor dependent on Yahweh's history with Israel. On the contrary, it is the presupposition for the fulfillment of the goal of Israel's history in the land." Rolf P. Knierim, *The Task of Old Testament Theology: Method and Cases* (Grand Rapids: Eerdmans, 1995), 197.

the theological significance of God's providential ordering of things for our understanding of creation's history and the human generations that follow. When the second creation account establishes providential links between rain and wild growth and between Adamkind and cultivated growth, the reader learns that God's providential ordering of things in creation *shapes the meaning of human life and existence* in the post-creation world. Thus we should understand the history of creation that follows Genesis 2 not simply as history defined in broad terms or as a history whose content and peculiar character is one we supply by filling in the blanks. Rather, the history that follows the first creation account is to be understood as a *providential* history—that is, a history whose meaning is shaped by God's providential ordering of things in time and space. That which divine speech *creates* in Genesis 1:1–2:3 is ordered and governed by God's acts of *providential affiliation* in Genesis 2:5–25. The history of Adamkind that follows 2:5–7 is thus a particular kind of history that shares in what might be called ordinary history but is not simply identical with or reducible to it.[18] This is the model the Old Testament provides us for interpreting history at the outset of the creation narratives—a model Moses and the prophets do not depart from but presuppose and build on.[19]

Particularly interesting in this regard are Gerhard von Rad's observations regarding the providential character of history in the patriarchal narratives. He argues that the result of the shaping of the patriarchal narratives reflects a theological stance that deals "more with God than with men. Men are not important in themselves but only as the objects of divine planning and action." In view of this tendency we must ask "where and in what sense Abraham, Jacob, or Joseph are meant by the narrator to be understood as models, by virtue of their own actions or of divine providence." While some of these narratives encourage imitation and discipleship, in von Rad's view these narratives "are in the minority."[20] Von Rad concludes that "the patriarchal narratives are remarkably free of that urge to transfigure and idealize the figures of earlier times, which plays such a great role in popular literature.

18. See the discussion of the relation between saga and history in the patriarchal narratives in von Rad, *Genesis*, 31–43.

19. Reflecting on the providential character of the patriarchal histories, Gerhard von Rad writes that "the conviction of a historical plan conceived by Yahweh and the assurance with which this plan is contrasted with human action is very reminiscent of the authority of the prophets, who in other circumstances claimed to know the long-term divine plan for history." Von Rad, *Genesis*, 38–39.

20. Von Rad, *Genesis*, 36. This is in keeping with von Rad's earlier statement that as the theologian *par excellence* of the patriarchal histories, "the Yahwist presents one story of divine guidance and disposition; God's providence is revealed in all areas of life, the public as well as the private" (30).

The patriarchal narratives do not fall short of the rest of the Old Testament in drawing a picture of man which Israel found only through *a long conversation with Yahweh*. It is the picture of a man who is directed to hear the divine address and who is sheltered by the guidance of this God."[21]

In short, the patriarchal narratives offer a "canon" or providentially constructed rule for reading history in Genesis,[22] a rule produced by the community of faith's witness to the reality of a life lived under God's providence.[23] To distinguish this history from the history that biblical historians reconstruct, through either archaeological evidence or historical critical tools, I will use the term *historia* in contexts where I wish to stress the providential character of biblical history.

The first toledot of Genesis not only reflects an interest in the providential character and context of human history but also intrinsically links the Priestly account of creation (P) in Genesis 1:1–2:3 with the Yahwist account (J) in Genesis 2:5–25.[24] The structural unity between creation and human history formed by this ordering was ruptured by Adam's fall.[25] This resulted in the futility of human history or human generations described in the prologue of Ecclesiastes, though not the order of creation per se.[26] As a result, the Cosmopolis that formed the original unity of both the City of God (heaven) and the City of Adamkind (earth) has now broken down.[27] Creation is no longer a *eutopia* but a *dystopia*, because human beings in their rebellion against God have constructed an alternative ordering of things in which creation's original order and telos no longer norms the order of human history and its telos.

21. Von Rad, *Genesis*, 36, 37, emphasis added.

22. Von Rad, *Genesis*, 37–38.

23. Von Rad, *Genesis*, 41: "These narratives have a very high degree of compactness because they compress experiences that faith brought to the community slowly, perhaps over centuries. And this is primarily what gives the narratives their proper characteristic witness. So much is clear: if the historicity of the patriarchal narratives now rests essentially upon the community's experiences of faith, then that fact has far-reaching consequences for exegesis."

24. On the chiastic structure of Gen. 2:4 and the way it links the two creation accounts, see the discussion in Collins, "Discourse Analysis," 271–72.

25. "The hermeneutic implied in Genesis 1 presupposes a bipolar reality in which cosmic order and human history confront each other. In this confrontation, history appears to have fallen out of the rhythm of the cosmic order, whereas the cosmic order reflects the ongoing presence of creation. The cosmic order remains loyal to its origin. This ongoing presence of creation is, therefore, an ultimate presence." Knierim, *Task of Old Testament Theology*, 193.

26. See the discussion of the prologue to Ecclesiastes in Seitz, *Elder Testament*, 221–42.

27. On the idea that socio-political order and cosmic order relate to each other as microcosm and macrocosm, see E. M. W. Tillyard, *The Elizabethan World Picture* (New York: Vintage Books, 1959), 87–100. For a broader treatment of this theme set within the context of modernity, see Stephen Toulmin, *Cosmopolis: The Hidden Agenda of Modernity* (Chicago: University of Chicago Press, 1990), esp. his discussion of John Donne's poetic expression of grief for the loss of Cosmopolis in early modernity on pp. 62–69.

At the same time, the created order of things remains loyal to its Creator, as Rolf Knierim insightfully observes:

> An appropriate interpretation of the hermeneutic implied in Genesis 1, there-fore, must distinguish between two types of beginning in the act of creation: the beginning of cosmic time on the one hand, and the beginning of human history on the other. The fact that creation marks the beginning of human his-tory does not mean that after that beginning it ceases to exist as a reality of its own. All of creation continues to exist as an ever-present reality alongside and vis-à-vis human history. Thus, creation cannot be understood only as the begin-ning of human history and as standing in the service of that history. Rather, it must be understood as the place and moment which contains the criterion for the meaningful correlation of cosmic reality and human history, and at the same time the critical evaluation of human history in light of the ever-present cosmic reality which exists in accordance with its beginning. . . . The cosmic order remains loyal to its origin.[28]

To sum up, the first toledot in Genesis 2:4 negotiates the transition in con-text from the history of creation (scriptural days) to the history of Adamkind (human days). This teaches us that the divine establishment of an ontology of structured space in 1:1–2:3 is normative for the "generations" of the providen-tially governed human history that follows.[29] Though an original fracture has come about through the fall of humanity in Adam, the order of creation remains faithful to its Creator, continuing to serve as a norm for the new creation God will bring about through Israel's election and the promise given to Abraham.[30]

Creation, Time, and Figural Reading

The life Israel lived under God's redemptive providence was shaped by the figural ordering of time inherent in Israel's scriptures, especially the ordering

---

28. Knierim, *Task of Old Testament Theology*, 193.

29. On the presentation of creation as "structured space" in Gen. 1:1–2:3, see Knierim, *Task of Old Testament Theology*, 186–91.

30. Knierim writes, "There can be no doubt that the priestly writer sees creation and human history as systematically related, and that, in this relationship, creation appears as the salvific reality to which history genuinely belongs, from which it actually separated, and in view of which it is evaluated." Creation appears as a "salvific reality" in the postfall world because its ordering of things is what Israel's redemptive election is intended to renew and fulfill within human history: "If this view of creation is correct, then the liberation and election of Israel cannot be regarded as the purpose of creation. On the contrary, the purpose of Israel's history of liberation was to point to and to witness to the fundamental reality, to God's liberation of the world into the just and righteous order of his creation. Israel was called to actualize this purpose in its own existence." Knierim, *Task of Old Testament Theology*, 207, 210.

found in the creation account of Genesis 1:1–2:3. The structuring of time in creation provides the basis for the logic of the relation between word (*verbum*) and thing (*res*) intrinsic to figural reading and for figural ways of ordering time. While it has been popular for many years to construe the Old Testament's forward temporal movement as primarily linear in character, the presentation of creation in Genesis 1 complicates the character of time's movement. To be sure, the creation days are ordered toward the telos of Sabbath rest. But it is also true that this eschatological movement is embedded within a repetitive or liturgical ordering of time, an ordering that is a figure not of futility but of constancy. The temporal movement inherent in the human history of the second creation account should not be opposed to a so-called cyclical (and therefore futile) ordering of time in the first account. Rather, we should understand it as movement embedded within an ordering of things that remains constant in the midst of human history and change, constraining and interpreting novelties that arise in the forward movement of time.[31] There is movement toward a telos, but the creational structuring of time in Genesis 1:1–2:3 provides the authorizing framework in which eschatological movement toward that telos is situated and from which it takes its bearings.[32] Understood and interpreted apart from the cyclical structuring of time in Genesis 1:1–2:3, linear time displaces the fundamental character of cyclical time and sets up a metaphysics of the *novum*, or the "new." In this metaphysics for understanding time, event B follows event A, and the presence of event B means the absence of event A, since nothing in history remains constant or permanent without the prior context provided by the creational structuring of time in Genesis 1:1–2:3.[33]

A providentially framed account of biblical history as *historia* is governed by God's figural ordering of time, an ordering not to be identified with temporality

31. Westermann writes:

This is basic and decisive for the understanding of history. The western view of history considers only the variables to be constitutive; this is the presupposition in the concept of historical development as well as in the underscoring of the historically unique. When P introduces his historical work with the genealogy of Gen 5 he is saying that history never consists merely in historically demonstrable processes, developments and an apparently unique course of events. Rather, there are at work in every event elements of the stable, always and everywhere the same, which are common to all humankind at all times and which render questionable a science of history that prescinds from these constants. (Westermann, *Genesis 1–11*, 347)

32. Ray Van Leeuwen notes that "Knierim rightly insisted that cyclical time (day and night, winter and summer) was for Israel more fundamental than linear time, for the simple reason that cyclical, cosmic time patterns are what make history, with its unique and contingent events, possible." Quoted in Seitz, *Elder Testament*, 228n16.

33. For how this metaphysics of the *novum* has negatively impacted our understanding of God's relation to time, see Radner, *Time and the Word*, 67–68, esp. note 45.

as linear movement. Moderns typically understand temporal movement of this kind as temporal succession that moves linearly from past to present and into the future, never folding back on itself by means of figurally constructed relationships between present, past, and future. Of course, if history never folds back on itself in the figural sense just mentioned, then a figural reading of Scripture becomes difficult, if not impossible, amounting to little more than exercises in anachronism. But the strict historical sequentialism inherent in linear models for construing Scripture's ordering of time is at odds with Scripture's own testimony to the nature of biblical history.[34] The logic of providential affiliation on which figural reading rests cannot be identified with the chronology of the clock, though its genetic origins share to some extent in that form of sequencing. In contrast to the metaphysics of the *novum*, biblical figuration links together disparate temporal contexts through the construction of figural relationships, such that one can move back and forth between earlier and later contexts. Chronology is reversible, as it were, and reciprocal movement becomes possible. More importantly, the Old Testament's own unique theological voice is not consigned to something called *past time* that no longer presses in on the present. Instead, the Old Testament continues to abide in and through our present as a living voice, rather than being reduced to historical introduction or prolegomena for the New Testament.

Substituting linear movement for the Old Testament's own unique account of time has been the source of many problems in modern biblical scholarship. Not least of these issues is an account of the two testaments where God's providential dealings with biblical Israel cease to shape and inform his dealings with the church. The unidirectional character of linear models for construing the temporal relations between biblical figures inevitably leads to the conclusion that "the true meaning of any type lies in the future, never the past. Hence the church . . . transforms herself into an 'anti-type' rather than remaining herself a type of something else; and her progressive dispensation means that her form must be more 'perfect' than the type referring to her. This obviously breaks down the ability of Old Testament types to 'judge' the church."[35] Most

---

34. See the comments of Knierim, whose discussion of the distinction between cyclical and historical time in the creation narratives rightly recognizes the difficulty involved in distinguishing them: "The labels 'cyclic time,' referring to cosmic time, and 'historical time,' referring to human history, are chosen only for the sake of brevity. We are aware that 'historical time' also has a cyclic component, as Westermann has shown. Furthermore, there is reason for ascribing a historical dimension to 'cyclic time' as well." Knierim, *Task of Old Testament Theology*, 192n51; see also Westermann, *Genesis 1–11*, 347.

35. See Radner, *Time and the Word*, 78. Similarly, Calvin resists the reduction of Old Testament Israel to "a herd of swine" that has been "fattened up by the Lord on this earth, without any hope of the heavenly immortality" (John Calvin, *Institutes of the Christian Religion*, ed.

modern accounts of the Old Testament's "salvation history" operate with a more or less linear construal of that history, one that progressively moves toward a telos. The end or fulfillment in view is typically the New Testament, rather than the person and work of Jesus Christ. Rather than remaining integral to the person and work of Christ (Luke 22:20), on this reading, the new covenant is conflated with the New Testament. As a result, the people of Israel, along with their history, are identified with the old covenant (read: Old Testament), an epoch or period properly belonging to the past and now functioning as an extended foreword to the New Testament. By way of contrast, the figural ordering of time associated with the Old Testament's abiding theological voice positions the modern church in the "figural time" of the divided church and broken body of Old Testament Israel, rather than something evangelical moderns refer to as the "past" era of the old covenant.[36] The theological implications this has for our understanding of division in the church are significant but largely marginalized by the "horizontal Platonism" at work in the old covenant / new covenant schema dominating most approaches to the Old Testament in our day.[37]

To overcome the force of these alien pressures on the Old Testament's figural ordering of time, we must recover the theological significance of creation for figural reading. This in turn means the recovery of the early church's conviction that the fixed archē of creation remains foundational for our understanding of time.[38] Otherwise the redemptive providence at work in the world outside the Garden becomes a leaving behind of creation, rather than a fulfilling of its original purpose and telos. The eclipse of creation by linear constructions of salvation history thus goes hand in hand with the eclipse of figural sequencing of time, and by extension the logic of figural reading. Yet the fact that the redemptive movement of time in human history

---

John T. McNeill [Philadelphia: Westminster, 1960], 1:429). For Calvin, the theological significance of Old Testament Israel and its land blessings was not something that stood in abeyance until the apostolic construction of the New Testament witness. Rather, they were figures of the heavenly city in their own right (450–51).

36. Radner notes that "figural understandings of Scripture are, in a basic sense, subversive of 'sequentialist' experiences of history: they place, for instance, a pneumatically governed Christian Church within the movement of abandoned and destroyed Jewish Jerusalem, a temporal reversal that defies strictly sequential historical patterns." Ephraim Radner, *The End of the Church: A Pneumatology of Christian Division in the West* (Grand Rapids: Eerdmans, 1998), 303n55.

37. See Kendall Soulen, "YHWH the Triune God," *MT* 15, no. 1 (1999): 25–54, esp. 52n22.

38. For the interpretation of this archē in terms of Christ the eternal Word, see Don Collett, "The Christomorphic Shaping of Time in Radner's *Time and the Word*," *ProEccl* 27, no. 3 (2018): 276–79; cf. also Paul Blowers's excellent study of the early church's understanding of creation in his *Drama of the Divine Economy*.

beyond the Garden continues to be governed by the foundational constancy and stability of creation, especially its cyclical or repetitive ordering of time, is evident in the modeling of Israel's three annual pilgrim feasts on the created pattern of the seven-day week cycle.[39] This creational cycle formed the basis for the Feast of Unleavened Bread, or Passover (Exod. 12:18–19; Lev. 23:5–8; Deut. 16:2–3); the Feast of Weeks, or Pentecost (Lev. 23:15–16; Deut. 16:9–10); and the Feast of Ingathering, or the Feast of Booths (Lev. 23:34–36; Deut. 16:13–15).[40] In this way God taught Israel that its redemption is modeled on the continuing constancy and stability inherent in Genesis 1:1–2:3 and its structuring of time. The theological effect of this recurring seven-day liturgical pattern in Israel's major feasts is to interpret the Exodus redemption as a figure of new creation.[41]

A further link with the Priestly account of creation in Genesis is also found in Leviticus 23, this time with reference to the logic of word (*verbum*) and thing (*res*) intrinsic to the practice of figural reading. There are five sets of instructions in Leviticus 23. The first concerns the Sabbath, Passover, and the Feast of Unleavened Bread (vv. 1–8); the second concerns the Feast of Weeks (vv. 9–22); the third concerns the solemn day of rest (vv. 23–25); the fourth concerns the Day of Atonement (vv. 26–32); and the fifth concerns the Feast of Ingathering (vv. 33–43). Each of these instructions for the ritual-liturgical practices of Leviticus 23 is introduced with divine speech: "And the LORD said to Moses" (vv. 1, 9, 23, 26, 33). The repetitive use of these formulaic introductions underscores the central role of divine speech as an interpretive key to the meaning and content of the rituals of the feasts.[42] In other words, divine speech is the point of departure for understanding the feasts, not the ritual or figural things that characterize these holy days. What these ritual realities or

39. On the priority of the creational ordering of time for liturgical ways of ordering time in Leviticus, see Walter Vogels, "The Cultic and Civil Calendars of the Fourth Day of Creation (Genesis 1:14b)," *SJOT* 11, no. 2 (1988): 163–80. See also L. Michael Morales, *Who Shall Ascend the Mountain of the Lord? A Biblical Theology of the Book of Leviticus* (Downers Grove, IL: InterVarsity, 2015). Morales notes that in the Priestly account it is not Adamkind who rules over time but the two lamps or lights of the sun and moon, underscoring the fact that God orders time in creation "to which humanity is subject" (45).

40. See Jin K. Hwang, "Jewish Pilgrim Festivals and Calendar in Paul's Ministry with the Gentile Churches," *TynBul* 64, no. 1 (2014): 89–107, esp. 90, 95.

41. The redemptive significance of the Old Testament temple and its inner furnishings and appointments is also modeled on the ordering of things found in creation, a fact that accounts for the shared vocabulary between the language of the Priestly account and that of the book of Leviticus. See Morales, *Who Shall Ascend the Mountain of the Lord?*, 197–203.

42. See Joel White, "'He Was Raised on the Third Day according to the Scriptures' (1 Corinthians 15:4): A Typological Interpretation Based on the Cultic Calendar in Leviticus 23," *TynBul* 66, no. 1 (2015): 109–10.

figural things mean is structured, identified, and determined in terms of divine speech, much like the relation between word and thing in the first creation.[43]

Word and Thing in Creation, Prophecy, and Figural Reading

In Genesis 1, the things of creation not only are brought into existence through divine speech but also are ordered and illumined by the light of that Word, the Agent (or Beginning) through whom God created, ordered, and illumined the world of created things (Gen. 1:2–3).[44] The material sequence presented in the Priestly account stresses the priority of the Word for both the creation and the interpretation of things in Genesis 1:3–31. This way of ordering things continues in the new creation that the prophets of Old Testament Israel proclaimed. Prophecy is not only word but also vision, for the prophet not only "hears" words but also "sees" things (Isa. 2:1; Jer. 1:1–2, 11–14; Ezek. 1:1–4; Amos 1:1; Mic. 1:1; Zech. 1:1, 8). Prophecy thus accomplishes its sense-making through both words and figural things, according to the model provided by the Priestly account of creation. Like the ordering of time in the Priestly account, the ordering of time in biblical prophecy should not be reduced to linear movement. Rather, we should think of it as "providential affiliation through time, as later and earlier witnesses are canonically associated."[45] The gravitational pull of the figural things in prophecy generates its own world of meaning by gathering together significant persons, places, and events from disparate historical contexts, bridging their temporal gaps by treating them as features of one and the same theological reality.[46]

But while the images or figural things the prophet sees are typically drawn from the realm of creation and redemptive events in Israel's history, the

43. The classic account of the significance of "words" (*signa*) and "things" (*res*) for biblical sense-making may be found in Augustine's *De doctrina Christiana* (*On Christian Doctrine*). See the essays in Augustine, *"De doctrina Christiana": A Classic of Western Spirituality*, ed. Duane Arnold and Pamela Bright (Notre Dame, IN: University of Notre Dame Press, 1995).

44. Divine speech or the *logos* in Gen. 1:1 is presented as archē, which is not merely the idea of temporal beginning but the foundational agency by which God brought creation into existence (cf. John 1:1–3).

45. Seitz, *Prophecy and Hermeneutics*, 122: "In sum, temporality is not only forward movement, as that is typically understood. It is also providential affiliation through time, as later and earlier witnesses are canonically associated. In this way canonical editing seeks to draw out the implications of God's sovereign purpose from the perspective of a later, mature, configured understanding."

46. See Christopher R. Seitz, "Scriptural Author and Canonical Prophet: The Theological Implications of Literary Association in the Canon," in *Biblical Interpretation and Method: Essays in Honour of John Barton*, ed. Katherine Dell and Paul Joyce (Oxford: Oxford University Press, 2013), 176–88.

prophetic word remains primary, because it gives insight (*theoria*) into the figural things the prophet sees. Thus the prophetic word and the figural things it makes use of do not correlate as two equal pillars, because the light of the first (the prophetic word) exposes the order of the second (figural things) and also *determines* their meaning.[47] Prophecy links up with the future through word and figure, but in this act of figural linkage the eternal Word as Beginning (archē) retains ontological priority, according to the model provided by the sequencing of eternal Word and created things given in the creation account of Genesis 1:1–2:3. Stressing the primacy of the prophetic word is but another way of stressing the primacy of the literal sense for Scripture's figural-theological sense.

Conclusion

An account of creation structured and illumined by divine speech forms the basis for the original unity of creation and human history in the Old Testament—a unity ordered and sustained by providence, though now ruptured by human sin and rebellion. Its witness to these unique and foundational realities is not replaceable by rival ancient Near Eastern accounts of creation, nor does the New Testament supersede it. Here it is surely the case that the Old Testament "got there first." However, we should not forget that the life Israel lived under God's providence was also inextricably bound up with the disclosure of God's character and divine identity. Although Israel's scriptures may and in fact have been construed in many different ways, according to many different unifying realities or centers, we should not allow this to obscure the fact that the fundamental purpose of the Torah and the Prophets is to disclose the divine identity and character of Israel's LORD. Viewed in this light, the scriptures of Israel are more properly styled a "character history" in which metaphysical self-disclosures of Israel's LORD are made manifest in his economic dealings or providential ways with Israel.[48] The Torah and the

47. An analogy may also be drawn between Scripture and the figural things of the bread and wine used in the Eucharist: "Scripture and sacrament do not correlate as two equal pillars of the church. They are different in kind, and the first exposes the order of the second, as well as determines the usage of the second as a realm of ascesis or becoming in Christ." Radner, *Time and the Word*, 106, proposition 16.12.

48. On the non-Kantian character of the distinction between God *ad intra* and God *ad extra* in the act of divine self-disclosure, see Katherine Sonderegger's *Systematic Theology*, vol. 1, *The Doctrine of God* (Philadelphia: Fortress, 2015), 36–42. The nature of this disclosure is not to be confused with Kant's notion of a limiting or regulative concept that merely discloses the limits of rational knowledge (reason), rather than providing a positive disclosure of noumena (metaphysics). God's self-disclosure in Scripture not only reveals the limits of human knowledge

Prophets find their ground in a particular theological ontology, from which they cannot be separated, because the narratives of Torah not only reflect what the Lord has done but also disclose who the Lord is. Stated differently, the figural "ways" of the Lord in creation and providence disclose his identity or name (Exod. 33:13, 18–19; 34:5–7), a disclosure that takes place within an ordering of time that is at once both figural and liturgical,[49] accessed and interpreted through Scripture's literal sense. Thus the relation of the Lord's character to the issues of theological ontology, Scripture's literal and figural senses, and the rule of faith will form the subject matter of the following chapter.

---

but also provides an ontological disclosure of his character and being (see Sonderegger's comments on 68–69).

49. The intrinsic relation of figural and liturgical logic is not only embedded in the Old Testament's account of creation and prophecy but also evident from the fact that suspicion of figural reading in the church usually translates into distrust or even rejection of liturgical forms of worship found in the various prayer-book traditions of the church.

2

Figural Reading and Scripture's Literal Sense

There are few more perplexing and yet important problems in the history of biblical interpretation than the issue of defining what is meant by the *sensus literalis* of a text. The great scholars of the synagogue and the church wrestled intensely with the question. At times within this history a consensus regarding its meaning appears to have been reached, only once again to break apart for succeeding generations. In my judgment much of the present confusion within the exegetical discipline centers on this same problem.

Brevard S. Childs, "The *Sensus Literalis* of Scripture"[1]

Throughout the church's history, the Bible's literal sense has always been the primary basis for the practice of theological exegesis.[2] To be sure, renderings

1. Brevard S. Childs, "The *Sensus Literalis* of Scripture: An Ancient and Modern Problem," in *Beiträge zur alttestamentlichen Theologie: Festschrift für Walther Zimmerli Zum 70. Geburtstag*, ed. Herbert Donner, Robert Hanhart, and Rudolf Smend (Göttingen: Vandenhoeck & Ruprecht, 1977), 80.

2. This is not to imply, of course, that ecclesial interpreters of Scripture have always lived up to this exegetical ideal. For an overview and analysis of the church's struggle to clarify the relation between Scripture's literal sense and its theological sense, see esp. James S. Preus, *From Shadow to Promise: Old Testament Interpretation from Augustine to the Young Luther* (Cambridge, MA: Harvard University Press, 1969); cf. also Alastair Minnis, *Medieval Theory of Authorship: Scholastic Literary Attitudes in the Later Middle Ages*, 2nd ed. (Philadelphia: University of Pennsylvania Press, 2010); Christopher Ocker, *Biblical Poetics before Humanism and Reformation* (Cambridge: Cambridge University Press, 2002). Preus's study of medieval hermeneutics is a particularly helpful guide to understanding the hermeneutical issues at stake in reading the Old Testament *as* Christian Scripture, suggesting that while the medieval church struggled to do justice to both the Old Testament's literal sense and its christological referent, the former was often played off against the latter, resulting in a construal of the Old Testament's *sensus literalis* that threatened to demote its witness to a pre-Christian, preliminary status.

of Scripture's literal sense in the premodern church were capable of embracing a range of extended meanings or senses—for example, allegorical, tropological, and anagogical. Nevertheless, a general consensus decreed that these senses may be used to establish doctrine only insofar as they are founded on the literal sense. To reference only a few of the more prominent examples, both Augustine and Aquinas regard Scripture's allegorical or theological sense as an integral extension of its literal sense, and this sense remains foundational for the construction of exegetical argument.[3] At the same time, the issues involved in defining just what is meant by Scripture's *sensus literalis* have long been a source of struggle and dispute in the church. At the heart of this struggle lies the relation between Scripture's literal and theological sense, as well as the kindred issues of Scripture's figural sense and the rule of faith. Accordingly, this chapter will provide a brief introduction to the church's traditional account of the inner relation between Scripture's literal and theological senses. This relation has typically been mediated by the representative character of the church's threefold account of the figural senses, as well as the theological rule for reading Scripture generated by these senses. But as I hope to show, the landscape of biblical interpretation in our day is largely defined by the changing fortunes of figural and ruled readings of Scripture in the contexts of intellectual and ecclesial history. My overall goal will be to ask whether an exegetically responsible use of figural and ruled readings of the Old Testament illuminates its peculiar theological character and witness, and if so, what that might look like in practice.

At the same time I will also argue that what this account looks like should not be exclusively identified with a particular period in the church's history—for example, the "golden age" of the patristic-medieval church or the reforms fostered by the Reformation and the Enlightenment. In this regard it is wise to give ear to the admonition of John Webster, who rightly notes the presence

---

3. See Thomas Aquinas, *Summa Theologiae*, trans. Fathers of the English Dominican Province (Westminster, MD: Christian Classics, 1981), I.1.10; cf. also Augustine, "Letter 93: Augustine to Vincent," in *The Works of St. Augustine: A Translation for the 21st Century, Letters 1–99*, ed. John E. Rotelle, trans. Roland Teske, S.J. (Hyde Park, NY: New City Press, 2001), 376–408. In his work *De potentia Dei* (*On the Power of God*), Aquinas states that the dignity of divine Scripture is marked by the fact that it embraces many senses (*multos sensus*) under one letter (*sub una littera*). Thus for Aquinas, the literal sense is fully capable of embracing extended senses (cf. also Augustine, *On Christian Doctrine*, trans. D. W. Robertson Jr. [New York: MacMillan, 1958], bk. 3, chaps. 27–28; *The Confessions*, trans. Henry Chadwick [Oxford: Oxford University Press, 1991], bk. 12, chaps. 31–32). However, Aquinas also goes on to argue (rightly) that such "other senses" (*alios sensus*) are to be permitted, provided they preserve the authorizing context of the letter (*salva circumstantia litterae*). Thomas Aquinas, *The Power of God*, trans. Richard J. Regan (Oxford: Oxford University Press, 2012), Question 4, Answer 1.

of a perennial temptation for those who attempt to recover usable resources from the past:

> A temptation for theologians of retrieval is to subscribe to a myth of the fall of theology from Christian genuineness at some point in its past (fourteenth-century nominalism, the sixteenth-century Reformation, seventeenth-century Cartesianism, or wherever "modernity" is considered to have first presented itself). . . . Such a stance can indicate the same illusion of superiority as that sometimes claimed by critical reason. Moreover, it can fail to grasp that the problem is not *modern* theology, but simply *theology*. All talk of God is hazardous. Modern constraints bring particular challenges which can be partially defeated by attending to a broader and wiser history, but there is no pure Christian past whose retrieval can ensure theological fidelity.[4]

While Webster's comments are directed toward systematic theologians, they are clearly applicable to biblical exegetes as well. Up until recently it was common in historical critical circles to regard the era ushered in by the Enlightenment as the gold standard for constructing and defining Scripture's literal sense.[5] While this mentality is far from absent in our time, an opposite tendency has arisen, styling itself *ressourcement*, which leans toward viewing the early church's version of the literal sense as a sort of golden age for biblical exegesis.[6] My goal will be to avoid both these tendencies, adopting instead a critically confessional perspective on modern approaches to exegesis, as well as more recent movements such as *ressourcement* and the theological interpretation of Scripture.[7] Inasmuch as no age in the post-apostolic history of the church serves as the pinnacle or consummation of exegetical wisdom, a figural approach to reading the Old Testament holds itself free to learn from all.

4. John Webster, "Theologies of Retrieval," in *The Oxford Handbook of Systematic Theology*, ed. John Webster, Kathryn Tanner, and Iain Torrance (Oxford: Oxford University Press, 2007), 596.

5. For an account of the problems involved in identifying historical critical concerns with the Enlightenment, see John Barton, *The Nature of Biblical Criticism* (Louisville: Westminster John Knox, 2007), 117–36.

6. This statement is a generalization of the *ressourcement* movement, to which there are notable exceptions. Webster rightly notes that while theologies in this tradition "eschew saying anything new," this is not because they content themselves with "formulaic repetition" of the past, still less with "endorsing everything the tradition has ever said." Rather, "they operate on the presupposition that resolutions to the questions which they address may well be found already somewhere in the inheritance of the Christian past." Webster, "Theologies of Retrieval," 592–93.

7. For a readable introduction to the recent movement calling for theological interpretation of Scripture, see Daniel J. Treier, *Introducing Theological Interpretation: Recovering a Christian Practice* (Grand Rapids: Baker Academic, 2008); cf. also Stephen E. Fowl, *Theological Interpretation of Scripture* (Eugene, OR: Cascade, 2009).

The Literal Sense and the Early Church

One of the most disputed issues in church history surrounding the literal sense concerns its relation to the practice of figural reading. The issues surrounding this question are not merely academic but also crucial for the life of the church. For if it is true—as classical Christian exegetical tradition maintains—that the ability of Scripture's figural vision to enclose future readers is founded on its literal sense, then Scripture's ability to order our own place in time through its canonical form ultimately stands or falls on this issue. As others have observed, to speak of the Bible's capacity to figurally enclose our world—the world of post-biblical history, indeed, *all* historical worlds—no longer represents a live option for children of the Enlightenment, both modern and postmodern.[8] The problem is not merely a function of the widespread loss of biblical literacy in our day, although that's part of it. The problem ultimately lies in the erosion and loss of Scripture's figural sense, which disclosed the power of its inspired words to make sense of the various historical worlds we as creatures inhabit in and through time.

In the practice of biblical interpretation a great deal hinges on the question of *how* interpreters should conceive and construct the literal sense in relation to the figural or allegorical sense; this is especially true with respect to the early church's construction of the literal sense. The premodern church's approach to the Bible's literal sense was famously summarized in terms of a fourfold sense called the *Quadriga*: the literal-historical sense, the allegorical sense, the tropological sense, and the anagogical sense. Literal sense at its most basic level refers to the *littera* or "letter" of the biblical text. While the early church variously construed Scripture's literal sense as the verbal sense, the authorial sense, or the historical sense,[9] these three ways of describing the literal sense were typically regarded as its *integral* parts and not isomorphic entities. For this reason we may say that the literal sense is shorthand for what is more properly called the literal-historical sense—that is, the words of Scripture in their "original" or historical context. We may also refer to the literal sense as the verbal sense construed in terms of "the ways the words run" in Scripture[10]

---

8. See the introductory reflections in Hans Frei, *The Eclipse of Biblical Narrative: A Study in Eighteenth and Nineteenth Century Hermeneutics* (New Haven: Yale University Press, 1974), 1–16.

9. See Kathryn E. Greene-McCreight, "Literal Sense," in *Dictionary for Theological Interpretation of the Bible*, ed. Kevin Vanhoozer, Craig Bartholomew, Daniel Treier, and N. T. Wright (Grand Rapids: Baker Academic, 2005), 455–56.

10. The phrase represents David Yeago's translation (following Bruce Marshall) of the Latin phrase *salva circumstantia litterae* in Aquinas's *De potentia Dei*. See David Yeago, "The New Testament and Nicene Dogma," *ProEccl* 3 (1994): 161.

and alternatively as the authorial sense intended by its human author. That being said, it is important to stress that we should not identify Scripture's literal sense with either its verbal or its authorial sense. Rather, we should include also the original historical context and linguistic conventions by which Scripture's words are rendered, as well as the larger network of historical realities within which those words are embedded. Because the historical dimension that accompanies the literal sense is an integral part of the providence by which Scripture's theological sense is rendered, the history in view in the literal sense is identical not simply with biblical history as reconstructed by modern scholars but with a providentially constructed history or economy (*oikonomia*).

Another way of describing the place of the literal sense in the early church would be to think of it as an integral witness to the divinely ordered providence by which Scripture renders its theological sense.[11] Speaking of the literal sense in this way reminds us that while Scripture refers to historical realities (for example, the events, persons, places, institutions, and historical traditions of its own day), it also speaks of theological realities in and through those historical realities. The literal sense speaks of itself (that is, the historical and original context native to its own day) but at the same time also speaks of something "other"—namely, the theological reality that gave birth to the literal-historical sense in the first place. It thus has the peculiar property of self-speaking and other-speaking *at the same time*.[12] In this way a twofold distinction for describing the literal sense arose in the church's grammar. The self-speaking of Scripture, or the word in relation to its own historical context, constituted the literal sense proper. But its capacity for other-speaking, or that same word in relation to its theological context, constituted

11. In a study of Aquinas's understanding of the relation between virtue and biblical interpretation, Eugene Rogers Jr. persuasively argues that, materially speaking, biblical hermeneutics for Aquinas is "a meditation on providence," since by means of providence God sets up the figural relationships whose theological sense is rendered by the words of Scripture. Thus Thomas's view of the literal sense is not so much a method as a meditation on God's providence. See Eugene Rogers Jr., "How the Virtues of the Interpreter Presuppose and Perfect Hermeneutics: The Case of Thomas Aquinas," *JR* 76 (1996): 78; cf. 66n4.

12. Citing Gregory the Great's *Moralia* on the book of Job, Aquinas notes that "Holy Writ by the manner of its speech transcends every science, because in one and the same sentence, while it describes a fact, it reveals a mystery." The church of premodernity also regarded the divinely ordained providential link between original and future contexts in Scripture to be a distinguishing feature of scriptural texts in distinction from secular texts and thus by extension the uniqueness of theological science in comparison with other sciences. See Aquinas, *Summa Theologiae* I.1.10; cf. also Denys Turner, "Allegory in Late Christian Antiquity," in *The Cambridge Companion to Allegory*, ed. Rita Copeland and Peter T. Struck (Cambridge: Cambridge University Press, 2010), 79–80.

its allegorical sense. Similarly, in the church's shorthand summary (*verba-res*) of the Bible's scope, the term *verba* has in view Scripture's words in relation to the providential background or network of historical realities referenced by its literal sense, while the summary as a whole speaks of those words in relation to their theological or allegorical sense.[13] In both cases, the distinction between self-speaking and other-speaking was not to be interpreted as a separation or strict division of labor, as though the literal sense speaks of historical realities, while the allegorical sense speaks of theological realities. For the early church, Scripture's literal sense is ultimately defined in terms of the theological reality or subject matter it speaks of and which gave birth to that sense in the first place, rather than its historical context per se. Biblical words are not merely historical words; they are also inspired. Because of this, the distinction between Scripture's literal-historical sense and its theological sense is relative rather than absolute, and a separation between the two in terms of subject matter would be at odds with the inspired nature of the biblical text.

Allegory is the term chosen by the early church to describe Scripture's capacity for other-speaking. The term comes from the conjunction of two terms: *allos*, meaning "other," and *agoreuein*, meaning "to speak in public," in the marketplace (*agora*), as opposed to speaking in private venues.[14] With roots in both the Greco-Roman rhetorical tradition and Scripture itself,[15] the early church chose the term *allegory* to capture how biblical language makes public (*agoreuein*) something other than itself (*allos*).[16] To more fully describe the characteristics of this other-speaking, the premodern church further subdivided the text's theological meaning, or spiritual sense, into allegorical, tropological, and anagogical senses, thereby rendering the literal sense in terms of a fourfold sense. Whether this fourfold sense or *Quadriga* was an expansion of an earlier twofold account of the literal sense or, conversely, the twofold account was an economic contraction of the fourfold sense is not important

13. On the basis of distinctions made by Aquinas in *Summa Theologiae* I.1.10, Thomist scholars further unpack the summary of Scripture's overall scope (*verba-res*) in terms of first-order signification (verbal signification), by which words signify things (*verba-res*), and second-order signification (natural signification), by which things signify other things (*res-res*).

14. See Rita Copeland and Peter T. Struck, "Introduction," in *The Cambridge Companion to Allegory*, ed. Rita Copeland and Peter T. Struck (Cambridge: Cambridge University Press, 2010), 2.

15. See Gal. 4:24, where Paul uses the Greek word for allegory to describe his reading of Gen. 21 and the theological significance of the promise given to Abraham.

16. Cf. Martin Heidegger, "The Origin of the Work of Art," in *Poetry, Language, Thought*, trans. Albert Hofstader (New York: Harper & Row, 1971), 19: "The work makes public something other than itself; it manifests something other; it is an allegory. In the work of art something other is brought together with the thing that is made."

for our purposes.[17] What is important to recognize is that because different taxonomies for describing the literal sense existed in the early church, allegory could be used to refer to "the whole of the spiritual meaning latent in the literal sense, or one division of a tripartite spiritual sense."[18] In other words, allegory could be used as an umbrella term for Scripture's theological sense as a whole,[19] or more narrowly defined as one distinction within a threefold division of that sense.

While Scripture's allegorical sense *properly* describes the *theological* meaning of its historical realities, rather than their *historical* meaning per se,[20] it would be a mistake to press this distinction too far and fall into the error of detaching Scripture's allegorical sense from its literal-historical sense. Since both the literal and allegorical senses are rooted in the economy of Scripture, it follows that the allegorical sense is mediated through the same providential economy and historical realities disclosed in the literal sense. Broadly construed, the allegorical sense is the theological meaning of the spiritual *res* or theological reality the words of Scripture are talking about. But if we differentiate the theological meaning of Scripture's literal sense according to the *Quadriga*'s threefold aspects, then allegory takes on a more specific sense. Thus if we choose to view Scripture's literal sense with reference to its doctrinal aspect, or what it teaches us about the Christian faith, then we are speaking of its allegorical sense. If we view its literal sense with reference to its ethical aspect, or the way in which Scripture reforms the inner life of the

17. The earliest formulation of the literal sense as fourfold is usually identified with John Cassian's *Conferences* 14.8, cited in Turner, "Allegory in Late Christian Antiquity," 72n2. Cassian's account orders the spiritual senses as tropological, allegorical, and anagogical, rather than the order found in most medieval versions of the *Quadriga* (allegorical, tropological, and anagogical). However, the fourfold sense is clearly anticipated in Origen's threefold account of the literal sense as the historical, moral, and allegorical sense, which in turn finds an adumbration in his teacher, Clement of Alexandria, who in the *Stromateis* I.xxviii argues that the sense of the Mosaic Law is to be taken in three ways: as displaying a type, laying down a command for the moral life, and giving a prophecy.

18. Copeland and Struck, "Introduction," in Copeland and Struck, *Cambridge Companion to Allegory*, 4.

19. Speaking in reference to the church's fourfold construal of the literal sense, Aquinas writes that "of these four, allegory alone stands for the three spiritual senses" (*Summa Theologiae* I.1.10, reply to objection 2). In his study of Origen, de Lubac likewise notes that "the same word *allegoria*—or *sensus mysticus*—designates at times only the first of the three senses that go beyond the letter," while at other times it designates all three senses taken together. This movement is made possible by the fact that Scripture's spiritual senses "are interior to each other and form a real unity. All three concern, indissolubly, that unique 'great mystery that is accomplished in Christ and in the Church.'" Henri de Lubac, *History and Spirit: The Understanding of Scripture according to Origen*, trans. Anne E. Nash (San Francisco: Ignatius, 2007), 204–5.

20. See Turner, "Allegory in Late Christian Antiquity," 80.

soul,[21] then we are speaking of its tropological sense. If we view Scripture's literal sense with reference to its eschatological or future aspect, or what it teaches us to hope for, then we are speaking of its anagogical sense. We should also note that these three senses are integral aspects of Scripture's literal sense, rather than external add-ons we supply by way of pastoral application. They are not simply helpful guides for structuring sermons in tripartite form but intrinsic to the theological realities Scripture is concerned with and to which it bears witness. For this reason it is best not to think of these senses as applicatory senses—though they obviously have pastoral significance—but as theological, ethical, and eschatological senses inherent in the literal sense. They are necessary aspects of Scripture's theological landscape, whereas its applicatory senses are contingent on the changing historical contexts preaching seeks to address.

In order to further clarify the nature of the relation between the Bible's literal sense and theological sense, it is helpful to reference a Latin mnemonic or memory device the premodern church used: *Littera gesta docet, quid credas allegoria; moralis quid agas, quo tendas anagogia.*[22] That is, the literal sense teaches us what has been carried out or given birth to in God's providence (*gesta*); the allegorical sense teaches us what we should believe (*credenda*); the tropological sense directs us in what we should do (*agenda*); and the anagogical sense teaches us what to hope for (*speranda*).[23] From this one can

21. For a helpful discussion of how Athanasius tropologically applied the words of the Psalms to the ethical reformation and shaping of the soul's interior life, see Paul R. Kolbet, "Athanasius, the Psalms, and the Reformation of Self," in *The Harp of Prophecy: Early Christian Interpretation of the Psalms*, ed. Brian E. Daley, S.J., and Paul R. Kolbet (Notre Dame, IN: University of Notre Dame Press, 2015), 75–96.

22. Mark S. Burrows attributes this phrase to Nicholas of Lyre (Burrows, "Jean Gerson on the 'Traditioned Sense' of Scripture as an Argument for an Ecclesial Hermeneutic," in *Biblical Hermeneutics in Historical Perspective: Studies in Honor of Karlfried Froehlich on His Sixtieth Birthday*, ed. Mark Burrows and P. Rorem [Grand Rapids: Eerdmans, 1991], 154n5). Henri de Lubac suggests that it probably originated with the thirteenth-century Scandinavian Dominican, Augustine of Dacia, and his work *Rotulus pugillaris*. Henri de Lubac, *Medieval Exegesis: The Four Senses of Scripture*, trans. Mark Sebanc and E. M. Macierowski (Grand Rapids: Eerdmans, 1998), 1:1.

23. The fourfold sense had a Jewish counterpart in the Middle Ages, which the Jews called *PaRDeS*: "This word, meaning 'paradise-garden,' is an acronym for four layers, often simultaneously present, in the biblical text: there is *Peshat*, the literal meaning; *Remez*, the allegorical meaning; *Derash*, the tropological and moral meanings; and *Sod*, the mystical meaning." *Peshat* was defined in a way that clearly distinguished it from the act of interpretation. It is constituted by "the givenness and autonomy of the text" and stands for "the total text and not its component parts." Michael Fishbane argues that "it is this very givenness and invariance of the text which constitutes its eternal nature . . . which is received by one generation after another for interpretation and commentary. . . . It is the text which stands vis-à-vis the interpreter. . . . It is that which claims us, and it is that to which we submit ourselves, on the level of *Peshat*."

more easily grasp that for the premodern church, the function of Scripture's theological senses was to clarify how its words promote instruction in the three cardinal theological virtues of the Christian life: *faith*, or what is to be believed (doctrine); *love*, or what is to be done (ethics); and *hope*, or what is to be hoped for (eschatology). This tripartite subdivision of Scripture's figural senses may have been motivated by an attempt to correlate its theological sense with the three traditional Christian virtues of 1 Corinthians 13:13. Taking his lead from the apostle Paul, Augustine argues that love is the Christian virtue that resides at the heart of Scripture's theological witness and its literal sense. Thus whatever does not promote love of God or love of my neighbor does not properly belong to the literal sense.[24]

The more basic distinction between Scripture's literal and theological sense probably originated as a hermeneutical reflection on the dialectic of letter and Spirit in 2 Corinthians 3:6. From this arose a twofold account of biblical sense-making or "double signification" composed of the literal sense (or verbal signification) and the figural sense (or theological signification).[25] This construction of biblical sense-making presupposed a particular construal of the terms *letter* and *Spirit* in 2 Corinthians 3:6, wherein Scripture's theological sense (the realm of the Spirit) is transferred to its readers through the figural affiliation of historical things testified to in biblical words (the realm of the letter). Because the historical things testified to in Scripture's literal sense represent or "figure" spiritual realities, the literal sense is not the figure itself but that which is figured by the figure, or that which the figure is talking about[26]—namely, the invisible, transcendent Lord, who discloses himself as

---

Fishbane, "The Teacher and the Hermeneutical Task: A Reinterpretation of Medieval Exegesis," *JAAR* 43, no. 4 (1975): 710–13.

24. See Augustine, *On Christian Doctrine*, bk. 1, chaps. 35–36.

25. Arguably, the "principal initiator" of the distinction between Scripture's literal and spiritual sense is Origen, who further distinguished its spiritual sense using a twofold distinction between its moral and mystical senses. Origen also appears to have used the terms *anagogical* and *allegorical* as synonyms for Scripture's mystical sense (de Lubac, *History and Spirit*, 159–66, 204). The twofold distinction between "words" and "things" as a means of describing spiritual or intelligible realities in hermeneutics, however, is older than Origen and goes back to Aristotle's work *De Interpretatione* (*On Interpretation*), where Aristotle distinguishes between verbal signification (words as linguistic signs) and natural signification (things as natural signs) (Ocker, *Biblical Poetics*, 32n5, 32n37). As argued in the first chapter of this book, an account of figural sense-making understood in terms of "words" illuminating and interpreting "things" is inherent in the account of creation found in Gen. 1:1–2:3.

26. Aquinas, *Summa Theologiae* I.1.10, reply to objection 3. The point frequently resurfaces in Aquinas's biblical commentaries. For example, commenting on Matt. 27:9 he writes that "the duty of a good interpreter is to consider not the words, but the sense of the words" (Aquinas, *Commentary on the Gospel of Saint Matthew*, trans. Paul M. Kimball [Camillus, NY: Dolorosa Press, 2012], 916). This is another way of saying that unless one grasps *what*

the Word who speaks in Scripture by literal figures or word images. Like allegory, figure speaks of a theological "other" testified to in the literal sense. Thus on the basis of texts like 2 Corinthians 3:6, the figural sense of the letter was often used interchangeably with Scripture's spiritual sense. With reference to Israel's scriptures, this sometimes gave the unfortunate impression that the text's theological sense was rendered solely through its figural sense, and this occurred apart from the literal sense or even in spite of so-called Judaizing or historicized readings of the literal sense.[27] In a well-known essay on Luther's hermeneutics, for example, Gerhard Ebeling credits Origen with *identifying* Scripture's theological sense with its figural or mystical sense,[28] thereby reducing the Old Testament's literal sense to a dead letter lacking any theological significance in its own right.[29] As we will see, striking the proper balance between Scripture's literal and figural senses stands at the center

---

the words of Scripture are talking *about*, whether properly or figuratively, words *per se* will not produce knowledge, because to know what the words of Scripture mean, one needs to know what the words are talking about. A similar outlook on biblical interpretation may be found in the works of Brevard Childs and Christopher Seitz, both of whom argue that exegesis drives the interpreter to render a theological judgment regarding what the text is talking about—that is, its subject matter. Thus Scripture "pressures" (Seitz) or "coerces" (Childs) the interpreter to render what might be called a "referential judgment" about its subject matter. Thus, Childs writes, "proper exegesis does not confine itself to registering only the verbal sense of the text, but presses forward through the text to the subject matter (*res*) to which it points." Brevard S. Childs, "Does the Old Testament Witness to Jesus Christ?," in *Evangelium, Schriftauslegung, Kirche: Festschrift für Peter Stuhlmacher zum 65. Geburtstag*, ed. J. Ådna, S. Hafemann, and O. Hofius (Göttingen: Vandenhoeck & Ruprecht, 1997), 60; Christopher R. Seitz, *The Elder Testament: Canon, Theology, Trinity* (Waco: Baylor University Press, 2018), 41–42.

27. For a critical discussion of the issues at stake in the Reformation and early modernity, see G. Sujin Pak, *The Judaizing Calvin: Sixteenth-Century Debates over the Messianic Psalms* (Oxford: Oxford University Press, 2010).

28. Gerhard Ebeling, "Die Anfänge von Luthers Hermeneutik," *ZTK* 48 (1951): 182–87, cited in Preus, *From Shadow to Promise*, 12n11. For an English translation of the lectures, which were delivered in November 1950 at the University of Lund, see Gerhard Ebeling, "The Beginnings of Luther's Hermeneutics," *LQ* 7, no. 2 (1993): 129–58; "The Beginnings of Luther's Hermeneutics," *LQ* 7, no. 3 (1993): 315–38; and "The Beginnings of Luther's Hermeneutics," *LQ* 7, no. 4 (1993): 451–68.

29. Whatever else one might say about Ebeling's view of Origen on this point, it certainly does not apply to Aquinas's understanding of the relation between Scripture's literal sense and spiritual sense. In his commentary on Job 1:6, Aquinas notes that "although spiritual things are proposed under the figures of corporeal things, nevertheless the truths intended about spiritual things through sensible figures do not belong to the mystical but to the literal sense, because the literal sense is that which is primarily intended by the words, whether they are used properly or figuratively" (Aquinas, *The Literal Exposition of Job: A Scriptural Commentary Concerning Providence*, trans. Anthony Damico [Oxford: Oxford University Press, 1989], 76). For more nuanced accounts of Origen's theological reading of the literal sense, see Karen J. Torjesen, *Hermeneutical Procedure and Theological Method in Origen's Exegesis*, PTS 28 (Berlin: de Gruyter, 1985); John David Dawson, *Christian Figural Reading and the Fashioning of Identity* (Berkeley: University of California Press, 2002).

of most if not all the church's struggles to articulate a biblical account of Scripture's literal sense, as well as most of the problems associated with its abuses. While this twofold distinction between Scripture's literal sense and its theological sense is an interpretive consequence of the Bible's relation to the triune LORD, the church's attempt to hold these senses together by clarifying the relation between them has sometimes had unfortunate, albeit unintended, consequences, as Childs's essay reminds us. Distinguishing too sharply between these two senses places undue pressure on their integral unity.[30] As a result, the theological or figural senses begin to take on a life of their own that is at best only loosely accountable to the literal sense or at worst treats the literal sense as the mere occasion for the theological sense, rather than its authorizing exegetical context.

The Literal Sense and the Reformation

This difficulty also arises from the fact that while the literal sense often discloses Scripture's theological sense in conjunction with its figural senses, the literal sense is also capable of rendering theological meaning on its own. This occurs when the text is either a word of promise or divine speech that does not make use of historically visible forms or figures in order to speak to the present or link up with the future. By offering hope for the future, the promises of God in the Old Testament provide comfort, not only for a people yet to come but also for the people of Israel in their own day. Put differently, God's promises speak to the present by offering hope for the future. Promise is rooted in the character of God and expresses itself directly in divine speech (Gen. 12:2–3), though, to be sure, it is also often accompanied by historically visible signs or forms (15:7–21). Thus while biblical language often renders its theological meaning in relation to the figural sense, it nevertheless retains its own integrity within that relation and so need not always do so. Understandably, this has led some interpreters of Scripture's literal sense to conclude that its figural senses are unnecessary or redundant.[31] In the name

30. John David Dawson rightly argues that "to say that literal meaning extends into figural meaning is to reject the idea that what is figural must be nonliteral, or that in figural, the literal can no longer be present. Instead, when a narrative is read figurally, the reader stresses a certain feature of the text that differs from, but does not contradict, the feature of the narrative that would be stressed in a literal reading." Dawson, *Christian Figural Reading*, 147.

31. Cf. the remarks of Aquinas in his *Summa Theologiae* I.1.10, reply to objection 1, where he follows Augustine in the view that "nothing necessary to faith is contained under the spiritual sense which is not elsewhere put forward by the Scripture in its literal sense." Commenting on this point, Minnis and Scott rightly note, "If we push this principle, so clearly stated by Aquinas, to its logical conclusion, allegory becomes at worst redundant and at best a pleasing

of protecting the unity and integrity of the Bible's literal sense, readers of Scripture during the Reformation preferred to speak of the one true sense of Scripture (*unus verus scripturae sensus*) over against the fourfold account or *Quadriga* mentioned earlier.

Luther in particular worried that the dialectic of "letter" and "Spirit" at work in the hermeneutical reading of 2 Corinthians 3:6 opens the door to the problematic notion that Scripture's figural or theological senses are something other than the literal sense, as though the two were somehow opposed to each other. In addition, because Scripture's literal sense often speaks in figures or metaphors (i.e., when Jesus calls Herod a *fox* or when we speak of the *Lion* of Judah), Luther argued that it is better to speak of the grammatical-historical sense (*sensus grammaticus*) as the one true sense of Scripture, rather than using the language of either literal or figural sense.[32] This approach appears to deny the figural sense a place in biblical interpretation, effectively preventing it from contributing to our understanding of Scripture's theological sense. Roman Catholic readers of Scripture who remain committed to the analogical relation between the literal and figural senses in the *Quadriga* continue to argue that Luther's reformation of the literal sense reduces the reality of things (*res*) to words (*verba*) and is a hermeneutical extension of nominalism. The end result is a form of *sola Scriptura* in which biblical language does its sense-making apart from an external theological ontology (*res*) or a metaphysic for Scripture.[33] In this way, some argue, the ontological claims Scripture makes about God and creation disappear into the language of history, thereby giving birth—inadvertently—to something called modern historicism, in which historical ontology either replaces or swallows up theological ontology.

There is a sense in which Reformation hermeneutics is nominalistic, if by that we mean the insistence that Scripture's theological sense *is* the literal

---

(and persuasive) optional extra." Alastair Minnis and A. B. Scott, *Medieval Literary Theory and Criticism, c. 1100–1375: The Commentary Tradition* (Oxford: Clarendon, 1988), 204, cited in Ocker, *Biblical Poetics*, 42.

32. Martin Luther, *Answer to the Hyperchristian, Hyperspiritual, and Hyperlearned Book by Goat Emser in Leipzig—Including Some Thoughts Regarding His Companion, the Fool Murner*, in *Luther's Works*, vol. 39, *Church and Ministry I*, trans. Eric and Ruth Gritsch (Philadelphia: Fortress, 1970), 139–224, esp. 181. See the discussion in Gerald Bruns, *Hermeneutics: Ancient and Modern* (New Haven: Yale University Press, 1992), 143–44; cf. William M. Marsh, *Martin Luther on Reading the Bible as Christian Scripture: The Messiah in Luther's Biblical Hermeneutic and Theology*, PTMS (Eugene, OR: Pickwick, 2017), 6–10.

33. Thomas Luxon goes as far as suggesting that this hermeneutical move on the part of Protestants logically entails atheism and promotes the secularization of Western culture. Thomas H. Luxon, *Literal Figures: Puritan Allegory and the Reformation Crisis in Representation* (Chicago: University of Chicago Press, 1995), 50.

sense. Luther moved away from the analogical way of construing the relation between the literal and figural senses in the *Quadriga* toward a univocal mode of construing the literal sense. This was because, like Calvin after him, he regarded the *Quadriga*'s notion of levels of meaning as open to abuse and in need of reform. The difficulty with multiplying distinctions when attempting to relate Scripture's literal and figural senses is that in exegetical practice, a distinction all too easily becomes a separation—the result being that Scripture's figural senses begin to take on a life of their own.[34] Multiplying distinctions also has the potential to introduce logical and reflective distance between Scripture's literal sense and figural sense. Once the allegorical genie is let out of the bottle, the movement toward the independence of the allegorical sense, or "free range allegory," becomes difficult to stem.[35] The Reformation therefore prefers to speak of Scripture's one true sense, though this one true sense embraces the realms formerly occupied by Scripture's figural or allegorical sense. The point to stress is that this does not require us to conclude that the Reformation drove out Scripture's theological *res* and replaced it with history, thereby inadvertently giving birth to all kinds of anti-metaphysical campaigns in Western culture, including historical criticism as an interpretive model for reading Scripture. Rather, like Aquinas before them, both Luther and Calvin sought to prevent Scripture's literal and figural-theological senses from coming apart. To prevent this, they stressed the immediacy of the theological sense in the literal-historical sense or, if you prefer, the immediacy of the figural in the literal. In exegetical practice, the Reformers understood the literal sense "to cover an extended meaning virtually identical in content to that covered by allegory," albeit in a way "more closely governed by the grammatical and historical *sensus* of the text."[36] So far from dismissing Scripture's allegorical

34. Childs voices a similar concern, suggesting that the medieval fourfold sense "proved to be deeply flawed" because the levels of the text were "conceived in a static and arbitrary manner which resulted in the fragmenting of its unity," blurring the integral contact of text and subject matter "through clever interpretive techniques." Over against the medieval failure to clarify the relation between various levels of meaning in the fourfold sense, Childs proposes "a *single* method of interpretation which takes seriously both the different dimensions constituting the text as well as distinct contexts in which the text functions." Styling his own approach a "multi-level reading of Scripture," Childs, like Calvin before him, aims at defining the literal sense in such a way as to resist the dissolution of its unity, while at the same time leaving room for its figural or theological senses. Childs, "Does the Old Testament Witness to Jesus Christ?," 61, emphasis added.

35. See Turner, "Allegory in Late Christian Antiquity," 73–74.

36. Richard Muller, "The Hermeneutic of Promise and Fulfillment in Calvin's Exegesis of the Old Testament Prophecies of the Kingdom," in *The Bible in the Sixteenth Century*, ed. David Steinmetz (Durham, NC: Duke University Press, 1990), 73.

or figural sense altogether, this approach suggests that much of the business formerly accomplished by the figural sense "had actually been relocated [and] brought under new management,"[37] rather than abolished, with the literal sense now construed as "the single true sense of the text" instead of the multilevel account on offer in the medieval fourfold.[38]

Patristic hermeneutics sought to give expression to the scope of the canon in terms of the two realities reflected in the compact formula *verba-res*, along with an exegetically authorized rule of faith for relating them. Scripture's theological reality is other than its words, just as the Creator is other than the creature. But from this ontological judgment it does not follow that Scripture's literal sense is something other than its figural or theological sense, because the Other who speaks in Scripture infuses its words by his Spirit. Here one must avoid getting trapped in a false dilemma whose argument is as follows: If the purpose of the literal sense is to disclose another world beyond itself, then it exists for the sake of something else. Having no life of its own, it is a dead letter. However, if it exists for its own sake, then it has nothing relevant to say about theological realities that are external to it. Thus the literal sense is either dead or theologically irrelevant. On the contrary, the truth is that Scripture's theological sense is an inner sense and communicative theological presence within Scripture's words (a literal *res*), as well as a sense that finds its origin in a theological reality external to the text (a theological *res*). The external triune reality that gave birth to the literal sense in the first place does not present a necessary threat to the integrity of the literal sense, though the potential for viewing the relation of literal and theological in a mechanical or

37. See Minnis, *Medieval Theory of Authorship*, xi. This open-but-critical attitude toward allegory's exegetical usefulness may be found, for example, in the following statement from Calvin's *Institutes*, bk. 2, chap. 5, sec. 19: "Allegories ought not to proceed beyond the point where they have the rule of Scripture guiding them; certainly they must not be used as the basis for any dogmas *per se*." In arguing the latter point, Calvin is simply reiterating a point both Augustine and Aquinas before him would also have affirmed—namely, that doctrinal argument must be based on the literal sense and not on its allegorical or figural sense *per se*. In other words, figures do not interpret figures; rather, words interpret figures.

38. According to Muller, the shift from medieval to Reformation exegesis was a shift "from a precritical approach that could acknowledge spiritual senses of the text beyond the literal sense to a precritical approach that strove to locate spiritual meaning *entirely* in the literal sense" (Richard Muller, "Biblical Interpretation in the Era of the Reformation: The View from the Middle Ages," in *Biblical Interpretation in the Era of the Reformation: Essays Presented to David C. Steinmetz in Honor of His Sixtieth Birthday*, ed. Richard A. Muller and John L. Thompson [Grand Rapids: Eerdmans, 1996], 14). Childs notes that Calvin preferred to speak of "the *verus scripturae sensus* which is both literal and spiritual, the single true sense of the text" (Childs, "*Sensus Literalis* of Scripture," 87). Arguably, this close identification of the literal sense with its spiritual or theological sense is already present in Aquinas. See Ocker, *Biblical Poetics*, 6–7, 40–43.

purely external manner is always there.[39] Nevertheless, while the theological reality disclosed in Scripture exists outside the literal sense, it is impossible to describe or identify that reality apart from the literal sense, precisely because of the inner relation between Scripture's literal sense and its theological sense.[40] This is the point the Reformation seeks to stress when it argues that Scripture's figural or allegorical sense is immediately present in the literal sense.[41] Given Scripture's inspired character, the stress Reformation hermeneutics places on this fact is fully appropriate.[42]

In Scripture we do not meet with historical figures per se but literal figures— that is, figures presented through the medium of Scripture's words or its literal

39. Samuel Taylor Coleridge opined that allegory promoted precisely this sort of mechanical and external relation between Scripture and its theological sense. As an alternative, he chose to speak of Scripture as a "symbol" that participates in the theological reality it discloses, rather than an allegorical sign that merely points away from itself. For a defense of Coleridge's symbolist poetics on incarnational grounds, over against the deconstructionist criticism of Paul de Man, see John David Dawson, "Against the Divine Ventriloquist: Coleridge and De Man on Symbol, Allegory, and Scripture," *JLT* 4, no. 3 (1990): 293–310.

40. According to Ephraim Radner, the inner relation between Scripture's literal and figural-theological sense is best conceived as a special class of metaphor called *synecdoche* in which the part is contained in the whole. Although rhetoricians typically distinguish synecdoche from metonymy, classifying them as two different types of metaphor, in practice it is often difficult to distinguish them, since both terms work with the notion of rhetorical *substitution* or *pars pro toto*. Roughly stated, the difference consists in whether the attribute that is substituting for the whole is *part of* the whole in an internal or participatory sense (synecdoche) or merely *associated with* it in an external or incidental sense (metonymy). Synecdochal figuralism is an attempt to find a language that will underwrite a metaphysics of participation but stop short of insisting on the analogical predication at work in Catholic versions of figuralism as the only way to accomplish that. Ephraim Radner, *Time and the Word: Figural Reading of the Christian Scriptures* (Grand Rapids: Eerdmans, 2016), 189–97.

41. A similar emphasis may be found in Reno and O'Keefe's claim that for patristic readers of Scripture "the text is the *res*" or "the text is the subject matter" (John J. O'Keefe and R. R. Reno, *Sanctified Vision: An Introduction to Early Christian Interpretation of the Bible* [Baltimore: Johns Hopkins University Press, 2005], 13, 27–28, 30, 116). By making such statements, the authors offer resistance to the introduction of reflective or logical distance opening up between the literal sense and its figural-theological sense. This distance then offers a mandate for historical criticism to make use of critical tools and to get "behind the text" in order to recover what it is talking about, the latter of which amounts to a form of salvation by scholarly works.

42. Radner has recently argued that figural reading can flourish in the neo-Platonic soil of participatory metaphysics and analogical predication or in the Ockhamite realm of "singularism" and univocal predication. See his summary remarks in *Time and the Word*, 159–62. Swimming against the current of both Catholic and Protestant historiographers of the Reformation, he argues that the shift to a new metaphysic in the fourteenth century did not render figural reading impossible, since the key issue for figural reading is a doctrine of creation rooted in divine omnipotence. Since, on his reading of matters, nominalism left this doctrine more or less intact, Radner finds "little relation between the supposed 14th century metaphysical shift and the conditions for the possibility of figural readings of the Bible" (118). The historical and theological case Radner makes for this contested claim is substantial (111–62).

sense.[43] Speaking of Scripture's literal figures is a shorthand way to express the Reformation's conviction, anticipated by Origen, Augustine, and Aquinas, that Scripture's figural sense remains internal rather than external to the literal sense, because the literal sense is our mode of access to and condition of understanding for Scripture's figural-theological sense. Origen draws no sharp distinction on historical grounds between Scripture's figures or types (τυποι), on the one hand, and its allegorical or theological sense, on the other hand, because the purpose of scriptural figures is to "figure" or represent theological realities.[44] Similarly, in *On Christian Doctrine* Augustine warns the reader that the linguistic signs or figures of Scripture are not ends in themselves but are given for the purpose of facilitating union with the theological reality that they both mediate and testify to.[45] Aquinas succinctly rephrases this in his statement that the literal sense is not the figure but "what the figure figures."[46] The inherent logic of these three examples from Origen, Augustine, and Aquinas amounts to the claim that the literal sense *is* the theological sense—that is, what Scripture is referring to or talking about by means of its literal figures. Interestingly, in his reply to Goat Emser, Luther criticizes Emser's construal of 2 Corinthians 3:6, arguing that it produces a "twofold Bible" with two different subject matters, rather than one. For this reason, "even though the things described in Scripture mean something further, Scripture should not therefore have a twofold meaning. Instead, it should retain the one meaning to which the words refer."[47] In sum, the move toward Luther and Calvin's univocal language is inherent in the tradition's claim that the literal sense is not the figure but "what the figure figures." This is simply another way of saying that the literal sense is one with its theological referent.[48]

The Catholic tradition's approach, which purports to follow Aquinas, describes the relation between Scripture's literal sense and its theological sense using analogical rather than univocal language (i.e., "the literal sense *figures* the theological sense"), while the Reformation preferred to say "the literal sense *is* the theological sense." Whether the Catholic preference for analogical predication in this matter does a better job than the Reformation did of preserving the instincts of Aquinas and the tradition on this point remains debatable. Origen, Augustine, and Aquinas are concerned to argue

43. I owe the idea for this phrase to Luxon's thought-provoking book *Literal Figures*.

44. Peter Martens rightly argues that for Origen "the proper interpretation of a scriptural τυπος ought to be a *nonliteral* one, i.e., an exegesis in search of what the figure figures." Martens, "Revisiting the Allegory/Typology Distinction: The Case of Origen," *JECS* 16, no. 3 (2008): 302.

45. Augustine, *On Christian Doctrine*, bk. 1, chap. 4; cf. bk. 3, chap. 9.

46. Aquinas, *Summa Theologiae* I.1.10, reply to objection 3.

47. Luther, *Answer to the Hyperchristian, Hyperspiritual, and Hyperlearned Book*, 179.

48. Ocker, *Biblical Poetics*, 6–7, 40–43.

that Scripture's literal figures disclose theological realities, or *mysteria*, not by means of an ontological fusion of the literal sense with the theological sense but by an ontological union that makes possible their hermeneutical identity. Whatever we conclude on these matters, it is important to recognize, over against the standard Catholic reading, that the Reformation did not abolish the distinction between the literal sense and the figural-theological sense; instead, it sought to resist their dissolution by arguing that this distinction is *internal* rather than *external* to the literal sense. Ultimately, it is the Reformation's conviction that the literal sense is the mode of access and condition of understanding the Bible's theological sense that motivates the claim that Scripture's figural sense remains internal to the literal sense. The Reformation does not abolish the distinction between Scripture's literal and figural senses, while at the same time recognizing that what the literal sense *figures* or refers to is ontologically different from the creaturely nature of biblical language itself, just as the Creator is other than the creature.

Allegory, Figural Reading, and the Literal Sense

But if the literal sense is the theological sense, why continue to speak of the figural or allegorical sense of Scripture? This question is especially pressing for those who view allegory as an interpretive category that exercises a largely negative or even destructive pressure on Scripture's literal sense. Extended into the realm of biblical interpretation, allegory distracts from the literal sense by directing our attention to some referential x outside the text.[49] Even worse, allegory does violence to the literal sense by draining it of its historical particularity[50] and reducing it to an empty linguistic sign that defers meaning by continually pointing away from itself,[51] never managing to mediate the reality it refers to, let alone make any contribution to our understanding of the reality to which it testifies. Taking her cue from Gordon Teskey's critical perspective on allegory, Louise Freeman sums up the issue well: "Taking for granted a disjunction between its referent and its signs, allegory as 'other' (*allos*) 'speaking'

49. Along with the pernicious influence of Locke's theory of substance on biblical interpretation, Frei argues that myth and allegory promote a "behind the text" approach to reading narrative (Frei, *Eclipse of Biblical Narrative*, 11, 98–99, 101). To combat this, Frei proposes a figural model rooted in "realistic narrative" in which words mean what they say (literal sense), *not* what they refer to (allegorical sense).

50. Gordon Teskey, *Allegory and Violence* (Ithaca, NY: Cornell University Press, 1996), 43–46.

51. See Paul de Man, "Semiology and Rhetoric," *Diacritics* 3, no. 1 (1973): 27–33, reprinted in *The Norton Anthology of Theory and Criticism*, ed. Vincent B. Leitch, William B. Cain, Laurie Finke, and Barbara Johnson (New York: Norton, 2001), 1515–26.

(*agoria*) creates dual spheres that are incommensurable with each other, the material and the ideal. While the intent of allegory at some level is to conceal the gap between the two, it always in fact underscores the separation."[52] Still others identify the theological other-speaking at work in allegory with an act of translation, to be construed primarily as an act of contemporization, transposition, or reformulation that erases or ignores the original meaning of the literal sense for the sake of later interests and the need to make the text speak to those interests. Allegory on this view "converts everything into itself" and epitomizes "a structure of subsumptive thinking."[53] Here, allegory stands for that which suppresses the voice of the literal sense and becomes a form of deterministic ventriloquism. To sum up, allegory *distracts* from the meaning of the literal sense (Frei), *spiritualizes* it to the point of abstraction (Teskey), endlessly *defers* its meaning (de Man), or *absorbs* its integrity and otherness into itself (Bruns).

A more recent, alternative proposal moves in the opposite direction, arguing that since figural or allegorical interpretation is not a method but is inherent in the use of language itself, we should simply speak of the figural rather than the literal sense.[54] The interpretation of historical realities in Scripture necessarily proceeds by construing a new or unfamiliar "this" in terms of a familiar or previously known "that."[55] The structure of biblical interpretation is inherently analogical and translational in character, because it proceeds by interpreting one thing in terms of another, which is just another way of saying that the interpretive character of biblical language is inherently figural or allegorical in character. Advocates of this approach to figural reading do not ask why one needs an allegorical sense if it is contained in the literal sense. Instead, they raise a different question: If all acts of interpretation are figural in character in the manner just described, then why continue to speak of Scripture's literal sense as distinct from its figural sense? Again, the answer ultimately turns on the indispensable role of the literal sense as both

52. Louise Gilbert Freeman, "The Metamorphosis of Malbecco: Allegorical Violence and Ovidian Change," *Studies in Philology* 97, no. 3 (2000): 316.

53. Bruns, *Hermeneutics*, 203–4.

54. "The whole basis of language and speaking, the very thing which makes it possible, is ambiguity or metaphor" (Hans-Georg Gadamer, "Dialectic and Sophism in Plato's Seventh Letter," in *Dialogue and Dialectic: Eight Hermeneutical Studies on Plato*, trans. P. Christopher Smith [New Haven: Yale University Press, 1980], 111). In this, Gadamer was anticipated by Nietzsche's claim that "what is usually called language is actually all figuration." Cited in Gerald Bruns, "On the Weakness of Language in the Human Sciences," in *The Rhetoric of the Human Sciences: Language and Argument in Scholarship and Public Affairs*, ed. John S. Nelson, Allan Megill, and Donald N. McCloskey (Madison: University of Wisconsin Press, 1987), 241; cf. 239.

55. For example, in Acts 2:16, Peter interprets the event of Pentecost in terms of the prophecy of Joel using the logic of "this is that."

a mode of access and a condition of understanding for Scripture's figural or theological sense. This is also why we should retain the nomenclature of the literal sense, even while recognizing that because the Bible was written with the people of God in view, our approach to Scripture's literal sense typically occurs within an ecclesial sphere or context. The influence of Ralph Loewe's work on the nature of *peshat* or the "plain sense" in Jewish exegesis has led some to speak of the *literal sense* in terms of the *plain sense* in a more or less interchangeable way.[56] On this reading, the plain sense is not the literal sense per se but the literal sense as it has been received and interpreted by faith communities—or what might alternatively be styled its ecclesial, traditioned, or received sense.[57] While there are other ways of construing the plain sense that retain both its theological and scriptural integrity,[58] in this book I have adopted the standard nomenclature of literal sense instead of plain sense. This is not because I fail to recognize that our ecclesial and social contexts inevitably condition how we hear and appropriate the literal sense but because speaking of Scripture's literal sense rather than its received sense underscores the objective reality and status of biblical texts.

The point to stress is that while the literal and figural senses may be *distinguished* from one another and their relative integrities articulated within a providential account of biblical sense-making, they "cannot be *separated* from one another in a clear or satisfactory way."[59] Moreover, figural or allegorical interpretation should be distinguished from destructive ways of construing the act of translation or interpretation inherent in the figural logic of "this is that." Here figural or allegorical does not mean a translation of the *other* into the *same* but represents an affiliation or juxtaposition of *this* with *that* which expands the meaning of *that* in light of the new historical context

56. See Ralph Loewe, "The 'Plain Meaning' of Scripture in Early Jewish Exegesis," in *Papers of the Institute of Jewish Studies London I* (Jerusalem: Magnes, 1964), 140–85. See Childs, "*Sensus Literalis* of Scripture," 81n3.

57. See the range of options for construing Loewe's work canvassed in Kathryn Tanner, "Theology and the Plain Sense," in *Scriptural Authority and Narrative Interpretation*, ed. Garrett Green (Philadelphia: Fortress 1987), esp. 62–66.

58. In distinction from those who construe the "plain sense" in terms of its ecclesial or received sense, others construe it as a property of scriptural texts interchangeable with the literal sense or the rule of faith generated by the theological pressures inherent in the literal sense. See, for example, Christopher R. Seitz, "Reconciliation and the Plain Sense Witness of Scripture," in *The Redemption: An Interdisciplinary Symposium on Christ as Redeemer*, ed. Stephen T. Davis, Daniel Kendall, and Gerald O'Collins (Oxford: Oxford University Press, 2004), 25–42; cf. Kathryn E. Greene-McCreight, *How Augustine, Calvin, and Barth Read the "Plain Sense" of Genesis 1–3* (New York: Peter Lang, 1999), 1–31, esp. 5–7.

59. See Thomas Böhm, "Allegory and History," in *Handbook of Patristic Exegesis*, ed. Charles Kannengiesser (Leiden: Brill, 2004), 1:213–26, here 213, emphasis added.

provided by *this*. This makes possible communion and commerce between the two, while at the same time retaining their discrete integrities without a critical loss on either side. While this figural model may be applied to acts of interpretation occurring within the Old Testament, we can also extend it to cover the relation between the two testaments. The theological judgment reflected in the figural union of a New Testament *this* with an Old Testament *that* presupposes a theological judgment about the hypothesis, subject matter, or reality uniting the two testaments, and thus offers a rule for relating the words of the Old Testament to the selfsame theological reality testified to in the new historical context of the New Testament era.

We should however mention a word about the continuing usefulness of *allegory* as a term. As the foregoing discussion suggests, in the church's lexicon, the terms *literal*, *grammatical*, and *figural* have been the most popular candidates for describing Scripture's theological sense. All these terms are useful, but unlike *allegory* none of them foreground the character of biblical language as theological other-speaking. The very meaning of the term lays emphasis upon the importance of Scripture's referential dimension for biblical sense-making, and for that reason its use should not be made redundant.[60] Allegorical hermeneutics reminds us that the problem with much of today's biblical exegesis is not that it is obsessed with "original" context but that such exegesis is not original enough. Allegorical exegesis accomplishes this by referring us to an original context outside Scripture provided by the invisible, transcendent LORD who inhabits yet transcends biblical language. By stressing the character of biblical language as other-speaking, it directs us toward the One who gave birth to the literal sense in the first place. The term *allegory* offers resistance to the postmodern collapse of ontology into language or, in classical patristic terms, the collapse of Scripture's theological *res* into its *verba* or words. Allegorical exegesis thus reminds us that in rendering its theological sense, Scripture relies on a specific ontology external to itself. By underscoring the significance of a theological other for biblical sense-making, allegory also resists the reduction of figure and metaphor to *mere* figure and *mere* metaphor, or literary fiction. Rather, as Janet Soskice rightly notes, figure and metaphor are reality-depicting; like allegory, they work with the

---

60. Making this point is the main burden of Brevard S. Childs's essay "Allegory and Typology within Biblical Interpretation," in *The Bible as Christian Scripture: The Work of Brevard S. Childs*, ed. Christopher R. Seitz and Robert C. Kashow (Atlanta: Society of Biblical Literature, 2013), 299–310, especially his observation that "the heart of the problem of allegory turns on the nature of the referentiality of the biblical text. Allegory is a figure of speech implying that its reference is something other than what is being said, and the crucial issue lies in determining the theological substance to which it points metaphorically" (304).

logic of analogy and reference.[61] Because meaning is never wholly produced or self-contained within biblical texts but originates outside the text in the inner, eternal life of the Trinity, there will always be some sense in which subject matter explanations and referential theories of meaning remain vital for biblical hermeneutics. Allegorical exegesis accounts for the referent of biblical texts in terms of a theological other or reality outside the text, driving home the point that Scripture's theological referent is indispensable for the efficacy of biblical texts.

Allegory foregrounds the link between Scripture's theological ontology and its inspired words, resisting the anti-metaphysical bent inherent in much that passes for biblical exegesis in late modernity. In such a context, the advantage of a term like *allegory* consists in its uncompromising insistence that the Bible's proper pedigree does not belong in the first instance to the realm of historical data but originates outside itself in the eternal, inner life of the Trinity. Precisely because theological exegesis is theological, it involves claims about the being and reality of God and therefore has an inescapable metaphysical or ontological aspect. If one does not like the word *being*, then one must come up with other vocabulary to express biblical claims about reality, claims that begin with Genesis 1:1 and the two-world ontology of triune Creator and creature it establishes from the outset of creation's history. Call it ontology, an order of things, or a claim about reality—all these are metaphysical claims and metaphysical language. The concern of allegory to reckon with the metaphysical dimension of Scripture also dovetails with the ontological aspect of the church's rule of faith, which underwrites the Old Testament's character as Christian Scripture. If Jesus is not one in being with the God of Israel, a Christian way of understanding Israel's scripture becomes impossible, and the collapse of that ontological judgment also means the collapse of Christianity's soteriological claims—for who can forgive sins but God alone?

Defining Figure and Metaphor

Because Scripture's figural senses are tied to the ongoing theological significance of Scripture's history, their significance for God's creatures is not limited to their original historical context but also extends backward and forward in

---

61. For this account of metaphor, see Janet Soskice, *Metaphor and Religious Language* (Oxford: Clarendon, 1985). Biblical metaphors disclose truth about Scripture's theological reality (the triune God), because their "referential force" and efficacy derives from their relation to that referent.

time. While other terms might have been chosen, the term chosen in this book to express the representative significance of biblical history for all of time is that of *figure*. Adapting a phrase from Ephraim Radner, we may say that a figure is something God providentially constructs for the sake of speaking of himself[62]—for example, the royal *person* of David, the redemptive *event* of the Exodus, the sacred *institutions* of the tabernacle and the temple, or the sacred *places* of Zion and Jerusalem. At the outset it is important to grasp that the meaning of a figure is built upon the specific historical context in which it arises, and so figural reading is not to be identified with non-historical modes of reading, though moderns often construe it in those terms.[63] To understand David's figural significance as the LORD's anointed in Psalm 2:2, for example, we need to understand something about the historical context in which the biblical figure of David arises in God's providence. Original historical context thus remains significant for figural reading, though unlike later modernity, the early church was not interested in isolating this dimension of Scripture's literal sense from its relation to the larger providential history by which Scripture was formed. On the contrary, the very possibility of figural meaning presupposes a providentially constructed background or context.[64]

Old Testament figures like Adam or David or figural events of Israel's Passover do not merely point away from their own temporal context to a Messiah yet to come. As specific figural persons and events situated within a larger providential nexus, their historical meanings also share in the entire cosmos of meaning at work in the Old Testament history of creation and Israel.[65] Neither do biblical figures primarily serve as witnesses to the inspired consciousness at work in authorial intention, apart from God's providential ordering of creation and history. Rather, they bear witness to a production of

62. See Ephraim Radner, *Hope among the Fragments: The Broken Church and Its Engagement of Scripture* (Grand Rapids: Brazos, 2004), 13.

63. In his description of Calvin's approach to figural reading, Frei notes that for Calvin, "figural meaning is a part of the specific historical context *in which the figure arises*, and not a pattern retrospectively applied to the earlier context from the vantage point of a later situation" (Frei, *Eclipse of Biblical Narrative*, 192, emphasis added). For Calvin, figural reading cannot be separated from the historical dimension inherent in Scripture's literal sense.

64. This is a slight reinterpretation or, better, a theological extension of Auerbach's contention that biblical narrative is "fraught with background" that is left unstated or not made visible in the foreground of the text. See Erich Auerbach, *Mimesis: The Representation of Reality in Western Literature* (Princeton: Princeton University Press, 1953), 12. For an account of the way in which this works itself out in the context of scientific discovery and insight, see Steven Johnson, *Where Good Ideas Come From: The Natural History of Innovation* (New York: Riverhead, 2010).

65. Cf. the discussion in Stephen B. Chapman, "Reading the Bible as Witness: Divine Retribution in the Old Testament," *PRSt* 31, no. 2 (2004): 171–75.

meaning that takes place within a providential network of ordered historical realities, which include inspired human intentions but are not simply identical with them. In figural sense-making, God's providential ordering of things is not an inference from authorial intention but its enabling condition. Viewed from this perspective, the way in which biblical figuration constructs meaning shares in the theological impulse toward providential affiliation and association at work in the historical formation of canon.[66]

Like metaphor, biblical figures draw together various levels of meaning and signification.[67] When the theological significance of related persons, events, and situations are gathered from temporally disparate contexts in biblical history, the gravitational pull of a particular biblical figure generates a cosmos of meaning in itself, a world or microcosm of meaning that is at once both theological and historical in its significance.[68] For this reason, while biblical figures and metaphors share a number of properties in common, it is important to recognize that a biblical figure is not a *mere* figure or a *mere* metaphor—that is, something we like to think of as a literary device or literary fiction. Although *figure* may be used in this sense, and literary fictions and devices of various kinds may be found in Scripture, these uses of the term are not in view in this book or, for that matter, the primary sense in which the early church interpreted *figure*. Rather, figure is a historical reality whose original integrity and sense is rooted in a providentially constructed history, the theological significance of which is mediated in and through Scripture's literal sense. Moreover, because metaphor typically depends upon an analogy with a natural or historical reality that enables metaphor to perform its function, it is best to understand metaphor as reality-depicting, rather than a literary fiction or device without any traction in history.

In this book, the meaning and theological function of figure and metaphor will be broadly interchangeable with other words such as *allegory*. Because these terms and others like them (e.g., *trope*) typically render a reality in terms of something other than themselves, and since all of them depend upon natural and historical meanings to do so, literary terms like *figure, metaphor,*

---

66. See Christopher R. Seitz, *Prophecy and Hermeneutics: Toward a New Introduction to the Prophets* (Grand Rapids: Baker Academic, 2007); Christopher R. Seitz, *The Goodly Fellowship of the Prophets: The Achievement of Association in Canon Formation* (Grand Rapids: Baker Academic, 2009).

67. William P. Brown, *Seeing the Psalms: A Theology of Metaphor* (Louisville: Westminster John Knox, 2002), 8.

68. Biblical figures such as Adam and David function in terms of what Paul Beauchamp would call *l'homme-récit*—that is, a specific individual in whose person the story of a people is carried. Paul Beauchamp, *L'un et l'autre Testament Tome 2: Accomplir les Écritures* (Paris: Seuil, 1990), 397.

allegory, and *trope* will be treated as roughly synonymous modes of theological other-speaking in Scripture. Thus we may variously speak of Scripture's theological sense in terms of its literal sense, grammatical sense, figural sense, allegorical sense, and metaphorical or tropical sense.[69] Similarly, when we speak of figural sense, figural exegesis, or figural reading in this book, we will not be drawing a sharp distinction between these terms and allegorical sense, allegorical exegesis, or allegorical reading. Just as allegory in the broad sense serves as an umbrella term for Scripture's theological senses, so also may figure.[70] Scripture's figural and allegorical senses are interchangeable,[71] because the world-enclosing, explanatory power of both is rooted in the fact that Scripture truly is a book about God and not simply history. Properly understood, figural reading and allegorical reading are modes of reading rooted in Scripture's literal sense that seek to render its theological sense.[72]

The Place of the Literal Sense in Figural Reading

A student once approached Brevard Childs to ask his opinion of Bernhard Anderson's bestselling book *The Living World of the Old Testament*, a highly popular introduction in its day that passed through four editions. Childs's witty response to the student's inquiry was to say, "It's better than the Bible." The anecdote serves to remind us that a popular approach or paradigm for

69. Scripture's *tropical* sense should not be confused with its *tropological* sense. The former is used for the metaphorical sense that is, when a word's ordinary and natural sense is "troped" from that sense into another sense (e.g., the *arm* of God). The latter often is rendered by making use of a metaphor or trope but is not identical with the metaphorical sense per se. Rather, *tropological* is typically used by the early church to speak of Scripture's moral or ethical sense, without necessarily making use of metaphor or trope.

70. This way of understanding the relation between figural reading and allegorical reading of Scripture goes back at least as far as Augustine, for whom the Latin noun *allegoria* was a comprehensive term for figural interpretation. See Preus, *From Shadow to Promise*, 14n17.

71. See Dawson, *Christian Figural Reading*, 15. Because of the modern equation of allegorical readings of Scripture with non-historical modes of reading, Dawson prefers to speak of figural rather than allegorical reading, while at the same time recognizing that this modern equation is misguided. To preserve the historical integrity of figural (and allegorical) modes of reading, he suggests that "figural" reading should be distinguished from the "figurative" or non-historical reading.

72. For the difficulties involved in distinguishing allegory from typology, see Martens, "Revisiting the Allegory/Typology Distinction," 283–317. Although Greek words like τυπος are found in Scripture (1 Cor. 10:6, 11), it was not until the nineteenth century that the term *typology* began to appear in English usage (300n66). The movement to distinguish typology from allegory in the mid-twentieth century was an attempt to translate the vertical nature of *theological* other-speaking in allegory and figure into a horizontal form of *historical* other-speaking, thereby rendering biblical figures safe for public consumption by modern biblical interpreters, both evangelical and mainline in their ecclesial orientation.

interpreting the Bible can easily replace the Bible itself. In like fashion, a host of interpretive categories and paradigms on offer in our day attempt to provide totalizing ways of construing Scripture's literal sense—for example, salvation history, narrative, story, drama, intertextuality, as well as prominent theological themes such as law-gospel, covenant, kingdom, and eschatology. These interpretive categories and theological themes are often useful in pedagogical contexts where convenient ways of summarizing Scripture's message are needed; and the point here is not to gainsay their usage in every context. When it comes to the practice of biblical interpretation, however, these categories can easily exercise a reductive pressure upon Scripture's own presentation and verbal profile, generating a canon within the canon that effectively replaces the biblical canon itself.

Although hermeneutical and theological differences exist between this book's approach to figural exegesis and the literary movement known as New Criticism, wariness with respect to the interpretive impact of totalizing categories upon Scripture's literal sense overlaps to some extent with New Criticism's doctrine of "the heresy of paraphrase." This interpretive strategy replaces the words of literary texts as the object of interpretation with paraphrases and plot summaries.[73] In recent years especially, reaction to historical criticism's atomistic reading practices have helped foster the rise of postcritical modes for reading that stress the importance of narrative and story,[74] both for how Scripture's literal sense is constructed and for how it delivers meaning to its readers.[75] But even comparatively helpful genre categories such as story, narrative, and metanarrative can be used to override Scripture's literal

73. See, for example, the discussion in chap. 11 of Cleanth Brooks's book *The Well Wrought Urn: Studies in the Structure of Poetry* (New York: Harcourt, Brace, 1947). In addition to other concerns, this is one reason why the rule of faith should not be directly identified with plot summaries, though such summaries may indeed give expression to theological judgments that have been exegetically authorized by the literal sense. On the *regula fidei* as plot summary, see Paul M. Blowers, "The *Regula Fidei* and the Narrative Character of Early Christian Faith," *ProEccl* 6 (1997): 199–228.

74. For a helpful discussion of the potential that "story" exegesis has for replacing Scripture's theological referent or subject matter with a mode of reading, see Francesca Murphy, *God Is Not a Story: Realism Revisited* (Oxford: Oxford University Press, 2007).

75. See Frei, *Eclipse of Biblical Narrative*; George Lindbeck, *The Nature of Doctrine: Religion and Theology in a Postliberal Age* (Louisville: Westminster John Knox, 1984). On the differences between a canonical approach to Scripture and recent forms of narrative ontology, see Brevard S. Childs, "Excursus III: The Canonical Approach and the 'New Yale Theology,'" in *New Testament as Canon: An Introduction* (Philadelphia: Fortress, 1985), 541–46; cf. also Brevard S. Childs, *The Church's Guide for Reading Paul: The Canonical Shaping of the Pauline Corpus* (Grand Rapids: Eerdmans, 2008), 35, 60. For an attempt to acquit Frei of at least some of Childs's legitimate concerns, see Don Collett, "Review Essay of Daniel R. Driver's *Brevard Childs, Biblical Theologian for the Church's One Bible*," *ProEccl* 23, no. 1 (2014): 99–112.

sense or "the way the words go" in the text.[76] Viewed in this light, it is not difficult to grasp why the heresy of paraphrase and the schematic categories just mentioned tend to discourage the close reading of biblical texts,[77] and in at least some cases actually pose a real threat to our ability to hear Scripture on its own terms, according to its own canonical indices and presentation.

For this reason figural reading stresses the hermeneutical primacy of the canon's own construal of the literal sense over against potential substitutes.[78] A proper focus on the Bible's literal sense in figural exegesis allows us to retain the primacy of Scripture's own interpretive matrix for rendering its historical meaning according to the way the words go in the text, thereby preserving the circumstances of the letter (*salva circumstantia litterae*). Taking our cue from Aquinas, therefore, we may say that good theological exegesis seeks to "save the circumstances of the letter" by preserving the way the words run in the text. The touchstone for figural exegesis has always been and must continue to be Scripture's literal-historical sense, lest our interpretive categories become a substitute for the literal sense itself. Scripture's literal sense is the bearer of God's providential ordering of things, and this is ultimately why its figural sense remains accountable to its literal sense. The literal sense provides our mode of access to Scripture's figural-providential order, as well as its condition of understanding. Creation and providence enable the figural ordering of time, but the literal sense enables our understanding of that order.

Arguably, this also helps avoid the reductionism that often accompanies paradigm-driven approaches to reading Scripture, and this is a significant

76. The phrase represents David Yeago's translation (following Bruce Marshall) of the Latin phrase *salva circumstantia litterae* in Aquinas's *De potentia Dei.*

77. The close reading of texts promoted by New Criticism is aptly summarized by Paul de Man's description of a rule for reading texts promoted by the American literary critic Reuben Brower, who taught at both Amherst and Harvard: "Students, as they began to write on the writings of others, were not to say anything that was not derived from the text they were considering. They were not to make any statements that they could not support by a specific use of language that actually occurred in the text. They were asked, in other words, to begin by reading texts closely as texts and not to move at once into the general context of human experience or history." De Man goes on to note that this "rule for reading" effectively prevented students from hiding their "non-understanding" of a text "behind the screen of received ideas that often passes, in literary instruction, for humanistic knowledge. This very simple rule, surprisingly enough, had far-reaching didactic consequences." He notes that he had "never known a course by which students were so transformed" (!). Paul de Man, "The Return to Philology," in *The Resistance to Theory* (Minneapolis: University of Minnesota Press, 1986), 23.

78. "To work from the final form is to resist any method which seeks critically to shift the canonical ordering. Such an exegetical move occurs whenever an overarching category such as *Heilsgeschichte* subordinates the peculiar canonical profile, or a historical critical reconstruction attempts to refocus the picture according to its own standards of aesthetics or historical accuracy." Brevard S. Childs, *Introduction to the Old Testament as Scripture* (Philadelphia: Fortress, 1979), 77.

benefit. For insofar as our interpretive categories do not allow the whole of Scripture to inform our reading, there is a real possibility that an abridged or downsized version of Scripture will take the place of Scripture itself in our understanding of it. Moreover, placing an interpretive concept or theme at Scripture's center results in another form of reductionism—namely, one that displaces the person and work of Jesus Christ, whose life stands at the historical center of both testaments. The gospel and the new covenant are not abstract realities with a life of their own but find their center and meaning in Christ's person and work. Substituting an interpretive category or theme for the person of Jesus Christ subtly displaces the proper historical locus of Scripture's unifying reality, or *hypothesis*, ultimately reducing the gospel of Jesus Christ to a concept or theme. This may work for a while, but no interpretive category or theological concept can serve as a substitute for the person and work of Jesus Christ. Such categories and concepts cannot carry the freight required to fully support a coherent reading of Scripture, and making them do too much work inevitably leads to their collapse and replacement by something else.

Adjudicating exegetical issues in figural reading presupposes a genre judgment about the nature of Scripture, especially its character as a providential construction, and thus the word *figure* also functions as an interpretive category in biblical interpretation. The danger is always present that overarching appeals to the interpretive contexts of providence and figure may also become substitutes for exegesis and close attention to Scripture's own construal of history. However, since all readers of Scripture work with genre judgments regarding Scripture's nature, its subject matter, and rules for relating these realities, the solution is not to be found in adopting some version or variant of the myth of "presuppositionless exegesis." All readers of Scripture work with a set of interpretive presuppositions and theological judgments. And one can mount a persuasive argument for the claim that far from inhibiting the act of interpretation, such presuppositions constitute the enabling condition for interpretation.[79] The proper approach to reading Scripture does not turn on our ability to escape our assumptions about its nature and the rules for reading by which we access its meaning. Rather, the question is whether these assumptions and rules do justice to what Scripture is about (i.e., its subject matter). The concern to prevent Scripture's own construal of its subject matter from being folded into overarching interpretive categories, or overloading the

---

79. See the extended arguments for this in Hans-Georg Gadamer, *Truth and Method*, 2nd rev. ed., trans. J. Weinsheimer and D. Marshall (London: Continuum, 2006; originally published in 1989), 278–306.

interpretive function of genre,[80] helps clarify why it is best to follow the lead of the church's exegetical tradition in privileging Scripture's literal sense as the touchstone for figural reading. Building an approach to Scripture founded upon its own literary structure and verbal sense helps keep biblical interpreters accountable to Scripture's own way of structuring history. It also serves as a continuing reminder that appeals to totalizing interpretive categories cannot serve as a substitute for exegesis and the historical questions inevitably raised by exegesis.[81]

Figural Reading and the Rule of Faith

The Bible's figural sense is both mandated and generated by a particular ontological vision of history inherent in Scripture's own self-witness, a vision within which Scripture's literal sense is fully located. Stated differently, Scripture's figural sense is a natural and integral extension of Scripture's *scope*, which includes biblical texts as well as the particular theological reality who evoked the witness of Scripture in the first place—namely, the triune God speaking in Christ by the Spirit. It is the triune God (*res*) who lays hold of us through the words of the text (*verba*). This is why the act of reading Scripture exerts a theological pressure upon us, inevitably moving us to reflect upon the particular character of the theological reality that best fits Scripture's verbal profile and brings out its coherence by generating "new habits of reference."[82] This *verba-res* relationship not only epitomizes the scope of Scripture but also lies at the heart of the logic by which its figural sense operates.[83] The phrase

80. Mike Floyd helpfully makes the point that appeals to genre should not be allowed to do too much work but should rather function as initial starting points rather than endpoints: "Genre *analysis* is therefore necessary whether or not the genre of a text is explicitly named in its title, because the naming is not an end in itself. Even if Shakespeare tells us, for example, that *Hamlet* is a tragedy, this fact alone will not deepen our understanding of the drama. The name of the genre is but a point of entry into the process of identifying the narrative patterns that inform this play's dramatic structure" (Floyd, "The מַשָּׂא [*Maśśā'*] as a Type of Prophetic Book," *JBL* 121, no. 3 [2002]: 407, emphasis added). When forming genre judgments about the character of Scripture, commitment to the primacy of its own structure and function calls for willingness on our part "to modify any general theory of literary value in order to do justice to the oddities of this particular text." Kathryn Tanner, "Scripture as Popular Text," *MT* 14, no. 2 (1998): 294.

81. See further the discussion in Seitz, *Elder Testament*, 71–84.

82. I am indebted to David Yeago for calling my attention to this phrase in Paul R. Kolbet's work *Augustine and the Cure of Souls: Revising a Classical Ideal* (Notre Dame, IN: University of Notre Dame Press, 2010), 150. The phrase occurs in Kolbet's summary of Augustine's *De doctrina Christiana*.

83. Augustine's semiotics was built upon a referential theory of theological meaning in which the words of Scripture functioned as linguistic signs (*signa*) that both signify *and* disclose

itself is exegetical-theological shorthand comprising the words of the biblical text, their theological subject matter or referent, and the grammar or rule for reading that properly relates both of them. Traditionally styled the *regula fidei*, the rule of faith is an exegetically authorized theological context for reading Scripture, derived in the first instance from reading Israel's scriptures in light of the risen Christ. As an exegetically grounded theological judgment concerning the unifying reality, or *hypothesis*, of Israel's scriptures, it functions as a rule for relating Scripture to its theological subject matter.[84] Because Scripture's external *res* (the triune God) gave birth to its inner *res*, a coherence or unity already exists, objectively speaking, between Scripture's literal sense and its theological referent. It is not the role of the rule to generate this coherence but to uncover it in conversation with the literal sense.

Because of the integral relationship between the words of Scripture and the triune Lord who evoked those words, attempts to read Scripture in terms of some other subject matter or rule of faith ultimately foreclose the possibility of coming to terms with what Scripture is actually talking *about*. Although we may learn many things about Scripture's history—including its cultural, social, and political contexts—in the end the reality it speaks of will remain a puzzle to us. For example, a hymnbook may be read to study the history of hymnody, just as a cookbook may be read to study the culinary habits of a particular people. We may read a hymnbook or a cookbook in these ways, but we generally have no trouble understanding that hymnbooks and cookbooks were not written for this purpose.[85] If we read any book, and most especially Scripture, "against the grain" in a way that is contrary to its aim, intention, or purpose (or what the fathers called its *skopos*), we will not be able to enter into its mind (*dianoia*) and come to terms with its overall unity and purpose. Reading Scripture as though it were merely a historical exercise not only fails to do justice to its theological *res* and subject matter but also ignores the purpose for which Scripture was given—namely, to serve as the inspired instrument of the triune God's self-disclosure in Christ by the Spirit. To discern the mind of Scripture (*dianoia*) one must read it according

---

theological realities (*res*). The relation between historical and theological meaning encapsulated in the *verba-res* relationship has thus been variously stated in terms of *signum* and *res*, word and thing, as well as the sacramental language of sign and thing signified (*signum et res significatas*). The close relation between biblical and sacramental accounts of sense-making arises from the fact that in Scripture, both word and sacrament are means of grace.

84. See Christopher R. Seitz, *The Character of Christian Scripture: The Significance of a Two-Testament Bible* (Grand Rapids: Baker Academic, 2011), 191–203.

85. Cf. the illuminating remarks of Christopher R. Seitz, "Review of Richard Bauckham's *God Crucified: Monotheism and Christology in the New Testament*," *IJST* 2, no. 1 (2000): 112–13.

to its purpose (*skopos*). This means that our approach to reading Scripture must be congruent with the theological nature of its subject matter and the purpose for which it was given. It is this relationship that the rule as a theological context for reading Scripture seeks to exegetically establish and ensure.

A recurring complaint about the revival of figural reading in our time, especially its interest in the rule of faith, is that as an interpretive enterprise, it is all theology and little or no exegesis. To be sure, there are grounds for concern. When it comes to contemporary suspicion on the part of biblical scholars concerning the rule of faith, at least part of the problem stems from the fact that the rule is not a fixed formula.[86] Indeed, it is precisely this underdetermined character of the rule that invites its exploitation by approaches that tend to weaken its literal-exegetical aspect by grounding it in either the interpretive categories derived from "story,"[87] the communal use of Scripture,[88] or the ecclesial tradition per se.[89] On the other hand, for those who rightly value the importance of figural imagination in exegesis, the rule can sometimes work in tandem with undisciplined and unbridled uses of human imagination, serving as a theological warrant for readers to override Scripture's literal sense with their own agendas. This is why a discussion of the proper role of the literal sense in relation to figural and ruled readings of Scripture is important, though it is not to suggest, of course, that one can provide an account that answers every historical difficulty associated with that relation. Providing a workable account of the literal sense need not fully quantify such issues, and in any case it is highly doubtful whether anyone in the church's history succeeded in doing so, as Childs's essay reminds us. Nevertheless some account must be given, for the church's theological stance rendered by the rule of faith is founded on this sense.

Conclusion

The importance of coming to terms with the nature of Scripture's literal sense for figural reading of the Old Testament should now be clear, especially when we reckon with the fact that the capacity of the literal sense to properly

---

86. Seitz, *Character of Christian Scripture*, 195.

87. Blowers, "*Regula Fidei* and the Narrative Character of Early Christian Faith," 199–228.

88. Hans Frei, "The 'Literal Reading' of Biblical Narrative in the Christian Tradition: Does It Stretch or Break?," in *The Bible and the Narrative Tradition*, ed. F. McConnell (Oxford: Oxford University Press, 1986), 36–77.

89. Craig Allert, *A High View of Scripture? The Authority of the Bible and the Formation of the New Testament Canon* (Grand Rapids: Baker Academic, 2007), 67–86, 173–76.

embrace figural senses discloses its power to speak a word beyond its own time and place in history. The Bible not only speaks figurally through its literal sense but also *must* speak figurally—not simply because Christians wish it to do so but because its subject matter is theological. Stated more plainly, the Bible must speak figurally because it is a book *about* God. Though it often renders its theological meaning in historically specific contexts, what the text means can never be delimited by those contexts alone because of the eternal nature and voice of the triune LORD who speaks in and through them. Figural reading is simply the recognition that biblical words and things have representative significance, not only for their own day but also for what lies in the past and what is yet to come in the future. Figural reading, like biblical prophecy, offers a totalizing vision of future, past, and present. Indeed, it swallows up all historical reality by enclosing all historical worlds within the scope of its theological vision. At the end of the day, figural reading is simply the historical extension of a theological judgment authorized by Scripture's own self-witness—namely, that the Bible is a book about God. It is not an imposition on Scripture but a consequence of the Bible's relation to its theological *res*, by which it speaks a word beyond its own day to enclose and position ours. To be sure, the rejection of Scripture's figural sense also means the rejection of interpretive methods based upon that sense, but the loss of figural reading is not merely the loss of a technique.[90] It also means our dislocation and disorientation in time, because it severs the link between the Bible and its theological referent, or word (*verbum*) and thing (*res*), which underwrites the Bible's world-enclosing power. The vertical linkage between Scripture and the triune LORD of history manifests itself in the figural sense, bearing witness to the Bible's ability to unify disparate historical contexts and speak in and through time.

Childs's 1977 essay on the literal sense formed the entry point into our discussion. Among the more important observations he makes is that the church's exegetical tradition teaches that Scripture's figural senses must be accountable to its literal sense. This chapter has attempted to clarify what is in view when we talk about Scripture's literal sense and its relation to the figural sense. Because these two modes for meaning-making are integral to the providential construction of biblical sense or biblical poetics, an adequate description of biblical sense-making must provide an account of both. Therefore it is not sufficient to mount a case for the continuing significance of human authorship and authorial intention for our understanding of the literal

---

90. Christopher R. Seitz, *Figured Out: Typology and Providence in Christian Scripture* (Louisville: Westminster John Knox, 2001), viii.

sense, over against its postmodern detractors.[91] While authorial modes for the construction of meaning in Scripture remain important, they cannot bear the full burden of biblical sense-making, simply because the providential affiliation of disparate historical contexts at work in the formation of Scripture locates the efficacy of those intentions within a figural ordering of time. For this reason it would be a mistake to *identify* the canonical intentionality that produced Scripture with the basic level of intentionality at work in authorial discourse or to isolate that level from figural modes of discourse.

Rightly proportioned and properly understood, such a move need not instrumentalize the role of human agency and intention in the production of biblical meaning, as though authorial intention were a mere means to an end without any distinctive contribution of its own to make toward the shaping of figural or theological meaning. This produces a species of textual "occasionalism" that reduces authorial intention to a mere placeholder or incidental occasion for constructing the figural-providential ordering of time in Scripture.[92] On this account, human speech per se does not participate in the truth of things; it serves as a sort of dispensable ladder that helps one get there.[93] Striking the right balance between authorial and figural modes of sense-making in Scripture is therefore crucial, albeit fraught with difficulty due

91. For a defense of authorial intention within the framework of speech-act theory, see Kevin J. Vanhoozer, *Is There a Meaning in This Text? The Bible, the Reader, and the Morality of Literary Knowledge* (Grand Rapids: Zondervan, 1998).

92. Occasionalism was a seventeenth-century attempt to provide a causal account of the interaction between mind and body, which took place within the larger context of battles over the role and meaning of "secondary causation" in providence and anthropology. In its theological form, occasionalism argued that our thoughts are able to "cause" bodily actions because our thoughts provide the "occasion" for God to act upon our bodies, thereby causing them to respond to our mental intentions. So defined, occasionalism effectively absorbs human agency (secondary causality) into divine agency (primary causality). This contrasts with the account of divine and human agency found in the Reformed notion of *concursus*, which argues that the integrity of creaturely causality is established, rather than absorbed or erased, by the sovereignty of divine agency. For a compact statement of the Reformed doctrine of *concursus*, see *The Westminster Confession of Faith* III.1: "God from all eternity, did, by the most wise and holy counsel of His own will, freely, and unchangeably ordain whatsoever comes to pass; yet so, as thereby neither is God the author of sin, nor is violence offered to the will of the creatures; nor is the liberty or contingency of second causes taken away, but rather established." For a discussion of Malebranche's "occasionalist" theory of causation, see Steven Nadler, "Malebranche on Causation," in *The Cambridge Companion to Malebranche*, ed. Steven Nadler (Cambridge: Cambridge University Press, 2000), 112–38; cf. also the discussion of Malebranche in R. S. Woolhouse, *Descartes, Spinoza, and Leibniz: The Concept of Substance in Seventeenth Century Metaphysics* (New York: Routledge, 1993).

93. For a modified account of occasionalism that seeks to preserve the immediacy of God's presence in creation and figural accounts of the literal sense, while at the same time avoiding the problem of determinism, see Radner, *Time and the Word*, 87–91, 98–99, esp. his comments on p. 91.

to continuing theological debates over the relation between divine providence and human agency. At various periods in history, the church has attempted to recover the primacy of the literal sense for accessing Scripture's theological sense by means of various strategies, not all helpful. Even in the case of useful reforms, the gains have often been short lived, with new imbalances arising in their wake. These programs for reform serve to illustrate that the fortunes of figural reading are bound up with the church's understanding of the relation between Scripture's literal and theological sense. With these concluding observations the first section of the book now comes to a close. In part 2 I will discuss an early thirteenth-century attempt to reform abuses of the figural sense by distinguishing metaphor from theological allegory, followed by a series of exegetical excurses. Part 3 will then close matters by offering a critical assessment of the reforms of the Reformation and modernity.

Part 2
Exegesis

3

Figural Reading, Metaphor, and Theological Exegesis

Is figural reading of the Old Testament an approach that has a place in the world of late modern exegesis, or is it a hopeless anachronism whose only contribution is to serve as an example of what *not* to do in biblical interpretation? Here it will be helpful to offer a few examples of figural reading drawn from Old Testament "Wisdom Literature" and Prophecy. Doing so will serve to illustrate the impact of one's account of figure and metaphor upon the interpretation of Scripture.[1] In order to further contextualize the issues in terms of the church's struggle with the place and role of Scripture's figural sense, I will begin by revisiting a debate over the theological status of metaphor in thirteenth-century scholasticism. Then I will turn to readings of the figure of Wisdom in Job 28 and Proverbs 8,[2] followed by a reflection on the significance of Hosea 1:2 for reading the Book of the Twelve. The goal of these readings will not be refuting alternatives so much as exploring the potential figural reading has for revitalizing theological exegesis in our time, in conversation with the church's continuing tradition.

Reforming the Literal Sense: Metaphor and Allegory

In the Augustinian abbey of St. Victor in twelfth-century northern France, a number of monks grew concerned over the rising tide of speculative excess

---

1. On the status of "Wisdom Literature" as a questionable interpretive category in the Old Testament, see Mark Sneed, "Is the 'Wisdom Tradition' a Tradition?," *CBQ* 73, no. 1 (2011): 53–71.

2. In this book the English gloss for the Hebrew word חכמה will be capitalized when referring to divine Wisdom, while lowercase spellings will typically refer to human wisdom, traditional wisdom, or wisdom in general.

in the realm of biblical interpretation. The source of the excess was traced back to the detachment of Scripture's figural senses (*allegoria facti*) from its literal sense (*allegoria verbi*), a concern prominently featured in Hugh of St. Victor's work, *The Didascalicon*.[3] The leading cause of this disintegration was located in the claim that speculative forms of monastic exegesis were confusing metaphor with Scripture's figural or allegorical sense. According to one account, Hugh of St. Victor attributes "the widespread tendency to allegorize arbitrarily and without constraint [to] the collapsing of the merely figurative into the allegorical: every time you spot a scriptural metaphor you have got an allegory; that seems to be the practice of many."[4] It is important to recognize that Victorine attempts to clearly distinguish metaphor from theological allegory arose as a reaction to certain abuses of the allegorical sense said to be present in the "spiritualizing" exegesis of the monasteries. They were also motivated in part by the perceived need to distinguish the theological meanings rendered by Scripture's figural senses from the merely historical meanings rendered by metaphor in secular poetry. The Victorine argument basically runs as follows: While the metaphorical sense is always a legitimate part of Scripture's literal or textual sense, its allegorical or figural sense may or may not be a legitimate part of that sense, depending upon whether one is attempting to move from the literal sense to the allegorical sense (a legitimate move) or from the metaphorical sense to the allegorical sense (an illegitimate move).

Viewed from the later perspective on biblical interpretation made possible by the various tools on offer in modern historical method, it is tempting to regard this debate as yet another example of a tendency in medieval hermeneutics to multiply distinctions to the point of abstraction. The attempt to reform the literal sense by setting up a fixed theological boundary between metaphor and allegory would then be a matter of medieval excess stranded in an interesting but irrelevant piece of arcane history. Interacting with this reading of metaphor is worthwhile, however, because the poetry of Israel's Psalter and the witness of her prophets are filled with metaphors. If the former account of metaphor is right, then not only scriptural metaphors but vast stretches of Old Testament poetry have no theological significance as such.

3. For a useful English translation with introduction and notes, based upon the critical Latin edition of C. H. Buttimer, see Hugh of St. Victor, *"The Didascalicon" of Hugh of St. Victor: A Medieval Guide to the Arts*, trans. Jeremy Taylor (New York: Columbia University Press, 1961); for an interesting recent commentary, see Ivan Illich, *In the Vineyard of the Text: A Commentary to Hugh's "Didascalicon"* (Chicago: University of Chicago Press, 1993).

4. See Denys Turner, "Allegory in Late Christian Antiquity," in *The Cambridge Companion to Allegory*, ed. Rita Copeland and Peter T. Struck (Cambridge: Cambridge University Press, 2010), 79.

This has rather serious consequences for the theological use of metaphor in the Bible, not to mention the way it conflicts with modern accounts of metaphor as "reality-depicting," rather than a bare literary trope primarily aimed at producing aesthetic enjoyment and pleasure.[5] This account of metaphor has been styled the "ornamental" view of metaphor.[6] It regards the use of metaphor as a matter of verbal decoration and dress rather than a reality-disclosing literary vehicle that expands our knowledge of reality and enlarges our vision of the world. Moreover, as modern literary theorists have taught us, metaphor has the power to bring together various levels of signification.[7] Given this integrative force and function, the attempt to identify metaphor with literal signification over against its figural or allegorical signification is questionable at best.

Consider the argument that the move from biblical metaphor to theological construction is illegitimate, inevitably leading to speculative abuse of Scripture's figural or allegorical sense. This claim finds its basis in a particular reading of the distinction between metaphor and allegory in the account of double signification Hugh and others inherited from Augustine, which account Aquinas clarifies and refines in his *Summa Theologiae* I.1.10. The Victorine interpretation of this distinction rests upon the claim that metaphor is a semantic property of *words*, properly belonging to first-order signification (verbal signification). Allegory, however, is a semantic property of historically mediated theological *things*, properly belonging to second-order signification (figural signification).[8] On this reading, first-order signification describes the way in which biblical words signify historical realities in a given historical context, while second-order signification describes the figural relationships

---

5. See Janet Soskice, *Metaphor and Religious Language* (Oxford: Clarendon, 1985); cf. also Brian C. Howell, *In the Eyes of God: A Metaphorical Approach to Biblical Anthropomorphic Language* (Cambridge: James Clark, 2014).

6. See William P. Brown, *Seeing the Psalms: A Theology of Metaphor* (Louisville: Westminster John Knox, 2002), 1–14, esp. 5.

7. See W. Brown, *Seeing the Psalms*, 8.

8. See the discussion in Turner, "Allegory in Late Christian Antiquity," 78–79. For a different take on the issue, see the comparison of Hugh's account of metaphor with that of Aquinas in Christopher Ocker, *Biblical Poetics before Humanism and Reformation* (Cambridge: Cambridge University Press, 2002), 34–43. Ocker more sharply distinguishes the Victorine account of metaphor from that of Aquinas and apparently disagrees with the implicit assumption in Turner's thesis that metaphor for Aquinas does not function as a vehicle for the disclosure of theological truth. Ocker also suggests that Aquinas was much closer to the late medieval tendency to blur any sharp distinctions between verbal and natural signification or between the literal sense and the spiritual sense (6–7). Indeed, for Aquinas the literal sense *is* the spiritual sense, anticipating Calvin's later preference for speaking of these two senses in terms of the one true meaning of the text (*unus verus scripturae sensus*), without the need to appeal to either the fourfold sense or a theory of double signification.

between historical things, signifying theological realities. From this distinction it follows that metaphorical sense-making remains within the sphere of literal-historical meaning—something it shares in common with secular poetry—while allegory is a non-literal meaning that properly operates within the realm of theological meaning.[9]

At least one recent interpreter of Aquinas regards this rigid distinction as the theological basis for Aquinas's alleged refusal "to admit poets into the company of allegorists in the properly theological sense."[10] Aquinas thus becomes a crypto-Platonist who banishes poets from the Republic of enlightened theologians, only to have them later readmitted as the result of Dante's erosion of the clear distinction Aquinas made between metaphor and figure. According to this line of thought, Dante is thus guilty of confusing things that differ, and his poetic theology represents "a retrograde step" in the fall from Aquinas that set in sometime after the late thirteenth century. On this reading, the use of metaphor in poetry, including scriptural poetry, is to be clearly distinguished from the theological truth brokered by figure and allegory, such that "for Thomas, poetry, even scriptural poetry, as such has no exegetical or spiritual significance."[11] In the end this sets up a rather sharp distinction between the historical meaning of biblical poetry and Scripture's theological meaning, a distinction Aquinas would have found impossible.

When Scripture's literal sense renders its theological sense in conjunction with the figural or allegorical sense, it may also be said to be making an analogical use of language. For example, when we speak of "the arm of God," we make use of the natural analogy that exists between a human arm and human power in order to metaphorically render the theological reality of God's power. In the vineyard allegory of Isaiah 5:1–7 the writer makes use of the natural analogy that exists between a barren vineyard and unproductive land to depict Israel as spiritually barren and unfruitful. Here the barren vineyard functions as a metaphor for the spiritually unproductive Israel of Isaiah's day. If there is a

9. The concern behind the policing of this sharp distinction between metaphor and theological allegory was also bound up with an attempt to preserve a privileged place in theological science for Scripture's figural or allegorical sense, over against the use of metaphor in the secular sciences.

10. See Turner, "Allegory in Late Christian Antiquity," 82.

11. See Turner, "Allegory in Late Christian Antiquity," 81–82. Rather than suggesting that Dante represents a step backward vis-à-vis Aquinas's account of metaphor, it would be more accurate to suggest that Dante extends Aquinas's theological account of metaphor to secular poetry, in which metaphor is a subset of allegory, as it is in rhetorical tradition. In his study of allegory in the medieval period, C. S. Lewis reflects this tradition when he suggests that "every metaphor is an allegory in little." C. S. Lewis, *The Allegory of Love: A Study in Medieval Tradition* (Oxford: Clarendon, 1936; repr., Cambridge: Cambridge University Press, 2013), 76.

distinction to be made between metaphor and allegory in these two examples, one might say that the vineyard allegory is an *extended* metaphor because it builds a short story around the metaphor of the vineyard, while "the arm of God" example is a more abbreviated instance of metaphor.[12] Here we should observe a distinction between metaphor and allegory, but this distinction concerns literary genre rather than a supposed contrast between the ability of metaphor and allegory to disclose theological or spiritual realities. To be sure, the Bible makes use of both analogical and non-analogical forms of language to render its theological meaning, as noted earlier. But if metaphor, like figure and allegory, rests upon the analogical use of biblical language, how can we say metaphor belongs to the literal sense while at the same time arguing that the figural or allegorical sense does not? Augustine wished to emphasize that biblical language is not simply for our pleasure or aesthetic enrichment; for him, it is a means to the end of enjoying God. Unfortunately, this observation inadvertently helped fuel a distinction in later biblical interpretation between the aesthetic function of metaphor in secular poetry and the disclosure of theological truth in Scripture. "Poetic theology" becomes an oxymoron, and the contribution made by biblical poetry to our understanding of Scripture's theological ontology is rendered suspect.

As a strategy for liberating "theological allegory from its confusions with the literary,"[13] this account of metaphor exacts a heavy price. This is because it not only threatens the theological unity of double signification in Aquinas but also evacuates metaphor in biblical poetry of any theological or ontological significance. It effectively severs the linkage between inspired words (*verba*) and theological things (*res*) Aquinas's account relies upon—which account, it should be added, finds its proper home in the theological context of the incarnation and the traditional analogy the fathers draw between Christ's incarnation and biblical language. It is this incarnational analogy that ultimately accounts for the theological unity of double signification in Aquinas's account of literal sense, rather than the apophatic account of human language and history inherent in the allegorical poetics of Plato's cave allegory, the latter of which effectively underwrites the non-biblical notion that poets are not truth-tellers but liars.

The distinction Aquinas draws between metaphor and figure in *Summa Theologiae* I.1.9 is not sharp; it certainly does not underwrite the thesis that

---

12. Although the vineyard metaphor refers to Israel rather than to God, the use of the word *vineyard* as a metaphor for Israel's barrenness is no more "proper" literally speaking than the use of the word *arm* as a metaphor for God's power. Vineyards do not properly refer to people and human arms do not properly refer to the Godhead.

13. See Turner, "Allegory in Late Christian Antiquity," 82.

metaphor is not a literary vehicle, properly speaking, for disclosing theological truth. The use of "less noble bodies" in similitude, metaphor, and
figure serves the practical purpose of making it easier for the unlearned to
grasp the fact that the description is not to be taken literally. But it does not
make the additional point that metaphor fails to disclose theological truth.[14]
Instead, we find Aquinas asserting the Augustinian point that one should
make use of non-metaphorical or non-figural passages that speak on the same
theological topic to clarify the meaning of metaphor, so that the theological
truth it discloses may be properly assessed. In other words, Aquinas does not
attempt to reform the abuse of metaphor by sharply distinguishing it from
Scripture's figural or allegorical senses; he refers biblical interpreters back to
the hermeneutical guidance provided by the literal-historical sense proper.

Thus when Aquinas goes on to argue in *Summa Theologiae* I.1.10 that the
literal sense is not the figure itself but that which the figure signifies—namely,
the theological sense of the reality it renders—it is difficult if not impossible
to avoid the conclusion that for him, metaphors, similitudes, parables, and
figures are all literary tropes used to disclose theological truth in Scripture.[15]
Moreover, while the different tropes discussed in *Summa Theologiae* I.1.9–10
properly belong to Scripture's verbal sense, what they disclose is at the same
time different from the verbal sense. Thus from a theological point of view,
the distinctions between these tropes are relative rather than absolute, and
literary rather than theological in character. They do not lend credence to de-
theologized accounts of metaphor aimed at clearly distinguishing metaphor
from allegory for the sake of reforming the literal sense. Aquinas instead
seeks to address the hermeneutical problems surrounding Scripture's use of
metaphor by encouraging readers to study non-metaphorical passages where
the same theological topic is discussed, in order to properly assess Scripture's
use of biblical metaphors according to the literal sense, especially with respect
to the metaphors' theological content and truth. This is but another way of
making the point that Scripture's extended senses—call them figural, allegorical, metaphorical, or parabolical—have no integrity independent from the

---

14. Aquinas, *Summa Theologiae* I.1.9, reply to objection 3. Whatever else one might say
about the distinction Aquinas draws between metaphor and figure, this section of the *Summa*
makes it clear that it does not turn upon the difference between literal and theological descriptions, respectively, since both metaphor and figure are employed in Scripture to disclose non-
literal or theological realities.

15. While Aquinas does not formally distinguish Scripture's parabolical sense from similitude in *Summa Theologiae* I.1.9, his discussion of parable in *Summa Theologiae* I.1.10 suggests
that its *formal* character is not to be isolated from the theological *function* of similitude, since
similitude serves the same judicial function as that of parable—namely, that of hiding the truth
from the unworthy.

literal sense. It is the literal sense that governs and interprets their meaning and use. For both Aquinas and Augustine, the literal sense provides its own set of controls for properly assessing the theological significance of the metaphorical sense, just as the literal sense also does in the case of figure and allegory.

A far more serious problem with this reading of the distinction between Scripture's metaphorical and figural senses is that it fails to account for the actual exegetical practice of Aquinas and others in the premodern church, most of whom regularly exegete biblical poetry in allegorical modes. Indeed, Aquinas's reading of the wisdom poem in Proverbs 8:22–31 follows the tradition, both before and after Athanasius, by reading that poem as an allegory of Christ's eternal generation. In closing this discussion, we turn to Aquinas's discussion of the metaphors of conception and birth in Proverbs 8:22–31. Let us consider the following passage from the *Summa Theologiae* I.27.2:

> **Reply to Objection 2:** The act of human understanding in ourselves is not the substance itself of the intellect; hence the word which proceeds within us by intelligible operation is not of the same nature as the source whence it proceeds; so the idea of generation cannot be properly and fully applied to it. But the divine act of intelligence is the very substance itself of the one who understands.[16] The Word proceeding therefore proceeds as subsisting in the same nature; and so is properly called begotten, and Son. *Hence Scripture employs terms which denote generation of living things in order to signify the procession of the divine Wisdom, namely, conception and birth; as is declared in the person of the divine Wisdom, "The depths were not as yet, and I was already conceived; before the hills, I was brought forth"* (Prov. 8:24). In our way of understanding we use the word "conception" in order to signify that in the word of our intellect is found the likeness of the thing understood, although there be no identity of nature. (emphasis added)

Aquinas argues that the prima facie meaning of terms like *conception* and *birth* is literally false, because of the ontological difference between human begetting and what it means to speak of Christ as "begotten" Wisdom (Prov. 8:22–24). However, this does not prevent Aquinas from reading the metaphors of conception and birth in this wisdom poem in terms of theological or figural allegory, contra the reforming zeal on the part of some to clearly distinguish metaphor from Scripture's figural-theological sense.

Similarly, in *Summa Contra Gentiles*, book IV, Aquinas engages a certain fourth-century bishop named Photinus and his followers, who denied Christ's divinity while at the same time allowing for his miraculous birth.

---

16. Cf. the discussion in Aquinas, *Summa Theologiae* I.14.4.

Aquinas argues against the notion that begotten Wisdom in Proverbs 8 is a poetic ornament or metaphor to be sharply distinguished from theological allegory. He writes:

> For, when Solomon says: "The depths were not as yet, and I was already conceived" (Prov. 8:24), he makes it clear enough that this generation existed before all bodily things. Hence, it follows that the Son begotten by God received no beginning of being from Mary. To be sure, they endeavored to debase these and other like testimonies by their perverse exposition. These, they said, should be understood after the manner of predestination. . . . But they are refuted by this: Not only in predestination, but in reality as well, He had been before Mary. For after the words of Solomon just quoted this is added: "When He balanced the foundations of the earth: I was with Him forming all things" (Prov. 8:29–30); but if He had been present in predestination only, He would have been able to do nothing. One gets this also from the words of John the Evangelist, for, when he had first set down: "In the beginning was the Word" (by which name the Son is understood as was shown) to keep anyone from taking this as predestination, he adds: "All things were made by Him: and without Him was made nothing" (1:1, 3); and this could not be true if He had not really existed before the world.[17]

Here human conception and birth both function as metaphors disclosing the theological reality of the Son's pre-existence. They are not simply verbal ornaments of the kind envisaged by those who distinguish metaphor from allegory on theological grounds. One might advance the counterargument that while exegetical tradition in the thirteenth century made a clear distinction between metaphor and allegory, it then proceeded to blithely set it aside in exegetical practice.[18] Another option would be to take the exegetical practice of the fathers (including Aquinas) more seriously, which would involve

---

17. *Summa Contra Gentiles* IV.4.11, trans. Charles J. O'Neil (Notre Dame, IN: University of Notre Dame Press, 1975), 45–46. Aquinas speaks here of the Son's eternal generation, not the incarnation. The point to stress, over against certain tendencies in Karl Barth's later writings (as well as Bruce McCormack's), is that the eternal person of the Word has a fully real existence and identity apart from the incarnation, albeit begotten in eternity. For the theological and hermeneutical issues at stake, see Darren O. Sumner, "The Twofold Life of the Word: Karl Barth's Critical Reception of the *Extra Calvinisticum*," *IJST* 15, no. 1 (2013): 42–57, esp. 51: "By grounding Christology in the notion that Jesus Christ (and not the *Logos asarkos*) is the electing God, as well as the elected human, Barth was ready to assign the *Logos* concept a sharply relativized place." Cf. also Don Collett, "The Christomorphic Shaping of Time in Radner's *Time and the Word*," *ProEccl* 27, no. 3 (2018): 287–88; Don Collett, "A Tale of Two Testaments: Childs, Old Testament Torah, and *Heilsgeschichte*," in *The Bible as Christian Scripture: The Work of Brevard S. Childs*, ed. Christopher R. Seitz and Robert C. Kashow (Atlanta: Society of Biblical Literature, 2013), 207n65; Don Collett, "Reading Forward: The Old Testament and Retrospective Stance," *ProEccl* 24, no. 2 (2015): 185n19, 192n35.

18. Cf. the remarks of Turner, "Allegory in Late Christian Antiquity," 81.

rethinking the theory that the tradition from Augustine through Nicholas of Lyre intended to set up a clear distinction between metaphor and theological allegory. Indeed, the resources for this project are already present in Aquinas's own writings.

Metaphor and Theological Disclosure in Job 28 and Proverbs 8

Both Job 28 and Proverbs 8 provide an ontological orientation for wisdom rooted in the unique identity and name of the LORD. By locating wisdom within what has traditionally been called the doctrine of God, these passages provide a theological framework or rule for reading wisdom literature that locates its origin in the LORD alone. Moreover, the poetry in both these texts makes use of architectural figures or metaphors to disclose theological truths and realities inherent in the Old Testament's witness to the unique and "peculiar" oneness of the LORD.[19] The wisdom poem in Proverbs 8:22–31 played a crucial role not only in the Arian controversy of the early fourth century[20] but also in the formulation of the Nicene confession that Christ is "begotten, not made."[21] Its theological function is to ontologically orient the human quest for wisdom in the eternally begotten Wisdom of the LORD. This function is underscored on a literary level by the fact that the poem occupies a central position in the three wisdom speeches found in Proverbs 1–9 (1:20–33; 8:1–36; 9:1–6).[22] In brief, the poem's argument is that wisdom originates in the LORD's begotten Wisdom (8:22), the architect of creation (v. 30) who precedes creation as the archē and agent through whom God brings creation into being (vv. 22–31).

A similar argument is present in the quest for a wise reading of the providence God sends upon Job in the book of Job. Although a number of candidates have been proposed when it comes to identifying the literary genre of

19. On the "peculiar" character of the Old Testament's presentation of divine oneness, see Christopher R. Seitz, "The Trinity in the Old Testament," in *The Oxford Handbook on the Trinity* (Oxford: Oxford University Press, 2011), 28–40.

20. See Jaroslav Pelikan, *The Christian Tradition: A History of the Development of Doctrine*, vol. 1, *The Emergence of the Catholic Tradition, 100–600* (Chicago: University of Chicago Press, 1975), 191–210.

21. In contrast to the early church's perspective on Prov. 8, there are few readers of Scripture in the world of evangelical modernism who would look to it as an exegetical witness to Christ in the Old Testament, let alone correlate its figural semantics with the triunely configured language of the Nicene Creed.

22. On the wisdom speeches in Prov. 1–9, see Bálint Károly Zabán, *The Pillar Function of the Speeches of Wisdom: Proverbs 1:20–33, 8:1–36, and 9:1–6 in the Structural Framework of Proverbs 1–9*, BZAW 429 (Berlin: de Gruyter, 2012).

Job, the book is perhaps best construed as a wisdom conflict,[23] at the center of which stands the wisdom poem of Job 28:1–28. Because the confession in 28:28 forms an *inclusio* with the prologue of Job (1:1, 8; 2:3), Job 28 is generally recognized as the narrative midpoint of the book.[24] The wisdom poem asks about the originating context for the acquisition of human wisdom, as well as how one finds or gains access to it (vv. 12, 20). These two questions are inextricably bound up with one another as two sides of the same coin. The fact that they are found at the book's narrative midpoint is not only significant but also a clue to the chapter's proper theological function in the book as a whole. The chapter orients the acquisition of human wisdom in terms of a particular theological ontology located in the archē and agency of "established" or begotten Wisdom.

How important is a theological account of metaphor for figural reading? Readings of the role of metaphor in Job 28 and Proverbs 8 offer cases in point. In order to probe the ontological significance of architectural figures and metaphors in these two wisdom poems, it will be useful to engage in a closer look at the exegetical semantics and interpretive issues involved in their modern reception. At the same time we should explore alternative readings that connect with the early church's theological instincts on these passages, especially since controversies over the figural character and ontological status of wisdom in both these texts have generated a fair amount of discussion in recent times. The pericopes serve as helpful test cases for illustrating the character of figural reading in the Old Testament, especially in conversation with modern accounts of the theological function of biblical metaphor. In this chapter, the theological context for wisdom set forth in Job 28, especially wisdom's originating context in verses 24–27, will serve as a point of entry to

23. For the many ways in which the genre of the book of Job has been construed, the reader may consult commentaries on the book. These genre judgments span the gamut from "parody" as a form of skeptical wisdom (Katherine Dell) to wisdom dialogue (Carol Newsom). See Katherine Dell, *The Book of Job as Skeptical Literature*, BZAW 197 (Berlin: de Gruyter, 1991), 109–57; cf. Carol Newsom, *The Book of Job: A Contest of Moral Imaginations* (Oxford: Oxford University Press, 2003), 3–31. Because the dialogues in Job 3–31 make it clear that a conflict over the source for a wise reading of Job's providence drives the debate, with the friends offering an ontology of tradition over against the ontology of revelation offered in Job 28 and the Elihu speeches, the genre category of wisdom conflict will be adopted, a category that satisfies Newsom's call for a genre "flexible enough to do justice to the 'multigeneric nature of the book.'" Newsom, *Book of Job*, 8.

24. Although the name Adonai in Job 28:28 appears nowhere else in the book, its alternation with the name Elohim in Job 28:23 clearly links it with the fear of Elohim in the prologue (1:1, 8; 2:3), where Elohim is also used interchangeably with YHWH (1:6–9, 12, 21; 2:1–4, 6–7; cf. also 5:8; 12:9; 38:1, 7). Apart from their possible significance for identifying different historical and literary sources in the book, the final form of Job apparently makes no theological distinction between the names Elohim, Adonai, and YHWH.

reflect on the character of the figure of "established" Wisdom and the relation between metaphor and theological ontology. After this, I will turn to a similar set of issues surrounding the interpretation of the architectural figure for Wisdom in Proverbs 8:30.

Job 28 and the Transcendent Character of Wisdom

The theological function of Job 28 in the book as a whole is closely linked with the question of the chapter's genre and voice. Commentators generally agree that Job 28 serves an orienting function akin to what Proverbs 8 does for the book of Proverbs, locating the source of human and traditional wisdom in the transcendent Wisdom of God. Along with other texts from the wisdom literature of Second Temple Judaism (e.g., Sir. 1; 24; Bar. 3:9–4:4), both chapters are often assigned the genre of "speculative wisdom,"[25] offering "interludes," "intermezzos," or "meditations" on divine Wisdom.[26] The meanings assigned to the Hebrew terms wisdom (ḥokmâ) and understanding (bînâ) in Job 28 is also characteristic of speculative wisdom.[27] In Job 28, the meaning of wisdom is not that of human understanding, skill, prudence, or erudition, such as one finds in non-speculative or non-metaphysical contexts for wisdom in the dialogues of Job (e.g., 4:21; 12:2, 12; 13:5; 15:8; cf. Prov. 4:5–7). The imagery for space and time employed in Job 28 is also characteristic of the genre of other speculative wisdom poems, such as Proverbs 8, with both poems assigning a cosmic scope to space and interpreting temporality in terms of the archē of creation.[28]

Citing Michael Fox's commentary on Proverbs, Carol Newsom suggests that in speculative contexts such as Job 28 and Proverbs 8, divine Wisdom functions as "the perfect and transcendent universal, of which the infinite instances of human wisdom are imperfect images or realizations."[29] Job 28

25. See Newsom, *Book of Job*, 171–72; cf. Katherine Schifferdecker, *Out of the Whirlwind: Creation Theology in Job* (Cambridge, MA: Harvard University Press, 2008), 46–47.

26. See Davis Hankins, "Wisdom as an Immanent Event in Job 28, Not a Transcendent Ideal," *VT* 63, no. 2 (2013): 230–31.

27. See Carol A. Newsom, "Dialogue and Allegorical Hermeneutics," in *Job 28: Cognition in Context*, ed. Ellen van Wolde, BIS (Leiden: Brill, 2003), 300.

28. Newsom, "Dialogue and Allegorical Hermeneutics," in van Wolde, *Job 28*, 300; cf. also Newsom, *Book of Job*, 172: "Both spatial and temporal tropes are used, especially those that span the cosmos (Prov 8:22–31; Job 28:12–14, 20–22; Sir 1:2–4; 24:3–7; Bar 3:29–31)." Cf. Newsom's later remark that from the perspective of the wisdom poem, "critical temporality is the *arche* of creation" (177).

29. Newsom, "Dialogue and Allegorical Hermeneutics," in van Wolde, *Job 28*, 300–301; cf. Newsom, *Book of Job*, 172.

does not speak of the pursuit of human wisdom or the acquisition of traditional wisdom per se. It intends instead transcendent wisdom, and "the poem
makes clear that its interest is in this transcendent dimension of wisdom,
not the meanings of 'skill,' 'prudence,' 'erudition,' etc., which the word may
have in other contexts."[30] Rather, this is Wisdom "in the specialized sense as
wisdom that transcends individual minds."[31] In contrast with other references to wisdom in the dialogues throughout Job, transcendent Wisdom here
functions as the primary interpretive category for creaturely wisdom.[32] Like
Proverbs 8, Job 28 offers theological reflection on wisdom that does not exist
"at the level of the narrative but in the metanarrative,"[33] or at the level of
meta-wisdom. Its distinctive voice or "dialect" generates a "meta-linguistic"
perspective on the dialogues of Job akin to Bakhtin's idea of *heteroglossia*.[34]
Rather than providing an answer to the three friends in the first instance,[35] it
offers instead an orientation on wisdom—that is, an ontology of wisdom—
though the character of that ontology remains a matter of interpretation and
debate. I will argue here that the perspective on wisdom in Job 28 ultimately
renders its distinctive voice not in terms of socio-cultural realities that are
ontologically other than the text but in terms of a theological reality whose
voice and life originate in a world external to or other than the economic
realm of creation and language, while at the same time inhabiting both those
realms as the archē and agent of creation.

   Is the claim that Job is the voice speaking in Job 28 consistent with its
orienting function as a speculative wisdom poem, interlude, intermezzo, or
meditation on wisdom? While the argument that the narrative perspective on
divine Wisdom in Job 28 does not reflect the voice or outlook of Job himself
is plausible, it cannot be said to be compelling.[36] Rather than regard it as an
intrusion or narrative voice-over in the midst of the dialogues, Barth suggests
that it may form a parallel with or amplification of earlier passages in Job's

30. Newsom, "Dialogue and Allegorical Hermeneutics," in van Wolde, *Job 28*, 301.
31. Newsom, *Book of Job*, 176.
32. Newsom, "Dialogue and Allegorical Hermeneutics," in van Wolde, *Job 28*, 301.
33. Newsom, *Book of Job*, 181.
34. The language here is that of Newsom, "Dialogue and Allegorical Hermeneutics," in van
Wolde, *Job 28*, 300, though in keeping with the perspective on figural reading argued for in this
book, I have subjected her *text-text* model of narrative and metanarrative to a reinterpretation
in terms of the *text-res* model shared by the early church and recent canonical approaches such
as those found in the work of Brevard Childs and Christopher Seitz.
35. Schifferdecker, *Out of the Whirlwind*, 47.
36. See the discussion in Alison Lo, *Job 28 as Rhetoric: An Analysis of Job 28 in the Context
of Job 22–31* (Leiden: Brill, 2003), 22–78. Lo notes that Childs, Janzen, Whybray, and Good read
Job 28 as the voice of Job, while Westermann, Andersen, Sawyer, Petersen, Newsom, Hartley,
and Habel consider it to be an "interlude or an authorial comment rather than Job's words" (2).

replies.[37] By this, Barth presumably means texts like Job 12:13, where Job confesses that wisdom and understanding are rooted in God's transcendent wisdom. In order to undercut the intertextual relation between texts like Job 12:13 and Job 28:23, some commentators read Job 12:13 as a kind of cynical parody or "satiric allusion to traditional platitudes about transcendent wisdom," rather than a sincere conviction on Job's own part.[38] Along with the use of irony and other literary means for subverting the language of traditional wisdom, it is an instance of parody exemplifying the book's generic character as skeptical wisdom.[39] However, the presence of introductory statements in chapters 26–27 and 29 set apart chapters 26–28 and 29–31 as two distinct speeches made by Job.[40] Further, the sixfold structural matching of Job's final reply in chapters 26–31 with the reply of Elihu in chapters 32–37 also supports the claim that we should take chapter 28 as a continuation of the words of Job in chapter 27.[41]

The point to stress is that whether the perspective of Job 28 is that of Job himself or the book's narrator, it is not merely a voice, language, or tongue that speaks from a different social or cultural location. Rather, the perspective is one that speaks from a different ontological orientation on the pursuit of divine Wisdom. Theologically reinterpreted, the concept of *heteroglossia* frames the wisdom debate in the dialogues and the figure of established Wisdom in Job 28:27 in terms of a particular theological context. Here *heteroglossia* is not a species of social or historical other-speaking but, like allegory, a distinctly theological form of other-speaking.

37. Karl Barth, *CD* IV/3.1:426.

38. Newsom argues that while the Job of the dialogues views his quest as a quest for justice, the perspective of Job 28 allegorically "transforms" that perspective into a futile quest for wisdom, doing "interpretive violence" to Job's point of view in the process. The distinction she draws between Job's point of view in the dialogues and the point of view in Job 28 not only tends to distinguish the concepts of justice and wisdom too sharply but also requires her to treat the confession of Job in 12:13 as a parody of transcendent wisdom (Newsom, *Book of Job*, 176–77; cf. 217–18; cf. also Schifferdecker, *Out of the Whirlwind*, 47, 47n69). At the same time, Newsom recognizes that the allegorical act of interpretive translation at work in Job 28 "also illumines important dimensions of Job's speeches," making explicit "the assumptions *embedded* in Job's passionate quest" (Newsom, *Book of Job*, 177, emphasis added). Job knows that wisdom and justice cannot be separated. Hence it becomes necessary for God to appear in court in order that the required judicial wisdom may be manifest (31:35). For this reason it would be better to recognize the intrinsic connection between Job's quest for justice and his quest for wisdom in the book, describing Job's quest as a quest for "judicial wisdom" rather than sharply distinguishing the two.

39. See Dell, *Book of Job as Skeptical Literature*, 125–33.

40. Norman Whybray, *Job* (Sheffield: Sheffield Phoenix, 2008), 12.

41. For the argument see Christopher R. Seitz, "Job: Full-Structure, Movement, and Interpretation," *Int* 43, no. 1 (1989): 5–17, esp. 12–13.

Theological Ontology and the Figure of Wisdom in Job 28

Job 28 asks two questions: Where is Wisdom to be *found* (v. 12), and where does it *come from* (v. 20)? Job 28:23 answers that the LORD alone knows its way and that it derives from the figure of Wisdom established by the LORD before creation (vv. 24–27). Yet as many commentators have noted, there would seem to be a tension present in Job 28. On the one hand, verses 12–13 teach that Wisdom does not exist on earth, not even in the primal deep of creation (*təhôm*) or the sea (v. 14). It is therefore inaccessible to created beings. It follows then that the source of human wisdom does not derive from an immanent event within creation, because human wisdom's origin is transcendent. On the other hand, Job 28:28 proceeds on the assumption that human beings access this Wisdom through the fear of the LORD.[42] The quest for wisdom in Job 28 is not merely an exercise in futility, nor does it necessarily end in incoherence and hopeless contradiction. Rather, the issue turns on the context in which transcendent Wisdom will be found (v. 12), a question inseparably related to two other questions—namely, where Wisdom *originates* or comes from (v. 20) and how one gains *access* to it.

In Job 28:25–27, various metaphors are used to speak of the fact that Wisdom is established prior to creation for the purpose of weighing, measuring, decreeing, and ordering the course or "way" of things in the house we call creation. These terms are literal figures or, better, architectural figures. The Hebrew term כון in verse 27 is an architectural figure, rendered in most English translations as "establish" (ESV, NASB, NRSV) or "prepare" (KJV), the latter of which follows the rendering of the Septuagint and the Vulgate.[43] In metaphorical and human contexts elsewhere in the dialogues, the word's semantic range also includes acts of conception and birth (15:35; 31:15), and the concern with Wisdom's originating context in Job 28 naturally evokes the connotation of birth.[44] For this reason the divine action of establishing Wisdom in verse

42. Speaking of the wisdom poem, Schifferdecker writes, "Its subject matter is the inaccessibility of wisdom, which cannot be found on earth nor acquired with the greatest treasure. . . . [Job's] friends have been trying to use human wisdom to answer Job's dilemma. The poem asserts that authentic, transcendent wisdom is inaccessible to unaided human beings, animals, and cosmic entities alike. Only God knows wisdom, and only the pious person can hope to acquire it" (Schifferdecker, *Out of the Whirlwind*, 47–48).

43. The Jewish versions render it as "measured" (TNK), though an earlier version renders it "established" (JPS). See *The Jewish Publication Society Tanakh Translation* (Philadelphia: The Jewish Publication Society of America, 1985); *The Holy Scriptures According to the Masoretic Text: A New Translation* (Philadelphia: The Jewish Publication Society of America, 1917).

44. On the use of the hiphil conjugation for כון in Job 28:27 to speak of conception and birth in metaphorical and human contexts, see Job 15:35 and 31:15. In Job 15:35, the hiphil imperfect for כון speaks of a womb that has "produced" (TNK), "fashioned" (NIV), "establishes"

27 is closely akin to the begetting of Wisdom in Proverbs 8:22,[45] though the Hebrew verb קנה rather than כון is used there.[46] God established Wisdom to determine the weight of the wind and the measure or scope of the waters, to decree the advent of rain and the way for the storm of thunders (Job 28:25–26). These verses do not identify Wisdom with an attribute of God or an abstract principle that guides his creative activity. Nor do they locate Wisdom in the realm of creation per se, for in these verses "creation supplies the conditions through which wisdom appears to God, but wisdom is not of the order of those things that God's activity creates, such as the wind, water, rain and thunderbolt."[47] Though clearly manifest in these things, Wisdom's appearance

---

(CEB), or "bears as offspring" deceit (NJB). In Job 31:15, the polel conjugation is glossed in English by words closely associated with birth imagery: Did not God "fashion" (NAS), "form" (TNK), "shape" (CJB), or "conceive" (NETS) us in the womb? Because the use of this Hebrew verb in Job 28:27 is not qualified, as it is in these cases, by syntactical relations to contextual markers like "womb" or "belly," I prefer to retain the rendering of "established" for כון in Job 28:27. It should be noted, however, that Job 28 is clearly addressing the question of Wisdom's origin or originating context, which is a question closely related to the question of birth. For this reason, along with the usages found elsewhere in the dialogues in 15:35 and 31:15, the establishing or founding of Wisdom in Job 28:27 naturally carries with it the connotation of begetting or birthing.

45. Commenting on the meaning of "create" in Prov. 8:22, Hilary of Poitiers writes,

Lest any one should suppose that this beginning of the ways, which is indeed the starting-point for the human knowledge of things divine, was meant to subordinate an infinite birth to conditions of time, Wisdom declared itself established before the ages. For, since it is one thing to be created for the beginning of the ways and for the works of God, and another to be established before the ages, the establishing was intended to be understood as prior to the creation; and the very fact of its being established for God's works before the ages was intended to point to the mystery of the creation; since the establishing is before the ages, but the creation for the beginning of the ways and for the works of God is after the commencement of the ages. But now, lest the terms "creation" and "establishing" should be an obstacle to belief in the divine birth, these words follow, Before He made the earth, before He made firm the mountains, before all the hills He begot me. Thus He is begotten before the earth, Who is established before the ages; and not only before the earth, but also before the mountains and hills. (Hilary of Poitiers, On the Trinity, bk. 12, chaps. 35–37, in NPNF², vol. 9, trans. E. W. Watson and L. Pullan, ed. Philip Schaff and Henry Wace [Buffalo, NY: Christian Literature Publishing Co., 1899])

46. Translating קנה as "begat" or "begot" is to be preferred in Prov. 8:22, rather than "acquired" or "possessed." See C. F. Burney, "Christ as the ΑΡΧΗ of Creation," JTS 27 (1926): 160–77. The range of translational options for Hebrew verbs occurring in contexts of origin such as Job 28:27 and Prov. 8:22, for example כון and קנה, tend to fall into two clusters or semantic domains, with translators typically opting for English glosses that express the related ideas of begetting and creating or the related ideas of acquiring and possessing.

47. See Hankins, "Wisdom as an Immanent Event in Job 28," 222. While Hankins differs with the perspective of this book on the transcendent character of Wisdom in Job 28, as well as others such as Janzen and Newsom, he rightly recognizes that Wisdom is not portrayed as a divine attribute or principle in Job 28:23–27 but as a figure distinct from both creation and the LORD. However, he does not understand this distinction to be internal to the Godhead but a

in the act of creation is not to be conflated with them. Rather, Wisdom finds its origin in an immanent action within God by which the originating forms or metric for creation were established (e.g., scale, measure, decree, way).

Wisdom's origin prior to creation coheres with the responses to the questions "Where shall Wisdom be found?" and "Where does Wisdom come from?" in Job 28:12 and 28:20. Invoking the language of Genesis 1:24–26, both Job 28:13 and 28:21 reply that it is not found "in the land of the living" and is hidden from "the birds of the skies," while 28:14 takes us even further back in the creation account of Genesis to the primeval deep of *təhôm* (Gen. 1:2). The function of 28:1–11 and 28:12–19 is not to disconnect Wisdom from any source or cause altogether but to underscore the fact that although Adamkind cannot find it, God has access to it because he established it before the primeval waters of *təhôm* (28:14; cf. Gen. 1:2), prior to creation itself. The figure of Wisdom does not originate in the order of things God created in the economy of time, because it was by the agency of Wisdom that the LORD established a measure or metric by which to create the world.[48] Wisdom is not a divine attribute, abstract principle, or static blueprint but the archē and agency established before creation by divine action, the foundation and means in whom and through whom God brings created reality into existence.

Gerald Janzen rightly observes that Job 28:23–28 argues that "only in divine action can one identify the 'place' of wisdom."[49] The question turns on the context for this divine action. Is this action established in an eternal realm prior to creation,[50] or does it find its place or location in a divine action concomitant with, or consequent to, the creation of the world? Stated in theological terms, does Wisdom find its origin in the economy of creation or

figure independent of both God and creation: "Wisdom appears to God in the co-presence of creator and creation, but wisdom is part neither of God nor of creation" (222). For Hankins, the "emergence" and "otherness" of Wisdom in Job 28:23–27 is irreducible "to any clear causal foundation" (224). Interestingly, this exegetical judgment is bound up with Hankins's argument that Wisdom in Job 28 should be interpreted in terms of a particular type of metaphor whose function is "appositional" or "disjunctive." Applying this theory of metaphor to Job 28:23–27, he concludes that the relation of Wisdom to God is not direct but disjunctive. Wisdom is identified neither with God nor with creation but with a third, independent reality. Both its relation and its accessibility to God (v. 27), like that of human beings (v. 28), are indirect rather than direct.

48. Dhorme's commentary on the book of Job notes that the Hebrew preposition *bet* is used for agency in Job 28:25 in a manner akin to the *bet* of agency in Isaiah 40:12. See Édouard Dhorme, *A Commentary on the Book of Job*, trans. Harold Knight (Nashville: Nelson, 1984), 412.

49. J. Gerald Janzen, *Job*, IBC (Atlanta: John Knox, 1985), 189.

50. Writing around AD 175, Theophilus of Antioch argues that nothing can be co-eternal with God without itself also being considered divine. See Theophilus of Antioch, *Ad Autolycum* 2.4, trans. Robert Grant (Oxford: Clarendon, 1970), cited in David Fergusson, *Creation* (Grand Rapids: Eerdmans, 2014), 18.

in the immanent life of the triune God? In Job 28:23–27, Wisdom is a reality that both originates in God and yet "appears" to God in the economic act of creating the world. The dual description in Job 28:27 of Wisdom as a reality that God both "establishes" and "finds" leads Janzen to reject the idea that Wisdom is a divine attribute: "One would have supposed that wisdom is 'in' God as a divine attribute; yet this verse suggests that even God must 'find' wisdom by following a path that brings God to a place where it exists. This strange figure, however, is illuminated by the verses which follow."[51] Yet only if Wisdom is first of all immanent within God, "original and originating in God,"[52] is it possible for Wisdom to appear in acts that are concomitant with, or consequent to, the divine activity of creating the world. Otherwise Wisdom's appearance to God in 28:27 is reduced to a purely epiphenom-enal, economic manifestation whose place or location properly belongs to the economic realm of creation, rather than the inner life and mystery of the Godhead.[53] However, to recognize that Wisdom appeared to God in creation does not require readers of Job 28:23–27 to choose between the images of *establishing* and *finding*, for Wisdom appeared in creation precisely because God established it as the Archē and Agent of creation beforehand. Comment-ing on this passage, Norman Habel writes,

> In the process of ordering and establishing the limits of his cosmic design God discerned Wisdom. Thus Wisdom both precedes creation (Prov. 8:22ff.), and is revealed to God in the very creation process itself. Wisdom is apparently, therefore, the ordering principle of this creation process, the hidden design and designer behind all things. There is a mystery in eternal Wisdom that transcends definition and can be portrayed only by metaphor. Here the poet describes that mystery as a primordial discovery of the Creator. He acquired her before the creation (v. 22) and discerned her in the process of creation (vv. 25–26).[54]

Janzen's observation that the ocular metaphors in Job 28:24–27 function in the sense of "seeing to" or "attending to" opens up the possibility of an

---

51. Janzen, *Job*, 197.

52. Janzen, *Job*, 189.

53. The position of Davis Hankins attempts to escape this conclusion by offering a third option. On the one hand, Job 28:23–26 presents God in classical theological terms as the actor who brings about the creation of the world, rather than merely being an observer. Then in Job 28:27, Wisdom "appears" in the spontaneous combustion generated by the juxtaposition or "collision" of God with creation, the end result being that the causality that produced Wisdom cannot be reduced "to any clear causal foundation," whether in God or in creation. See Hankins, "Wisdom as an Immanent Event in Job 28," 224.

54. Norman Habel, *The Book of Job: A Commentary*, OTL (Philadelphia: Westminster, 1985), 400.

alternative reading that reframes the issue just mentioned along contextual lines. While the use of these metaphors typically invokes the idea of "seeing" as "looking," their use in both Hebrew and English is not limited to this sense.[55] Arguably, the "seeing to" in view in verse 24 functions in a sense more or less parallel with that of verse 27—namely, to provide for, produce, or establish the reality of something,[56] a sense also found in English usage. "*See to it* that you do your homework" means to produce, establish, or create its reality by working on it. When was Wisdom established? The answer Job 28:24–27 gives is that it was when God "saw to" the production of everything under heaven (v. 24) by establishing a scale for the wind, a measure for the waters, a decree for rain and the course of thunderstorms (vv. 25–26)—that is, before creation, rather than during or after creation. It was "then" that he "saw to" or "established" the reality of Wisdom (v. 27). That the "seeing" (ראה) in the first clause or stich of 28:27 is being used in this sense is suggested by its parallel with the Hebrew verb for "establish" (כון) in the verse's second stich. If the "seeing" in 28:24 speaks of a divine action by which God provided for or established the reality of creation, why would the "seeing" in 28:27 mean to "find" or "discover," especially given its parallel usage with the Hebrew verb כון?

On this reading, the point of 28:27 is not to negotiate a shift in context from establishing realities in the economic realm of creation to establishing the reality of Wisdom in a context prior to creation. Rather, the same context is in view throughout—namely, that of divine planning in eternity, rather than the execution of that plan in time. After all, the images of a scale, measure, decree, or course do not refer to the act of creation per se but to the instruments an architect uses to determine the magnitude and trajectory for realities that have not been actualized in time. They are architectural figures that presuppose an agent and precede the act of creation proper. While recognizing this avoids the dissonance that arises when we interpret the "seeing" in 28:27 as the result of Wisdom's appearance in time, there is more than one way to address that tension, as our prior discussion suggests. Whatever the case, the inner coherence of these verses argues against the notion that the divine action by which Wisdom was established can be reduced to a purely economic event in time. The distinction between Wisdom and God is an identity-in-distinction,

55. The Hebrew term נבט in Job 28:24 is used in Job 6:19 in the sense of "looking for" or hoping to "see" something, while Job 36:25 and 39:29 use it in the sense of seeing something from afar, implying the ability to perceive things before they arrive (cf. "I saw this coming"), a prescience that allows one to discern the meaning of things prior to the immediate experience of their reality.

56. This sense for the Hebrew verb ראה is found in Gen. 22:8, 14; cf. 16:13.

which Jewish readers of wisdom literature also recognize, though they speak of Torah as the agency or mediator of Wisdom rather than the Christian Logos: "In human practice, when a mortal king builds a palace, he builds it not with his own skill [דעת] but with the skill of an architect [root אמן]. The architect moreover does not build it out of his head but employs plans and diagrams to know how to arrange the chambers and the wicket doors. Thus God consulted [lit., looked into] the Torah and created the world."[57]

In the context of Job 28:23–27, Wisdom is other than creation but is not other than God, because it is established by an immanent and transcendent action within God prior to creation. Yet while Wisdom is other than creation, it manifests itself in creation. How then does one access it?

Accessing Wisdom in Job 28

The question where Wisdom is found in Job 28 is a question of source and also of access. This means that the question of finding in 28:12 naturally leads to the question of access in 28:20. Yet Job 28 also teaches that this Wisdom is not found on earth, because its origin does not lie within the economic realm of creation but in an immanent divine action belonging to the transcendent and eternal life of God. It follows that Wisdom is either altogether inaccessible to human beings or made accessible via revelation from God, who alone knows its way and "makes known" its place.[58] Broadly speaking, the book of Job offers two answers to the question "How does one access Wisdom?" One of these takes its bearings from an ontology of human wisdom and tradition, and the other from the ontology of divine revelation.[59] Just here an additional dimension of the wisdom conflict in the book of Job emerges. The dimension takes the form of a conflict between the wisdom of Job's three friends,

57. *Midrash Rabbah: Genesis*, trans. Harry Freedman (London: Soncino, 1951), 1.

58. The Peshitta brings out the causal sense of the hiphil verb in the first clause of 28:23, which may then be extended to the qal verb in the parallel second clause as follows: "God *causes understanding* of the way to it, and he *makes known* its place." This reading not only is grammatically permissible but also emphasizes God as the revealer of Wisdom to Adamkind, who otherwise find Wisdom inaccessible. See Tremper Longman III, *Job*, BCOTWP (Grand Rapids: Baker Academic, 2012), 326n20; cf. Brian J. Alderman and Brent A. Strawn, "A Note on Peshitta Job 28:23," *CBQ* 129, no. 3 (2010): 449–56.

59. Ragnar Andersen suggests that 42:5 contrasts the "hearsay" (Hörensagen) of oral tradition with the speech-theophany of chaps. 38–41. On this reading, the "hearing" Job speaks of in 42:5 is not direct word revelation from God but is oral tradition on wisdom, whether that from local wisdom traditions or more global international wisdom traditions with which Teman, and possibly Eliphaz the Temanite (2:11), appear to have been associated (Jer. 49:7–8). See Ragnar Andersen, "The Elihu Speeches: Their Place and Sense in the Book of Job," *TynBul* 66, no. 1 (2015): 92.

on the one hand, and the perspective of Job 28 and the speech theophany in chapters 38–41, on the other, with the Elihu speeches sandwiched in between (chaps. 32–37). Though biblical scholarship continues to disagree regarding the status of Elihu and the place of his speeches in the book, a good case can be made for the claim that the book presents him as a prophet of the LORD's advent in Job 38. On this reading Elihu is a transitional figure who stands between the friends' arguments for traditional wisdom in chapters 3–25 and the divine revelation of Wisdom in the speech theophany of chapters 38–41.[60] Elihu's claim that the Spirit or Breath of God gives wisdom and understanding (32:8–9) looks back to chapter 28 (v. 23), while also anticipating the divine revelation of Wisdom that follows (chaps. 38–41). For this reason, as well as others,[61] the position of the Elihu speeches in the location following chapter 28 and the end of Job's words in chapter 31 makes good sense.[62]

Janzen opines that "the chasm between divine wisdom and the human condition is not ontologically determined and unbridgeable but has arisen historically and therefore, perhaps, may *historically* be bridged."[63] While the nature of this historical bridge remains unclear in Janzen's commentary, it bears a certain family resemblance to aspects of arguments advanced by Job's three friends in the dialogues, over against the perspective of Job 28 and the speech theophany in Job 38–41. If we read Job 12:13 as a sincere statement on Job's part, then in keeping with the perspective of Job 28, Job understands that since wisdom resides with God, it is the LORD alone who knows its way and makes known its place. Yet Job's friends claim to have searched it out: "Behold, this we have searched out. It is true. Listen, and know it for yourself" (5:27). Their access to this wisdom forms the basis for their attempts to

60. On the different approaches of Elihu and Job's three friends to the issues of revelation and tradition, see Andersen, "Elihu Speeches," 75–94; cf. also Scott C. Jones, "Job 28 and Modern Theories of Knowledge," *Theology Today* 69, no. 4 (2013): 486–95; Choon-Leong Seow, "Elihu's Revelation," *Theology Today* 68, no. 3 (2011): 253–71; Newsom, *Book of Job*, 177–79. Andersen concludes his essay with the observation that "the Elihu speeches actually overturn an unnatural distinction between prophecy and wisdom tradition. The true wisdom teacher, like the true prophet, is taught by God" (94).

61. The wisdom of Elihu should not be reduced to a flat repetition of the wisdom of Job's three friends, nor a mere exercise in youthful arrogance. For Calvin's view of Elihu as "the mouthpiece of God" in the book of Job, see Susan Schreiner, *Where Shall Wisdom Be Found? Calvin's Exegesis of Job from Medieval and Modern Perspectives* (Chicago: University of Chicago Press, 1994), 131–38; Al Wolters, "Job 32–37: Elihu as Mouthpiece of God," in *Reading and Hearing the Word of God from Text to Sermon: Essays in Honor of John H. Stek*, ed. Arie C. Leder (Grand Rapids: Calvin Seminary and CRC Publications, 1998), 107–23; cf. also the views of Seow, "Elihu's Revelation," 270–71; Andersen, "Elihu Speeches," 93–94; and Newsom, *Book of Job*, 205–7.

62. See Seow, "Elihu's Revelation," 262–63.

63. Janzen, *Job*, 200, emphasis added.

provide a wise reading of Job's providence in the dialogues. Where is Wisdom to be found, and how does one access it? The answer the two oldest friends give comes down to the wisdom inherent in oral tradition (8:8–10), going back through the fathers to the first man Adam (15:7–10). Given that Job is not the πρωτος ανθρωπων or first discoverer of wisdom, to attain wisdom he will need to rely upon the wisdom of tradition mediated by elders who have gone before him, rather than limiting wisdom to himself (15:8; cf. 20:4–5).

As others have pointed out, the placement of Job 28 after the last word from the friends in the dialogues (chap. 25) serves to make explicit something already implicit in the dialogues—namely, "an exposé of the limits of the human capacity to know" and the friends' ability to search out wisdom. The chapter's literary position undermines the confidence the three friends place in their discernment and tradition, demonstrating that their views on wisdom's origin are misguided. Though they claim to know the "place" of wisdom's origin, Job 28 locates it in "a place beyond places."[64] The stock analogy between wisdom and precious metals represents the view of traditional wisdom, which chapter 28 subjects to deconstruction.[65] Contra traditional wisdom, the value of Wisdom is not identifiable with the worth of gold or silver. Job 28:1–19 displaces the link between tradition and Wisdom, while verses 20–28 locate it in the Wisdom God establishes before creation. The Wisdom Job speaks of in verse 27 cannot be established by searching the traditional wisdom of the fathers, contra Bildad in Job 8:8, who instructs Job to "inquire, please, of the former generation; *establish* what the fathers have *searched* out." The reason is because the Wisdom needed to provide a wise mediation of Job's trial has been established or begotten before creation.

The use of the same Hebrew verb for "establish" (כון) in Job 8:8 and 28:27, as well as the common motif of "searching out" wisdom (חקר) in Job 8:8 and 28:27 (cf. 28:3), establishes a grammatical and intertextual relation between Job 8:8 and 28:27. The questions of sourcing (establishing) and finding (searching) Wisdom go together, with Job 8 and Job 28 offering different answers. Stated differently, Job 28:24–27 critiques the attempt to locate the place or source of Wisdom in the wisdom of tradition per se (8:8), locating it instead in the revelatory agency of God's established Wisdom, a Wisdom begotten before creation. The ontological distinction between Creator and creature of which Janzen speaks can be bridged, but it will not happen by trying to move, Tower of Babel–like, from history to God. Rather, the gap will be bridged

64. Newsom suggests that the friends appear to be equating traditional wisdom with transcendent Wisdom. See Newsom, *Book of Job*, 178–80.
65. Janzen, *Job*, 196.

by the revelation of God's begotten Wisdom coming to meet us in creation and history. That ontological difference was already bridged when the Word spoke creation into existence, and it will be bridged by the same means in the new creation God is building by his work of redemption. As one commentary rightly observes:

> Like a master craftsman, God weighs, measures, etches, and makes grooves (vv. 25–26). All of this sounds very much like what one does when one builds a house; but in these lines, God's project is not a house but a storm. In ancient Israel and among its Canaanite neighbors, a thunderstorm was not merely a meteorological phenomenon, but a mode of revelation. That concept is also central in the Book of Job, as a storm wind is the mode of the theophany in the book's climactic divine speeches. In Job 28, the content of this revelation is presented in vv. 27–28, both of which follow from God's actions in vv. 25–26. The grammar of vv. 25–28 shows their interdependence: when . . . when . . . then . . . and . . .[66]

The God who understands the "way" of Wisdom (28:23) also makes a "way" for the voice of the thunderbolt (v. 26). The Hebrew phrase used at the end of 28:26 is used again at the end of 38:25.[67] This establishes a literary link between God making a way for the *voice* of the thunderbolt in the wisdom poem (28:26) and the revelation of Wisdom made possible by the *voice* of the theophany in the whirlwind speeches (chaps. 38–41).[68] Like Elihu's words in 37:2–4, which speak of the agency of the voice by which God thunders,[69] 28:26–27 looks forward to the revelation of Wisdom in the voice-theophany of chapters 38–41, while also looking back to 8:8, critiquing the attempt to place or locate Wisdom in traditional wisdom, over against the revelatory agency of established Wisdom described in 28:27.[70]

66. Jones, "Job 28 and Modern Theories of Knowledge," 494.

67. Cf. also 28:8 with 41:34, which is 41:26 in the Masoretic Hebrew text. See *Biblia Hebraica Stuttgartensia*, ed. Karl Elliger and Wilhelm Rudolph (Stuttgart: Deutsche Bibelgesellschaft, 1977). See Schifferdecker, *Out of the Whirlwind*, 47–48.

68. The text of Job 28:26 literally speaks of the thunderstorm of voices or the voice of the lightning bolt, looking forward to the voice of the storm wind or whirlwind in 38:1, 25, while also looking back to Elihu's speech in 37:4.

69. The agential character of this voice is grammatically underscored by the use of the Hebrew preposition *bet* in 37:2, 4.

70. Throughout the book of Job, Job seeks an audience with God, while his friends do not. Rather than talking about God in the third person, Job specifically addresses God in 7:7, 8, 12–14, 16, 17–21; 9:27–28, 30–31; 10:2–14, 16–17, 18, 20; 13:19, 20–27; 14:3, 5–6, 13, 15–17, 19–20; 16:7, 8; 17:3, 4; 30:20–23. See Dale Patrick, "Job's Address of God," *ZAW* 91 (1979): 269; Dariusz Ivanski, *The Dynamics of Job's Intercession* (Rome: Pontifical Biblical Institute, 2006), 178; Manfred Oeming, "Ihr habt nich recht von mir geredet wie mein Knecht Hiob,"

The speech theophany in Job 38–41 is a revelation of the *speaking* Wisdom and the voice of God. According to classical rhetoricians, we cannot imagine a speech without also imagining a person to utter it, and therefore "any character created in words was the performance of a persona."[71] Here we find an acoustic mode of divine self-disclosure in the form of a divine voice accompanied by figural phenomena—that is, the natural form of a storm wind or whirlwind. While this form of presence is not bodily or somatic in the narrow sense, "it would be wrong to say that this voice lacks a body all its own."[72] Rather, the voice is its own kind of body, distinct from a physical or somatic presence. Barth rejects the idea that Job 38:1 is a theophany, arguing that we may say that Job has "seen God" just insofar as "God has spoken to him and Job has heard his word." Job's case is resolved, not by disclosing the reason for his trial but through the speaking voice of God—that is, through the Word of God as that which constitutes Wisdom itself. In his revelation to Job, God's hidden presence remains hidden or invisible: "It is not in removal of His concealment but from within it, not in setting aside His unknowability but . . . both in it and in confirmation of it, that God reveals and makes Himself known to Job."[73] Stated differently, Job experiences an ontological disclosure of God's invisibility, yet by means that are not prejudicial to that invisibility. Although the storm wind centers upon divine speech, it does not seem necessary to follow Barth by denying its theophanic character, provided we properly retain the priority of the Word for interpreting theophanies, as well as figural phenomena in general.[74]

Evangelicalische Theologie 60 (2000): 103–16; ET: "You have not spoken rightly *to me* as did my servant Job." If we understand the perspective of Job 28 to be that of the voice of Job, then this is yet another way in which Job is distinguished from his three friends in the dialogues. He not only persistently seeks an audience with God but also seeks for God to let him in on what is going on, because he knows that God alone can reveal that to him, rather than the tradition his three friends base their hope in. See Barth, *CD* IV/3.1:424–25, 427. Unlike Adam, Job does not seek to hide from God (31:33–35; cf. 13:18–25) but "seeks all the more intensely a meeting with God face to face" and "for a wisdom which God would share with him or disclose to him." Janzen, *Job*, 191.

71. See Quintillian, *Institutio oratoria* 9.2.31–32, cited in *Renaissance Figures of Speech*, ed. Sylvia Adamson, Gavin Alexander, and Katrin Ettenhuber (Cambridge: Cambridge University Press, 2007), 98, 111. The idea is similar to Bakhtin's acoustic concept of a character as a "voice-idea" that expresses not simply a proposition but "the integral point of view and position of a personality" or persona. See Newsom, "Dialogue and Allegorical Hermeneutics," in van Wolde, *Job 28*, 299–305, for an application of this idea to the book of Job.

72. Hankins, "Wisdom as an Immanent Event in Job 28," 232.

73. Barth, *CD* IV/3.1:426–27.

74. See now the brilliant discussion of 2 Kings 6 and Exodus 3, as well as Barth's construal of divine invisibility and creational forms, in Katherine Sonderegger, *Systematic Theology*, vol. 1, *The Doctrine of God* (Minneapolis: Fortress, 2015), 66–130. The approach to figural reading in this book may be construed as a species of the "theological compatibilism" Sonderegger

Theology and Tropology in Job 28

All this does not mean that Job 28 is not interested in human or traditional wisdom. It does mean, however, that Job 28 is interested in that kind of wisdom only insofar as it concerns the question "whether or not human wisdom and transcendent wisdom *are* continuous,"[75] a relationship suggested by the final verse of the wisdom poem in Job 28:28. In other words, it is not human wisdom per se but its relation to transcendent wisdom that Job 28 is concerned with. Stated theologically, the concern of Job 28 is to situate ethics within a particular ontological situation, a concern that also finds articulation in Barth's reading of Job in his *Church Dogmatics*.[76] In the words of John Webster,

> Barth's *Dogmatics* is, amongst other things, a moral ontology—an extensive account of the situation in which human agents act. . . . It is primarily devoted to the task of describing the "space" which agents occupy. . . . [His] ethics tends to assume that moral problems are resolvable by correct theological description of moral space. A Christianly successful moral ontology must be a depiction of the world of human action as it is enclosed and governed by the creative, redemptive, and sanctifying work of God in Christ, present in the power of the Holy Spirit. Consequently, such an ontology is not centred on the human agent, and especially not on moral reflectivity. . . . Barth pushes *this* kind of focus on moral selfhood out of the way in order to introduce in its place what is to him a more theologically—and humanly—satisfying account of the moral life as genuine action in analogy to *prior divine action*.[77]

It is precisely this *prior divine action* that Job 28:23–27 situates moral selfhood and becoming *within*—that is, in the divine action of establishing Wisdom prior to creation—as the agency by which creation would be brought into existence. Thus the wisdom poem in Job 28 does not represent a turn from metaphysics to practical ethics.[78] Instead, it frames practical ethics and the tropology of moral becoming and formation in terms of a particular

---

argues for, which preserves the ontological distinction between the LORD and figures drawn from creation by means of the identity-in-distinction logic of metaphor. For the way mythological discourse collapses this distinction, see Ellen Davis, "'And Pharaoh Will Change His Mind . . .' (Ezekiel 32:12): Dismantling Mythical Discourse," in *Theological Exegesis: Essays in Honor of Brevard S. Childs*, ed. Christopher R. Seitz and Kathryn E. Greene-McCreight (Grand Rapids: Eerdmans, 1998), 224–39.

75. Newsom, "Dialogue and Allegorical Hermeneutics," in van Wolde, *Job 28*, 301.

76. Barth's reading of Job may be found in *CD* IV/3.1:383–88, 398–408, 421–34, 453–61.

77. John Webster, *Barth's Ethics of Reconciliation* (Cambridge: Cambridge University Press, 1995), 1–2, emphasis added in final sentence.

78. This is the position of Jan Fokkelman. See Jones, "Job 28 and Modern Theories of Knowledge," 486.

theological ontology—namely, the ontology of established or begotten Wisdom. Put differently, Job 28 offers its readers a "moral ontology" that defines the ontological situation and preconditions that make possible the moral space in which moral agents act. As such it both enables and maps out the moral "space" in which moral action is possible. The tropological character of human action is not superfluous but derivative rather than primary in character. Anthropology does not precede but follows theology, because its authorizing context or "rule" of intelligibility derives from a particular theological ontology that Job 28:23–27 establishes. Insofar as we are talking about moral theology, the situation in which "the fear of God" becomes wisdom (v. 28) is to be construed as an inquiry into the ontological character of the moral space in which the pursuit and acquisition of wisdom occurs in the creaturely order of things.

The figural interpretation of Wisdom in Job 28 requires a particular sequence or ordering of things in which the established Wisdom of God precedes not only the world but also the moral *ascesis* or transformation involved in becoming more fully and properly human creatures. Occupying moral space in God's creation not only requires a proper posture or characteristic way of being (*ethos*) but also requires a particular ontological orientation and frame of reference on wisdom.[79] In a helpful study of the Hebrew word for judgment (*mišpāṭ*), Willem Beuken argues that the term supports at least two broad senses in the Old Testament. One of these refers to an order of things brought about by God or human beings,[80] while the other refers more narrowly to God's commandments. Beuken also suggests that an integral relation exists between these two uses, with the first sense (God's ordering of things) establishing the context in which the second sense (God's commandments) is enabled to flourish.[81] God's providential ordering of things is thus an enabling precondition for the flourishing of his commandments in creation.

79. For this older, Aristotelian way of understanding *ethos*, see David Lachterman, *The Ethics of Geometry: A Genealogy of Modernity* (New York: Routledge, 1989), xi. Lachterman rightly argues that any ethical practice or "ought" that prescribes a particular behavior, whether in the discipline of mathematics or other practical contexts, presupposes a particular external ordering of things as the source of intelligibility for this "ought."

80. See W. A. M. Beuken, "*Mišpaṭ*: The First Servant Song and Its Context," *VT* 22 (1972): 1–30; cf. also the helpful discussion in Schifferdecker, *Out of the Whirlwind*, 111–20, esp. 112, 116; cf. 2–3, 52, 93–95, 164–65; Rolf Knierim, *The Task of Old Testament Theology: Method and Cases* (Grand Rapids: Eerdmans, 1995), 198–205, esp. his observation that "the world of Psalm 104 is not untrue because of Job's situation" (201).

81. These two dimensions of *mišpāṭ* are broadly correlated with God's role as king *and* judge. As King over creation, the LORD establishes an order of things in which his commandments may flourish. As Judge, he enacts and enforces that order. See the discussion in Schifferdecker, *Out*

The vast majority of usages of *mišpāṭ* in Job refer to God's ordering of things. For example, Job 40:8 refers to Job's objections against God's judgment (*mišpāṭ*) as equivalent to an objection to God's providential ordering of things in Job's trial. There are also usages that refer to an ordering of things by human beings—for example, the ordering involved in the presentation of Job's case before God (13:18; 23:4). *Mišpāṭ* does not typically refer to God's commandments in the book of Job, though they may be implied (34:4). The Hebrew word translated as *way* in Job (*derek*) also supports a twofold sense along the same lines,[82] with many uses of the term referring to an order or ordering of things (e.g., 28:26).[83] The linkage between *way* and an order of things is especially striking in Job 12:24, which links the lack of a *way* (*derek*) with formlessness, waste, or wilderness (*tōhû*), a place of disorientation where God's ordering is absent (cf. 26:7) and "there is no way" (בְּתֹהוּ לֹא־דָרֶךְ). The upshot is that in order for wisdom to flourish in the world of human action and becoming, a particular order of things is required in order to ontologically orient that flourishing and provide an enabling condition for its life.

Proverbs 8:30 and the Architectural Figure of Wisdom (*'Āmôn*)

The theological ontology for Wisdom in Proverbs 8 also ontologically orients the acquisition of human wisdom (4:5–7) in the *revelatory* agency of the LORD's begotten Wisdom (8:22), the mediator of God's self-revelation in the world of creation.[84] A study of the exegetical semantics surrounding the figure of begotten Wisdom in Proverbs 8 suggests that, like Job 28, the architectural figures and metaphors utilized in this wisdom poem do not speak of the personification of a divine attribute. They refer to the agency that produced the divine order, logos, or rationality built in to the structure of created reality. The theological use of metaphor in Proverbs 8 thus serves as a second case study,[85] revealing something of the same interpretive vision for Israel's scriptures we

---

of the Whirlwind, 111–20, which interacts with Sylvia Scholnick, "The Meaning of *Mišpaṭ* in the Book of Job," *JBL* 101 (1982): 521–29.

82. On *derek*, see Markus P. Zehnder, *Wegmetaphorik im Alten Testament: eine semantische Untersuchung der alttestamentlichen und altorientalischen Weg-Lexeme mit besonderer Berücksichtigung ihrer metaphorischen Verwendung*, BZAW 268 (Berlin: de Gruyter, 1999).

83. Job 34:27 appears to be a reference to God's commandments, though in the context it is difficult to distinguish this usage from the order of things God has established to enforce his commandments.

84. Brevard S. Childs, *Biblical Theology of the Old and New Testaments: Theological Reflection on the Christian Bible* (Minneapolis: Fortress, 1992), 189.

85. The following discussion of Proverbs 8 is adapted from Don Collett, "A Place to Stand: Proverbs 8 and the Construction of Ecclesial Space," *SJT* 70, no. 2 (2017): 166–83.

see in the early church's exegetical struggle to come to terms with the figural shape of the Old Testament's witness to monotheism, a struggle that takes its point of standing *within* the horizon of Israel's scriptures and not through an appeal to the New Testament in the first instance.

Here the figural witness of the Old Testament depend upon its correlation not with the New Testament in the first intance but rather with the triune God disclosing himself in Christ through word and figure in Israel's scriptures. Thus even after its juxtaposition with the New Testament to form the biblical canon, the Old Testament did not assume secondary status but remained first-order theological talk, fully capable of providing the church with a place to stand and offer her christo-trinitarian claims. Obviously, the shape of the ecclesial space in which we now stand is very different in this respect from the world of the early church, a difference bound up with resistance in our day to the patristic conviction that the Old Testament's figural language has significance for our understanding of the ontological identity of Israel's LORD.[86] Assessing the nature of this resistance to the ontological significance of the Old Testament's figural language is thus a prerequisite for our study, in order that the operative "theological a priori" concerning metaphor and figure at work in modern exegesis may come to light.[87]

Although there are many issues that might be pursued in this connection, recent exegetical debates over the meaning and translation of *'āmôn* in Proverbs 8:30 offer an instructive point of entry into some of the more theologically interesting issues raised for figural reading by this wisdom poem. While also important, kindred issues surrounding the proper translation and interpretation of the Hebrew verb *qānâ* in Proverbs 8:22 have been frequently pursued in the history of interpretation, and in any case serve to underscore theological issues similar in kind to those raised by the translation and interpretation of *'āmôn* in Proverbs 8:30. This chapter will therefore not venture into the exegetical debate over how the Hebrew verb *qānâ* in 8:22 should be

86. See, for example, Bruce Waltke, *The Book of Proverbs: Chapters 1–15*, NICOT (Grand Rapids: Eerdmans, 2004), 126–33. Waltke argues that "reading Proverbs on its own terms leads to the conclusion that Solomon identifies Woman Wisdom with his teachings, not with a hypostasis (i.e., a concrete, heavenly being who represents or stands for God and is independent from him)." Presumably aware that the early church fathers defined *hypostasis* in a way that differs from his own construal of that term, Waltke tends to be dismissive of patristic figural readings of Proverbs 8:22–31, arguing that "a grammatical-historical exegesis of Proverbs 8 does not support patristic exegesis" (127–28).

87. For a discussion of the theological a priori that produced the Arian doctrine of Christ as creature, along with the role of Prov. 8:22–31 in the Arian controversy, see Jaroslav Pelikan, *The Christian Tradition: A History of the Development of Doctrine*, vol. 1, *The Emergence of the Catholic Tradition, 100–600* (Chicago: University of Chicago Press, 1975), 191–210, esp. 194–200.

rendered, whether *created*, *begotten*, *acquired*, or *possessed*, though the arguments C. F. Burney offers for translating *qānâ* as "begat" or "begot" are to be preferred.[88] Instead, I will focus upon issues of exegetical interest in Proverbs 8:30 that are especially significant for the early church's hypostasis reading of begotten Wisdom in Proverbs 8:22–31. Reflection upon these issues will conclude in the judgment that the theological frame of reference within which they are contextually situated speaks *against* reducing the figure of begotten Wisdom either to an attribute of the LORD or to the literary personification of an abstract hypostasis.

On the one hand, the attribute reading has the merit of recognizing the ontological status of begotten Wisdom, yet this interpretation struggles to come to terms with the character of Wisdom as an active personal agent in the poem. On the other hand, while the personification reading comes much closer to recognizing the character of Wisdom as a *personal*, even *active* agent, it typically refuses to assign any distinctive theological significance to that agency for our understanding of the nature and character of God's oneness in Israel's scriptures. Both these readings leave no room for the fact that the "peculiar" form of monotheism in the Old Testament,[89] while resistant to the notion of a plurality of deities, is nevertheless capable of supporting the distinction of persons *within* the one being of Israel's LORD (YHWH),[90] distinctions for which the verbal profile and figural language of 8:22–31 provide exegetical support. As a result, the contribution this wisdom poem makes to our understanding of the peculiar nature of monotheism in Israel's scriptures is either marginalized or lost altogether.

Over against such approaches, the semantics and syntax of Proverbs 8:30, as well as the frame of reference established by verses 22–31, exert what might be called an ontological pressure upon our understanding of the character of

---

88. Those interested in the fine case Burney mounts for so translating *qānâ* would do well to consult his 1926 essay in the *Journal of Theological Studies*. See Burney, "Christ as the APXH of Creation," 160–77. Burney's essay suggests that the Hebrew term *rēʾšît* in Gen. 1:1 and Prov. 8:22, along with the Hebrew verb *qānâ* in Prov. 8:22, exercised an ontological pressure upon Paul's christological confession in Col. 1:15–18. Along with Richard Bauckham's analysis of the theological function of "Word" and "Wisdom" in the Second Temple wisdom literature (see note 90 below), his arguments tend to undercut Waltke's claim that "Paul . . . does not build his high Christology on Proverbs 8 or on Jewish Wisdom literature." Waltke, *Book of Proverbs*, 130.

89. See Seitz, "Trinity in the Old Testament," 28–40.

90. On this, see Richard Bauckham, *Jesus and the God of Israel: God Crucified and Other Studies on the New Testament's Christology of Divine Identity* (Grand Rapids: Eerdmans, 2008), 1–17. Bauckham argues that in Second Temple literature, Wisdom is "not someone else" in the sense of being a second deity but intrinsic to the LORD's identity (16–17). See further the discussion of the "New Religionsgeschichtliche schule" by Bogdan Bucur in "Justyn Martyr's Exegesis of Biblical Theophanies," *TS* 75, no. 1 (2014): 34–51, esp. 47n49.

divine identity in Proverbs 8. This pressure is evident in at least three different ways in the poem: (1) in the poem's figural-exegetical portrayal of begotten Wisdom as a specific and active personal agent; (2) in the theological ontology with which begotten Wisdom is identified in Proverbs 8:30; and (3) in the presentation of Wisdom's personhood as one that subsists through time. In closing, this study will suggest that Proverbs 8 remains crucial for our ability to appreciate, along with the church fathers, the Old Testament's continuing ability to rule and shape the church's christological confession when read in light of Christ, both apart from and in concert with the New Testament.

The Wisdom Poem and Proverbs 8

Proverbs 8:22–31 occurs within one of three wisdom speeches falling within the book's introductory section formed by chapters 1–9 (the other two being located in chaps. 1 and 9).[91] In contrast with the wisdom poem in 8:22–31, the two other wisdom speeches do not address the question of Wisdom's origins and relationship to the LORD, the God of Israel. For this reason most commentators acknowledge that the role of 8:22–31 in the larger context of the book is to specify the *origin* and *relationship* of Wisdom to the LORD.[92] In terms of the poem's inner relations with chapter 8, after the first exhortation (vv. 1–11), Wisdom moves to a description of the benefits she offers (vv. 12–21). These benefits are judged to be worthwhile because of the special relationship Wisdom has with the LORD himself (vv. 22–31), a relationship the wisdom poem justifies by specifying Wisdom's origin and relationship to the LORD. Having established this, the closing section (vv. 32–36) is then able to justly affirm that the benefits of life and favor she offers are not merely transient or temporal but enduring blessings that ultimately proceed from the LORD himself: "Whoever finds me finds life and obtains favor *from the LORD*" (v. 35).

Most modern commentators recognize that the debate over the translation of Proverbs 8:30 has theological implications for the nature of monotheism in the Old Testament. This is because the text directly impacts the question whether we should conceive of Wisdom as an active *agent* in creation or as merely *instrumental* in a more or less passive sense (cf. 3:19). Commentators have translated the Hebrew word ʾāmôn in 8:30 in a variety of ways, the most

---

91. Prov. 1:20–33; 8:1–36; 9:1–6. For a helpful study of the literary structure and exegetical issues raised by Proverbs 1–9, see Zabán, *Pillar Function of the Speeches of Wisdom*.

92. Alan Lenzi, "Proverbs 8:22–31: Three Perspectives on Its Composition," *JBL* 125, no. 4 (2006): 694; cf. Stuart Weeks, "The Context and Meaning of Proverbs 8:30a," *JBL* 125, no. 3 (2006): 436.

popular candidates being "artisan," "architect," or "master craftsman." All of these would seem to imply an active agency on Wisdom's part in creation, and not merely what might be called a passive instrumentality. Among the problems involved with rendering *'āmôn* in an active sense is the contextual question why "the active role of Wisdom is introduced *only at this late point* in the poem and mentioned nowhere else in Proverbs 1–9."[93] At the other end of the spectrum, others have responded to the lack of contextual precedent for assigning Wisdom an active role in creation. They thus have translated *'āmôn* with a passive sense, arguing that only a passive understanding of Wisdom's role in creation can do justice to the context preceding 8:30. Brief summaries of the arguments on both sides of this debate are helpful for illustrating the contextual issues at stake.

Passive Renderings of *'Āmôn*

Alan Lenzi argues for the translation of *'āmôn* as "master" in the sense of skilled sage or scholar, an idea that he regards as congruent with Wisdom's lack of active agency in the verses preceding 8:30. He arrives at this translation by emending the spelling of *'āmôn* along the lines of the noun used in Canticles 7:1.[94] He then reconstructs the meaning of *'āmôn* by appealing to the Akkadian cognate *ummânu*,[95] a move others before him have also followed in order to reconstruct *'āmôn*'s meaning.[96] Lenzi's decision to translate *ummânu* as "master" rather than "master architect" or "master craftsman" assigns a passive sense to the term, presumably because "master" taken in the sense of sage or scholar suggests passive contemplation rather than constructive activity.

On the other hand, Stuart Weeks argues that *'āmôn* is a proper name or title meaning "faithful one." He suggests that this reading of *'āmôn* strengthens

---

93. Weeks, "Context and Meaning of Proverbs 8:30a," 434, emphasis added; cf. Michael Fox, "'AMON Again," *JBL* 115, no. 4 (1996): 700.

94. This verse is 7:2 in the Hebrew text (Masoretic Text).

95. Lenzi, "Proverbs 8:22–31," 705–7.

96. See Ray Van Leeuwen, "Cosmos, Temple, House: Building and Wisdom in Ancient Mesopotamia and Israel," in *From the Foundations to the Crenellations: Essays on Temple Building in the Ancient Near East and Hebrew Bible*, ed. Mark J. Boda and Jamie Novotny (Munster: Ugarit-Verlag, 2010), 399–421, who argues that "despite some recent objections, in the light of Akkadian and Aramaic evidence, it is best to take אָמוֹן in Prov 8:30 as cognate with *ummânu*." He cites as supporting references Richard J. Clifford, *Proverbs* (Louisville: Westminster John Knox, 2016), 23–28, 99–101; Henri Cazelles, "*Aḥiqar, Ummân, and Amun* and Biblical Wisdom Texts," in *Solving Riddles and Untying Knots: Biblical, Epigraphic, and Semitic Studies in Honor of Jonas C. Greenfield*, ed. Ziony Zevit, Seymour Gitin, and Michael Sokoloff (Winona Lake, IN: Eisenbrauns, 1995), 45–55; and Jonas C. Greenfield, "The Seven Pillars of Wisdom (Prov. 9:1)—A Mistranslation," *JQR* 76, no. 1 (1985): 13–20.

the likely dependence of Revelation 3:14 on Proverbs 8:30.[97] Weeks's solution thus offers a slight variation on an earlier approach found in the revision history of the Septuagint, in this case that of Symmachus and Theodotion, who render the Hebrew in an active sense with the Greek participle ἐστηριγμένη, meaning "to set or stand firm." As a participle in the active voice, 'āmôn would thus be rendered adverbially as "faithfully" or "constantly."[98] Following an earlier tradition that renders 'āmôn in the sense of "faithfulness" or "constancy," Weeks argues that it functions as an attributive name or title, in the form of either an appositionally placed noun or a substantive adjective. The rendering allegedly avoids violating contextual concerns and is consistent with rendering 'āmôn as an attribute of wisdom, rather than an active co-agent with the LORD in creation.

Curiously, Weeks does not discuss Proverbs 9:1, in which the *activity* of building a house is attributed to Wisdom. This is presumably because Weeks does not regard the house-building in 9:1 to be contextually linked with or modeled upon a reading of 'āmôn in 8:30 that connects it with an active agent at work in the construction of creation. The interplay between the images of creation and house is commonly found in ancient Near Eastern portrayals of cosmic creation as house-building, and an active rendering of 'āmôn as "architect" or "artisan" allows this figural and contextual linkage to emerge by presenting Wisdom as the architect of creation in 8:30, followed by Wisdom as house-building in 9:1.[99]

Active Renderings of 'Āmôn

Apart from contextual concerns, the concern to maintain a passive voice for 'āmôn is also tied to a larger theological worry some interpreters have. The concern is that assigning an active sense to 'āmôn will not merely lead to a distinction of persons (e.g., the reading of the fathers) but to a separate creator alongside the LORD. Interpreters with a concern to protect the Old Testament's monotheistic claims follow the lead of Aquila and a number of rabbis by reading 'āmôn as 'ĕmûn, interpreting the vowel letter *vav* as *shureq*

97. Weeks, "Context and Meaning of Proverbs 8:30a," 434: "If Prov. 8:30–31 does indeed refer to Wisdom's continuing relationship with God, then an expression of constancy would not be out of place in v. 30a; in fact, such an expression would offer an excellent parallel to the emphasis on continuity in the following stichs."

98. For example, Otto Plöger takes the Hebrew root in a passive sense as "be firm," arguing that its grammatical form is that of an infinitive absolute functioning adverbially. See M. Fox, "'AMON Again," 700.

99. See Zabán, *Pillar Function of the Speeches of Wisdom*, 35.

rather than *holem-vav*.[100] The potentially active sense inherent in *'āmôn* is thereby more or less neutralized by rendering it in terms of a *passive* participle from the Greek (τιθηνουμένη) and translating it as "nursling" or "one who is nursed."[101]

Those who share a concern for preserving the claims of Old Testament monotheism while opting for an active sense for *'āmôn* are thus in a bit of a fix, fighting as it were in a two-front war involving *both* contextual and theological issues. For example, in his Baker commentary on Proverbs, Tremper Longman argues for the active sense of *'āmôn* as architect based upon Akkadian comparative philology.[102] Yet he also worries about the threat this reading might pose to Old Testament monotheism. Accordingly, his solution to the exegetical difficulties involved in 8:22–31 calls for a variation on the strategies canvassed above. The variation stresses two things: (1) the importance of keeping in view the figurative nature of the language in 8:22–31 and (2) appreciating the fact that as a personification of "Woman Wisdom" in Proverbs,[103] Wisdom functions as an attribute of the LORD and is thus not to be conceived of as someone (or something) distinct from the LORD.

In his *How to Read Proverbs*, Longman articulates his position on the figural character of Wisdom in Proverbs by arguing that "the location of her house makes clear that Woman Wisdom stands for God. She is a poetic personification of God's wisdom and represents God, as a part for the whole

---

100. Aquila's reading of the Hebrew may reflect an instance of *al tiqre* wherein the vowel letter *waw* was not read but substituted for by another vowel (*al tiqre* means "do not read" X but Y), thereby creating a deliberate alternate reading. The possibility also exists that Aquila based his substitution on a known or textually attested variant reading.

101. For objections to this rendering, see M. Fox, "'AMON Again," 701.

102. Tremper Longman III, *Proverbs*, BCOTWP (Grand Rapids: Baker Academic, 2006), 196; cf. also his *How to Read Proverbs* (Downers Grove, IL: InterVarsity, 2002), 105.

103. Longman, *How to Read Proverbs*, 104. The issue of whether the language of 8:22–31 has ontologically descriptive significance should not be confused with the misguided attempt to define the nature of the Godhead by wrongly assuming a one-to-one relationship between grammatical and sexual gender, especially since the begotten Wisdom in view in Prov. 8:22–31 exists prior to the reality of creation—that is, prior to the existence of created realities, such as bodies and natural sexual genders, whether male or female. Wisdom in 8:22 is earlier depicted in the feminine voice of a prophet who speaks (8:1–3; cf. 1:20–21), not because divine or transcendent Wisdom has a feminine sexual nature (an idea often found in pagan *sophia* traditions) but because the Hebrew noun for Wisdom is feminine in grammatical gender. The interpretive construct "Lady Wisdom," while a commonplace in Proverbs scholarship, tends to obscure this fact. Although what it means to speak of "begotten Wisdom" does not entirely escape these difficulties, the phrase is arguably closer to the semantics of v. 22. For a helpful discussion, see Christopher R. Seitz, "Reader Competence and the Offense of Biblical Language: The Limitations of So-Called Inclusive Language," in *Word without End: The Old Testament as Abiding Theological Witness* (Grand Rapids: Eerdmans, 1998), 292–99.

(synecdoche)."[104] As one reads on, however, it becomes apparent that this definition, especially the stress it places upon the metaphorical and figurative character of biblical poetry, is closely tied to a concern on Longman's part to protect the Old Testament's teaching on monotheism:

> We have already observed that Woman Wisdom is a personification of God's attribute of wisdom. This part of the poem is making the point that God created the cosmos by virtue of his age-old wisdom. The language about the creation of Wisdom is a powerful metaphor, affirming that God's wisdom preceded every other thing. It is figurative language; Wisdom is not a separate personal entity. That it is provocative language is not to be doubted and is confirmed by the fact that certain minor but articulate strands of Judaism and Christianity came to treat Wisdom as a separate divine being, even a bride of Yahweh himself.[105]

The argument seems to have in mind those who interpret Lady Wisdom as a separate deity, created at the beginning of time for the purpose of being the bride of Yahweh.[106] While monotheistic interpreters who share the concern to refute this reading have often resorted to the exegetical tactic of rendering the Hebrew verb *qānâ* as "acquired" rather than "formed,"[107] Longman regards this as heavy-handed. It is the result of what might be called genre amnesia, or as he puts it, forgetting "that we are interpreting a poem."[108] Failure to reckon with the genre effects of poetry and the metaphorical nature of its language has prevented interpreters from grasping that "Woman Wisdom is a personification of God's attribute of wisdom." On this approach, a better way to satisfy the concerns of monotheism is to take seriously the passage's genre as poetry, especially the implications this has for the "figurative" character of Woman Wisdom as a literary device. Once this is recognized, the nature of *'āmôn* as an attribute of the LORD rather than a separate deity becomes clear.

104. Longman, *How to Read Proverbs*, 33; cf. also 56, 74, and 104. His Baker commentary adopts the same view: see Longman, *Proverbs*, 196.

105. Longman, *How to Read Proverbs*, 104. On pp. 109–10, the link between this understanding of Wisdom in Proverbs and Longman's concern to preserve monotheism is strongly stated.

106. Longman, *Proverbs*, 196.

107. Longman, *How to Read Proverbs*, 104–5. Longman's Baker commentary on Proverbs renders *qānâ* as "begot" rather than "formed." See Longman, *Proverbs*, 195.

108. Longman, *How to Read Proverbs*, 105. The early church was also aware of "the proverbial character of the material," and thus may be said to have had a sense of the importance of genre as well. See Frances Young, "Proverbs 8 in Interpretation (2): Wisdom Personified," in *Reading Texts, Seeking Wisdom*, ed. David Ford and Graham Stanton (Grand Rapids: Eerdmans, 2004), 111. Interestingly, this awareness did not foster the conclusion that Wisdom is simply the literary personification of an attribute of the LORD.

One may readily agree that *'āmôn* should be translated as "architect" not simply because of its Akkadian cognate but also because of the pervasive use in wisdom literature of architectural metaphors and figures to depict creation in terms of house-building. This imagery often construes all of creation in terms of a house or temple that the LORD originally constructed in order to dwell with his creatures. The problem arises not so much with the active sense inherent in the gloss "architect" but with the decision to interpret *'āmôn* as an attribute of the LORD. The problem in 8:30 is not solved by arguing that *'āmôn* is an attribute of the LORD, because the third person possessive suffix in the preceding word אֶצְלוֹ suggests a distinction that reading *'āmôn* as an attribute obscures. This makes it difficult "to understand why the writer would have obscured his own meaning by using a redundant suffix pronoun."[109] Moreover, the prepositional phrase "at his side" continues the distinction pursued throughout the poem between Wisdom's voice, which is presented in the first person, and references to the LORD, which occur in the third person. If we should take *'āmôn* straightforwardly as an attribute of the LORD in 8:30, rather than a distinct hypostasis or *persona* within the Godhead, why not avoid the continuance of this grammatical distinction and drop the third person suffix altogether? After all, if *'āmôn* merely refers to an attribute of the LORD, then the third person suffix is redundant. The difficulty with reading *'āmôn* as an attribute of the LORD is that it obscures what the verbal profile of the text distinguishes.

On the other hand, if the writer intended to register a distinction between the LORD and *'āmôn*, then the use of the third person suffix not only makes sense but also coheres with the larger context by continuing the distinction between the LORD and Wisdom through the use of first and third person pronouns.[110] Moreover, the semantics of Proverbs 8:30 suggest a further distinction. The children of Adam, along with the rest of creation, occupy a position in the poem that suggests a life before rather than beside God, while the figure of Wisdom as a master architect is positioned as a life beside God. While these observations do not conclusively settle the issue, they do appear to be compatible with the "distinct but equal" status of Wisdom in the poem that the early church discerned. To be sure, one can make the counterargument that personification as a literary device typically adopts the use of personal pronouns. Hence this phenomenon is hardly unusual, especially within the

---

109. Weeks, "Context and Meaning of Proverbs 8:30a," 434n6.

110. Longman appears to be aware of this problem and suggests that *'āmôn* in 8:30 has a double referentiality to both the LORD and Woman Wisdom. This double referentiality, however, is simply the counterpart to his claim that Woman Wisdom is simply the literary personification of an attribute of the LORD and thus indistinguishable from the LORD himself. See Longman, *Proverbs*, 196.

genre of poetry. However, there are other exegetical phenomena in this poem that resist this logic and ultimately oppose being completely resolved by this explanation. Answering the biblical claims of monotheism calls for a different approach—that is, if the words of the text are to be our guide.

Wisdom as Instrumental Means and Personal Agency

Alan Lenzi argues that 8:22–31 was composed and added to the growing corpus of Proverbs 1–9 with an eye toward 3:19–20 in its final form,[111] suggesting that 8:22–31 interprets 3:19–20 and so constitutes an instance of intrabiblical exegesis in Proverbs. While the reference to Wisdom in Proverbs 3:19 makes an instrumental use of the Hebrew preposition *bet* to describe Wisdom's role in creation, suggesting that Wisdom in 3:19 is being described in terms of *instrumentality* rather than *personhood*, in 8:22–31 the writer presents Wisdom's role in creation in a different light by constructing Wisdom's relationship to the Lord in different terms. The contrast consists in the fact that in 3:19 Wisdom is presented as the instrument of God's creative activity, while in 8:22 Wisdom is not the instrument but the object of that activity: "The Lord begot *me*," that is, Wisdom.[112] In other words, Wisdom in Proverbs 8:22 is presented not as an instrumental means or tool by which God created but as a personal agency or "me," a reading that coheres with the presentation of Wisdom in 8:30 as a master architect or artisan.[113] The Hebrew phrases "there am I" in 8:27 (שָׁם אָנִי) and "I am at his side, a master architect" in 8:30 (וָאֶהְיֶה אֶצְלוֹ אָמוֹן) form an *inclusio* around the activity of creation described in 8:27–30.[114] The literary effect is to link the architectural activity and continuing presence of Wisdom with the mediation of God's creative activity.[115] In sum, 8:22–31 interprets 3:19–20 in terms of two phrases that expand upon the abbreviated description of Wisdom's instrumentality in 3:19. Whereas Wisdom's role in

111. See Lenzi, "Proverbs 8:22–31," 687–714.
112. Lenzi, "Proverbs 8:22–31," 696.
113. For a critical interaction with the positions of Bruce Waltke and Michael Fox on Prov. 8:30, see Zabán, *Pillar Function of the Speeches of Wisdom*, 28n44.
114. It is grammatically possible to render these phrases in either a present or a past tense, for example, "I was there" and "I was at his side (as a) master architect." On either rendering, the presence and activity of Wisdom in the act of creation are presupposed.
115. Lenzi, "Proverbs 8:22–31," 698. Even non-christological readers of Prov. 8:22–31 recognize that it portrays Wisdom as a mediator figure. For example, Gale Yee notes that "the whole movement of the poem—from Wisdom's begetting by God to her presence at God's side when he organized the world—throws into relief the mediative role of Wisdom between humankind and God, even though the character of this mediation is not specified." Gale Yee, "An Analysis of Prov 8:22–31 according to Style and Structure," *ZAW* 94, no. 1 (1982): 60.

creation in 3:19 is presented using the language of instrumentality, the figural language of 8:27–30 construes that role in terms of an active "personal presence" and agency.[116]

The shift in meaning that occurs as we move from the context of 3:19 to 8:22–31 is in keeping with the theological function of Proverbs 8 in the larger literary context of Proverbs 1–9. The three wisdom speeches in Proverbs 1–9 (1:20–33; 8:1–36; 9:1–6) function as foundational pillars in the house of Wisdom, whose voice is directed not to Israel in the first instance but to the children of Adam (8:4). In literary terms, the central location of the wisdom poem in 8:22–31 vis-à-vis the other two wisdom speeches in chapters 1–9 is closely akin to the location and function of Job 28 in the book of Job. Its position at the center of chapters 1–9 underscores the central role 8:22–31 occupies in shaping the ontological orientation of readers in their acquisition and pursuit of wisdom (4:5–7), rooting that wisdom in the unique identity and begotten Wisdom of the LORD (8:22). The acquisition of wisdom by which we build human houses and fill them with knowledge and understanding (24:3–4) occurs within a particular ontological ordering of things shaped by begotten Wisdom (8:22). In this way Proverbs 1–9 teaches its readers that the wisdom of human house-building originates with and is modeled upon the LORD's begotten Wisdom (8:22), the Architect of creation (v. 30) who precedes creation (vv. 22–26), the Agent through whom God brings creation into existence.

We should add to this the observation that the opening verses (vv. 1–11) of the first section of Proverbs 8 present Wisdom in first person terms as a speaking voice.[117] The second section (vv. 12–21) carries forward this first person, prophetic voice. Thus Wisdom in Proverbs 8 is conceived as a prophetic orator who mediates the wisdom implicit in Solomon's teachings to Israel. The question of Wisdom's identity in the poem is not framed in terms of the question "*What* is this speaking voice?" but in terms of the question "*Who* is this speaking voice?" That is, *who* is the one speaking, and what is the relationship of this "who" to Israel's LORD?[118] Whether one translates *qānâ* as "acquired" or as "begat," both renderings undercut the notion that the Wisdom in view in 8:22 refers to an attribute of the LORD. After all, what sense does it make to speak of the LORD acquiring or begetting an attribute? Supporters of the attribute reading will doubtless argue that this objection ignores the metaphorical, figural, or poetic nature of the language, an objection

116. Lenzi, "Proverbs 8:22–31," 705.
117. Cf. Prov. 1:20–21. Both ancient and modern commentators register the observation that the agency of Wisdom in Proverbs 8 is framed in prophetic as well as creational categories.
118. Lenzi offers his own take on this question by drawing upon the allusions to Exod. 3:14 and Isa. 48:16 in Prov. 8:27–30a. Lenzi, "Proverbs 8:22–31," 711–14.

already anticipated in thirteenth-century attempts to reduce metaphor to a literary rather than a theological category. For now, suffice it to say that these translations comport more fully with the hypostasis reading of the fathers than they do with the attribute reading. This is not to claim, of course, that the writer of Proverbs 8:22 had in mind the concept of person (ὑπόστασις), as this concept later came to be worked out in the trinitarian formulas of the early church. It is simply to register the observation that the syntax, language, and *concepts* used to describe Wisdom in Proverbs 8:22–31 *cohere*, both onto-logically and exegetically, with what the early church intended to signify by its use of the Greek term ὑπόστασις to render the Son's personhood,[119] as well as the Nicene claim that the eternal Logos or Son was "begotten, not made."

Wisdom and Theological Ontology: Proverbs 8:30 and Exodus 3:14

Although the preceding observations help to establish an exegetically plausible case for the early church's hypostasis reading of Wisdom's personhood in 8:22–31, over against the attribute reading,[120] those commentators who argue that the personification of Wisdom is merely a literary device, a reference to Solomon's teaching per se, or a metaphor functioning on a purely literary and imaginative level, will probably remain undaunted. The suggestion that the metaphorical character of Wisdom rules out any theological and ontological status for Wisdom is especially curious. Is it always the case that metaphors in poetic discourses or genres lack ontological status? Shall we think of biblical metaphors as quasi-Kantian phenomena that fail to mediate any descriptive knowledge of that which lies beyond our temporal experience? Before ad-dressing more fully the rationale undergirding non-referential accounts of biblical metaphor, the ontological status of Wisdom in Proverbs 8 should be explored in terms of the wisdom poem's own semantics.

To begin with, Proverbs 8:30 exegetically links the figure of begotten Wis-dom in 8:22 with a particular theological ontology rooted in the divine name of Israel's covenant LORD. Here the two Hebrew phrases in 8:27 and 8:30 offer their own distinctive contribution to the question of Wisdom's origins and relationship with the LORD. In response to the question of Wisdom's origin, 8:27 answers, "I was there," even before the waters of *təhôm*, the deep, were in place (cf. Gen. 1:2). In response to the question of Wisdom's relation to the

---

119. For a similar line of argument made on the basis of Paul's reading of Isaiah 45 in Philip-pians 2, see David Yeago, "The New Testament and Nicene Dogma," *ProEccl* 3 (1994): 152–64.

120. While I do not find the "attribute reading" persuasive, it does have the merit of avoiding a purely literary or historical reading of Wisdom's identity in Proverbs 8.

LORD of Israel, Proverbs 8:30 answers, "I was at his side." As argued earlier, these phrases link the activity and presence of Wisdom with the mediation of God's creative activity. However, the double use of the Hebrew verb "to be" (היה) in 8:30 is a bit odd, especially given the general tendency in Proverbs "to avoid the verb 'to be' in favor of juxtaposition or simple comparison."[121] As a number of commentators have pointed out, along with the Hebrew phrase in 8:27, the double use of the verb "to be" in 8:30 may be rendered in the present tense as "*I am* at his side" and "*I am* daily his delight,"[122] thereby constituting "an eloquent allusion" on a grammatical level to the divine name "I am who I am" in Exodus 3:14.[123] What significance might these observations have for the ontological status of Wisdom in Proverbs 8? Certainly, if it was not the intention of the writer of 8:30 to direct the reader's thoughts to the divine name in Exodus 3:14, then the decision to invoke a double use of the Hebrew verb היה was at best unfortunate and at worst a bit reckless, especially in the context of a discussion about Wisdom's origin and relationship to the LORD.

Subsistence and Personhood: Proverbs 8:27–31

The question of Wisdom's identity in Proverb 8 is closely tied to the question of its origins. What is the originating context for Wisdom's identity? Proverbs 8:22 locates this originating context, and therefore the identity of Wisdom in the agency of "Beginning" (archē), *prior* to the LORD's way (*derek*) in creation and time.[124] While the significance of 8:22 for Wisdom's origins has often been noted, especially its polemical function,[125] comparatively few modern commen-

---

121. Roland Murphy, *Proverbs*, WBC 22 (Nashville: Nelson, 1998), 52–53.

122. Weeks, "Context and Meaning of Proverbs 8:30a," 438n19.

123. The observation that Proverbs 8:30 is "an eloquent allusion" (*Eine beredte Anspielung*) to the divine name derives from Arndt Meinhold. See Lenzi, "Proverbs 8:22–31," 711n90; cf. R. Murphy, *Proverbs*, 52–53.

124. On the significance of beginning (archē) in Gen. 1:1 as a theological title describing agency within the Godhead, see Collett, "Christomorphic Shaping of Time in Radner's *Time and the Word*," 277–78; cf. also Van Leeuwen, "Cosmos, Temple, House," 408. Van Leeuwen rightly observes that when the Midrash Rabbah on Genesis exegetes rēʾšît (beginning) in Gen. 1:1 in terms of ʾāmôn (architect) in Prov. 8:30, "it is not imposing an alien wisdom upon Genesis 1, but making explicit aspects of the text's implicit metaphoric domain." Like the terms archē and ʾāmôn in Prov. 8:22 and 8:30, the architectural figure of "Beginning" in Gen. 1:1 depicts an eternal agent who establishes creation's temporal beginning. In these texts, archē and ʾāmôn do not merely speak of an instrument or tool but the eternal agent by which God created.

125. Lenzi argues that the triple occurrence of "water words" in 8:24, 27, and 28, as well as the birth imagery in 8:22–25, operates with an eye toward establishing a polemical relationship with the *Enuma Elish* and Ea, the Mesopotamian god of water and wisdom. See Lenzi, "Proverbs 8:22–31," 700.

tators have reflected on how 8:22–31 frames and conditions *all* time in terms of a movement from the LORD to the children of Adam.[126] Stuart Weeks rightly argues that "we must envisage a progression through three periods: before, during, and after the creation."[127] He argues against the traditional reading of 8:30 as the completion of a sixfold series of temporal clauses begun in 8:27, pointing out that in 8:30–31 these clauses are a unit tied together by catchwords. As such, verses 30–31 structurally demarcate the period of post-creation in the poem, whereas verses 27–29 refer to a period during creation.[128] The overall movement of the poem thus progresses through three periods: *before* creation (vv. 22–26), *during* creation (vv. 27–29), and *after* creation (vv. 30–31), with begotten Wisdom as a personal presence subsisting through all three periods. Wisdom in these verses reflects a resistance to that which does not endure—that is, a resistance to mortality. Along with our observations on 8:30, this resistance serves to link the figure of begotten Wisdom in 8:22–31 with an ontological reality that endures before, in, and through time.[129] At this juncture, it would appear to be at least reasonable, in light of the text's grammar, to give ear to the ontological overtones of the language and reconsider whether the reduction of biblical metaphors to literary categories or rhetorical ornaments can do full justice to the claims Proverbs 8 registers regarding Wisdom.

Dismissing these overtones in the name of figurative or metaphorical language presupposes a non-referential account of metaphor that should be questioned, as argued earlier in this chapter. Because biblical metaphor operates within the larger framework of Christian figural realism, there are good reasons to reject an account of metaphor's role in figural reading that reduces metaphor to an imaginative, verbal trope that undercuts its reality-depicting function[130]—that is, an account of metaphor that makes no ontological demands upon its readers. As ancient Greek rhetoricians understood, metaphor is itself a form of other-speaking, in that it relies on an analogy or relationship between two things in order to do its sense-making. For example, the biblical or literary metaphor "the Lion of Judah" relies upon the reader's knowledge of a relationship between the verbal metaphor *lion* and an ontological thing or reality (*res*) outside the text (the animal we refer to as a lion). Apart from the reader's knowledge of this relationship, the metaphor simply fails. Stated

126. The Hebrew of 8:30 frames the ongoing or "daily" rejoicing of Wisdom in comprehensive terms as the "all" of time.
127. Weeks, "Context and Meaning of Proverbs 8:30a," 437.
128. Weeks, "Context and Meaning of Proverbs 8:30a," 441.
129. Weeks, "Context and Meaning of Proverbs 8:30a," 437–38. As noted earlier, the judgment of Theophilus of Antioch is that nothing can be co-eternal with God without itself also being considered divine. See Theophilus of Antioch, *Ad Autolycum* 2.4.
130. See Soskice, *Metaphor and Religious Language*; cf. also Howell, *In the Eyes of God*.

differently, the text's literary referent depends upon a particular ontological referent in order to do its sense-making. In this sense, metaphor as a literary phenomenon is akin to the referential account of sense-making we find at work in allegory. It is therefore a *species* of allegory, or theological other-speaking, in that it depends upon an ontological reality or non-textual referent *outside* itself in order to render its sense.

This is why it will not suffice, whether in the name of metaphor or in the name of personification construed as a literary device, to rule out a priori the ontological status and framework in which the interpretive categories of wisdom, beginning, and begetting operate in Proverbs 8:22–31.[131] A de-ontologized reading of metaphor severs the relation between theological ontology and economy that holds metaphor and dogmatics together. However, because referential logic is built into metaphor, the status of Wisdom in Proverbs 8 cannot be resolved by remaining at the level of the literary presentation alone. Moreover, the exegetical semantics of the poem offer resistance to such a reading. The referential force of begotten Wisdom in Proverbs 8 is not merely a form of "textual" other-speaking, such as we often find in contemporary theories of intertextuality.[132] Nor is it simply a form of "historical" other-speaking, such as we often find in modern versions of scientific exegesis. On these approaches, biblical referentiality becomes a way of speaking of other texts in a vast web of linguistically constructed sense-relations,[133] or an instrumentalized means to the end of reconstructing a historical ontology outside the words of Scripture, which ontology has usually been thoroughly de-theologized. Over against such approaches, it needs to be asserted that the referential logic at work in figural sense-making is ontological other-speaking in a distinctly theological sense. Both the theological frame of reference established by Proverbs 8:22–31 and the language of Proverbs 8:30 exert what we might call an ontological pressure

131. The ontological status of interpretive categories or metaphors in Israel's scriptures (for example, Word, Wisdom, Beginning, and Begetting) are crucial to the New Testament's exegetical witness to Christ. See Seitz, "Trinity in the Old Testament," 28–40.

132. Intertextual models for constructing a theological account of biblical language generally fail to do justice to the *text-res* model at work in the early church, the latter of which is arguably better suited to addressing the problems inherent in hermeneutical accounts that construe biblical language in self-referential terms—that is, as a self-contained system of meaning. See Brevard S. Childs, "Critique of Recent Intertextual Canonical Interpretation," *ZAW* 115 (2003): 173–84, esp. his remarks on 182–83; cf. also the helpful summary of Childs's concerns in Daniel R. Driver, *Brevard Childs, Biblical Theologian for the Church's One Bible* (Tübingen: Mohr Siebeck, 2010), 152–59.

133. See, for example, the discussion in Martin Irvine, *The Making of Textual Culture: "Grammatica" and Literary Theory 350–1100* (Cambridge: Cambridge University Press, 1994), 244–47. Irvine suggests a *text-text* model, rather than a *text-res* model, for understanding the nature of language as "other-speaking."

upon our reading that speaks against reducing the figure of begotten Wisdom to a *mere* metaphor or literary device, bereft of any ontological purchase upon the character of the divine identity of Israel's one LORD.

Certainly one can appreciate the admonition that as a "highly figurative composition," Proverbs 8:22–31 should not be read in a strictly literal fashion that collapses the ontological differences between divine and human begetting.[134] We can also respect the warning that "Woman Wisdom is not a pre-incarnate form of the second person of the Trinity."[135] The trouble is that this way of putting the matter lacks theological and exegetical nuance. What, for example, is meant by the phrase "pre-incarnate form"? Presumably it means to say that one should not take the figural language of Woman Wisdom in Proverbs 8 and throughout the book in general as a sort of literal incarnation of Christ before the fact—and with this, we can fully agree. Christ's figural presence in the form of Old Testament Wisdom is not the same mode of presence as his incarnate presence. Drawing an analogy between biblical language and the incarnation, the early church argued that before the Word *assumed* a body, he first *clothed* himself in creation and the language of Scripture. Yet it is one thing to argue that these acts of "clothing" are figurally linked with Christ's incarnation and therefore participate in its reality, and another thing to argue that the Word *assumed* a human body prior to the incarnation. Because the figures of Scripture "give flesh" to Christ the eternal Word, scriptural figuralism is its own kind of incarnational reality, sharing in the theological logic and form of the incarnation, yet mysteriously distinct from it. In his book on Origen, Henri de Lubac attempts to register this distinction as follows: "In the literal meaning of Scripture, the Logos is thus not, properly speaking, incarnated as he is in the humanity of Jesus, and this is what allows us still to speak of comparison: he is, nevertheless, already truly incorporated there; he himself dwells there, not just some idea of him, and this is what authorizes us to speak already of his coming, of his hidden presence."[136]

Begotten Wisdom and Monotheism in Proverbs 8

One can also agree with the concern to respect the teaching of Israel's scriptures on monotheism. That being said, however, the ongoing distinction

134. Longman, *How to Read Proverbs*, 104.
135. Longman, *How to Read Proverbs*, 110.
136. Henri de Lubac, *History and Spirit: The Understanding of Scripture according to Origen*, trans. Anne E. Nash (San Francisco: Ignatius, 2007), 389. Cf. also the discussion in Collett, "Christomorphic Shaping of Time in Radner's *Time and the Word*," 287–88.

between the LORD and Wisdom in the poem registered by the use of first and third person pronouns, along with the other exegetical phenomena mentioned above, opens up another avenue that honors the Old Testament's commitment to monotheism while allowing the Old Testament's own presentation to shape our understanding of the character of that monotheism. At this juncture it is helpful to reference the comments of Christopher Seitz:

> The problem here is that the term "monotheism," when used in reference to the Old Testament, is nothing but a placeholder serving to rule out some obvious alternatives (Israel did not worship multiple gods in a pantheon) but in itself it is imprecise. At issue is the *kind* of monotheism said to mark the life of God with his people Israel. . . . For later Christian theological reflection, it is the very existence of the scriptures of Israel and their commitment to a peculiar kind of monotheism that gives rise to trinitarian convictions about the character of God, such that, lacking these scriptures and their specific literal-sense declarations, we would simply have no trinitarian talk at all, but rather something like the divinization of Jesus (with the help of borrowed titles having not much to do with him in reality). The precondition of trinitarian reflection, in other words, is precisely the Old Testament of early Christian reception and interpretation. Had there been no reception of these writings as the sole authoritative witness to the work and identity of God, during which period the New Testament writings were coming to form, the conditions would not have been in place for the kind of trinitarian theological thinking that emerged.[137]

At the end of the day, there is no need to protect Old Testament monotheism from possible polytheistic abuse by interpreting Wisdom as an attribute of the LORD or as a literary personification without significance for expressing the ontological identity of the God of Israel. There are good reasons to question whether such moves do justice to the exegetical pressures of the text. Moreover, the nature of Old Testament monotheism is *bound up* with these exegetical pressures. Israel's scriptures teach that the LORD is God—not in the way that other gods might be called God but in a unique and incomparable way (Deut. 4:35, 39; cf. Exod. 15:11; Mic. 7:18). Those scriptures disclose his identity in a manner that reveals the unique character of his oneness, a peculiar form of monotheism capable of supporting distinction of persons within that oneness, as Proverbs 8:22–31 teaches and the early church confessed.

The exegetical debate over Proverbs 8 offers a timely reminder that the early church fathers were confident in the ability of the Old Testament text, in relation with Christ the eternal Word, to position their present situation and the

---

137. Seitz, "Trinity in the Old Testament," 30–31.

church's christological confession without recourse to the New Testament in the first instance. Frances Young notes that in the debate over Proverbs 8:22–31, "no one in the fourth century challenged the fundamental approach to this text which we can already trace in the work of the second-century apologists. The christological referent of personified wisdom was a tradition never questioned" by either party to the debate, including Arius.[138] Rather, Proverbs 8 was "generally read as a passage about the being who was the instrument through whom God created the universe."[139] Here we meet with the early church's confidence in the Old Testament's continuing ability, in conjunction with the Spirit and the Word now made flesh, to exegetically authorize a place to stand in the mapping out of the church's christo-trinitarian confession. It is to this Old Testament witness that the rule of faith calls our attention in the first place, and it is for this reason that the witness of Proverbs 8 continues to shape the christological character of ecclesial space in the present.

Hosea 1:2: "The Beginning of (That Which) the Lord Spoke through Hosea"

Before closing this chapter, one additional example drawn from the witness of the prophets also offers a window on the potential that figural reading has for making visible the relation between archē and agency in the Old Testament—in this case, the archē of the prophetic word the Lord spoke through the prophet Hosea. Hosea 1:2 speaks of "The beginning of (that which) the Lord spoke through Hosea."[140] The Hebrew term תְּחִלַּת is rendered in English as "beginning," which the Septuagint translates as archē. Most commentators typically assume that the beginning in view describes a temporal beginning, and so its significance as an architectural figure for prophecy in the Book of the Twelve receives little or no discussion in commentaries. The Masoretic Hebrew text of Hosea contains an open paragraph marker in the middle of 1:2 that marks the first sentence off as a separate grammatical unit,[141] while also signaling that the following sentence should start on a new line. For this reason the first sentence in Hosea (1:2a) should be grouped with the superscription that precedes it in 1:1, rather than with what follows (1:2b: "And the Lord said to Hosea, 'Go, take to yourself a wife of harlotry'"). In other words, Hosea 1:2a functions as a subunit within the superscription in 1:1 that introduces Hosea.

138. Young, "Proverbs 8 in Interpretation (2)," 103.
139. Young, "Proverbs 8 in Interpretation (2)," 104.
140. The LXX converts the piel verb in the Masoretic Text to a noun, rendering the phrase as "the beginning of the word of the Lord through Hosea."
141. For a discussion of paragraph markers placed in the middle of sentences, see Emanuel Tov, *Textual Criticism of the Hebrew Bible*, 2nd rev. ed. (Minneapolis: Fortress, 2001), 53–54.

Because the unit formed by Hosea 1:1–2a occurs at the outset of Hosea's prologue in chapters 1–3, when the significance of "beginning" in 1:2a is recognized, its introductory reach is typically understood in temporal terms and limited to Hosea's prologue itself or to the book of Hosea as a whole. However, given the temporal scope envisioned by the names in Hosea's prologue (Jeroboam, Gomer, Jezreel), there are good reasons to question such restricted readings of the scope and function of Hosea 1:2a. As an interpretive synopsis of the Twelve, Hosea's prologue makes use of the figures of Hosea and Gomer to frame the LORD's relation to Israel in terms of a marriage. By forming an interpretive frame or *inclusio* around chapter 2, the marriage relationship of Hosea and Gomer in chapters 1 and 3 functions as a literary way of underscoring the figural message already set up in Hosea 1:2—namely, that Hosea's marriage to Gomer is intended to be a living parable of the LORD's covenantal marriage with Israel. Both the reference to Jeroboam in Hosea's prologue and the figures of Gomer and Jezreel serve to coordinate this marriage with the division of history that unfolds from Jeroboam I to Jeroboam II in 1 and 2 Kings, a history summed up, interpreted, and comprehensively styled "Jeroboam."[142]

The scattering of Israel in Hosea 1:4–5 through the day of visitation anticipates Israel's regathering in the great day of Jezreel in 1:11. This makes it clear that in Hosea's prologue, the image of Jezreel comprehends within itself simultaneous acts of judgment and redemption, an Old Testament figure of the cross-shaped logic inherent to the LORD's name and character (Exod. 34:5–7). In other words, the day of visitation associated with Hosea 1:4–5 is not the whole story but a down payment on the *greater* day of Jezreel (v. 11) when a united Israel will once again confess one another as the LORD's people (2:1).[143] The great day of Jezreel in Hosea's prologue finds a counterpart in

142. In *Bonds of Love*, R. Abma writes,
   Jeroboam ben Joash functions in the superscription of Hosea as virtually the *last* king of Israel. Both the correspondence in name to the *first* king of the divided Israel, the prototypical character of this name, and the developments after his death (2 Kings 15) could point in that direction. Jeroboam II may have been looked upon as the summation of kings in the northern kingdom, in the double sense of "conclusion" and "summary." He is the summary of these kings in the sense that he represents the full amount of evil that has characterized, and still characterizes, the kings of Israel, and he is the conclusion to these kings in the sense that the evil of the Israelite monarchs that he represents will inevitably bring the northern kingdom to ruin. . . . The name Jeroboam . . . functions as a *pars-pro-toto* appellation for the last kings of Israel. (R. Abma, *Bonds of Love: Methodic Studies of Prophetic Texts with Marriage Imagery (Isaiah 50:1–3 and 54:1–10, Hosea 1–3, Jeremiah 2–3)* [Assen, Netherlands: Van Gorcum, 1999], 136)
143. For a list of the differing ways this verse has been interpreted, see Abma, *Bonds of Love*, 166n128.

the great and fear-inspiring Day of the LORD in Joel (2:11, 31; cf. Zeph. 1:14), ultimately coming to rest at the close of the Twelve with Malachi's great Day of the LORD (Mal. 4:5),[144] bringing in its wake godly fear, repentance, and the healing of family division within Israel through the eschatological ministry of the prophet Elijah (Mal. 4:5–6).

In light of the figurally comprehensive ways these names function in Hosea's prologue, a theologically foundational reading of "beginning" in Hosea 1:2 makes sense. But just what does "beginning" in Hosea 1:2a introduce? Hosea 1:2b–1:9,[145] Hosea 1–3,[146] the entire book of Hosea, or the Book of the Twelve (Hosea through Malachi)? If "beginning" in Hosea 1:2 is not merely a temporal beginning for the Twelve—that is, the temporal starting point of the Twelve's history—but an archē that founds and constrains what follows, akin to the function of *bərē'šît* in Genesis 1:1 and Proverbs 8:22, then Hosea's prologue is doing something more than just introducing the book of Hosea. Adopting an archetypal reading of "beginning" in Hosea 1:2 means not only that Hosea is the "first" prophet through whom the LORD spoke in the Twelve[147] but also that the *word* the LORD speaks to Hosea is the *founding* agent or agency by which the witness of the Twelve is established. As archē, the word the LORD speaks to Hosea has foundation-laying significance for what follows in the Twelve. Here we find the same intrinsic relation between archē (Beginning) and divine speech (Word) found in Genesis 1:1–3. In this way, the archetypal reading of "beginning" in Hosea 1:2a suggests that Hosea's prologue provides a rule or authorizing frame for reading the Twelve as a whole.

Conclusion

A cryptic saying attributed to Hegel claims, "The Owl of Minerva flies at dusk." Given that the Owl of Minerva is a Greek figure for Wisdom, the point seems to be that Wisdom is a matter of retrospective realization (telos), rather than archetypal foundations (archē). Much bad biblical theology has been

144. According to Abma, the great day of Jezreel "plays upon" the notion of the great Day of the LORD in the Twelve, though the Day of the LORD is usually not given the positive connotation registered by the great day of Jezreel in Hosea 1:11. Abma, *Bonds of Love*, 165.

145. Hans Walter Wolff, *Hosea: A Commentary on the Book of the Prophet Hosea*, trans. G. Stansell, Hermeneia (Philadelphia: Fortress, 1974), 12.

146. Since 1:2a properly belongs to 1:1, and since 4:1 marks the start of a new unit in Hosea after 1:1 (using the parallel construct phrase "the word of the LORD"), Abma argues that the "beginning" in 1:2a introduces only Hosea 1–3. See Abma, *Bonds of Love*, 125.

147. Whatever one decides regarding the meaning of archē in Hosea 1:2, assigning a chronological sense to archē makes no sense, since in temporal terms, Amos's prophetic ministry began before Hosea's.

built upon this very assumption. It is not that history teaches us nothing, nor that creation is simply an instrumental means to a divine end, with no integrity or contribution of its own to make to the realization or actualization of human wisdom in time. Rather, the point is that the enabling condition for this process of temporal maturation finds its location in Wisdom as the eternal and pre-existent Archē of creation (cf. Gen. 1:1; Prov. 8:22; John 1:1–3; Col. 1:15–18), apart from which the telic character of human wisdom loses its foundation as well as its life-giving, motivating force. As the example drawn from Hosea's prologue suggests, the prophetic witness of the Old Testament also knows of the archē and agency of divine speech at work in Israel's midst, forming her as a new creation through acts of judgment and mercy rooted in the name and character of the LORD. In this way we learn that both creation and prophecy do their sense-making in terms of the Wisdom and Word of the LORD, the archē and agent by which God has inaugurated a new creation and formed a kingdom of priests for himself (Exod. 19:4–6; 1 Pet. 2:9).

Interpretive Postscript

Placing undue emphasis upon the distinction between metaphor and figure failed to provide a solution to the figural-allegorical abuses of twelfth-century exegesis. Arguably, the ironic outcome of this program of reform was the demotion of biblical metaphor to the status of poetic ornament. That such a result should not have been the case, especially since the differences between metaphor and figure do not turn upon their ability to disclose theological realities, nevertheless did not prevent subsequent students of Scripture from identifying metaphor with literary ornament, and thus by extension with something that has little or nothing to do with theological reality and truth. A classic modern example may be found in the sharp distinction John Locke draws between rhetorical figures, which do not yield truth, and discursive modes of philosophical argument in the form of propositions, which serve as the touchstone for truth.[148] One also wonders whether the attempt to read a sharp distinction between metaphor and allegory in Aquinas gets off on the wrong foot by misconstruing his account of first-order signification. While it is true that Aquinas speaks of this "first sense" as the literal-historical sense,

---

148. See the derisive comments on rhetoric, as well as the sharp distinction Locke draws between rhetorical figures and philosophical truth, in bk. 3, chap. 10, sec. 34 of *An Essay Concerning Human Understanding* (1690). There he argues that while rhetorical figures are aesthetic "ornaments" that bring "pleasure and delight," they do not disclose "things as they are" but actually "mislead the judgment." As such they are "perfect cheats." He concludes by observing that as far as truth and knowledge are concerned, rhetorical figures are "wholly to be avoided."

it is highly doubtful he intended to identify the literal sense with the transfer of *historical* meaning, and the figural or allegorical sense with the communication of *theological* meaning. For Aquinas this is a false dichotomy, since like Luther after him, he recognizes that, properly speaking, Scripture does not have two subject matters but one.

In the nature of the case, when we privilege something by pushing it up and foregrounding it, something else gets pushed down and falls into the background. While this belongs to the nature of the descriptive task and so on one level cannot be avoided, it is possible to avoid the mistake of deflating metaphor to the status of literary ornament in order to prop up the theological significance of figural signification. We also need not fall into the opposite error of undercutting the theological function of metaphor in order to prop up the theological importance of verbal signification. What we learn from this is that in attempting to account for the place of authorial and figural modes in the construction of biblical sense, it has always been possible to proceed along one of two false paths: either inflate the importance of figural signification by deflating the distinctive contribution language makes to the construction of Scripture's theological sense; or, in what is now a characteristically contemporary move,[149] inflate the importance of language and verbal signification while deflating or even erasing the significance of figural signification in Scripture.[150] The latter move can easily lead to the devaluation of the church's liturgical and sacramental theology, not to mention the eclipse of providence in biblical poetics. What we need is a providential account of biblical sense-construction that rightly proportionalizes the literal sense in relation to its figural sense. Scripture's theological sense is mediated through inspired words in a given historical context *and* through the relation of those words to a larger, providentially constructed network of figurally related things. Since the Bible bears witness to both modes, authorial and figural, it is wrong to exclusively identify its theological meaning with its figural sense, as though its inspired words made no contribution of their own to Scripture's theological sense but merely serve as empty pointers to the figural or allegorical sense. This not only runs the risk of erasing the distinctive contribution the literal sense makes to the

149. For Heidegger, only the act of dwelling in our linguistic practices discloses their meaning or sense. In language man dwells; therefore man does not speak language, but language speaks man. Language is the chamber in which being is disclosed, for "it is *language that speaks*, not, or not primordially, man" (George Steiner, *Martin Heidegger* [Chicago: University of Chicago Press, 1989], 22). See the essays on language and poetry in Martin Heidegger, *Poetry, Language, Thought*, trans. Albert Hofstader (New York: Harper & Row, 1971).

150. It is at least arguable that when joined with the inflated account of language in modernity, the Reformation's heavy emphasis on verbal signification gives rise to an account of biblical sense-making that threatens to overwhelm figural reading in biblical interpretation.

construction of the biblical sense but also undercuts its primary role as the interpreter of the economy of God's redemptive providence.

Failure to appreciate the governing significance of biblical words for our grasp of Scripture's figural senses also precludes the possibility of a disciplined approach to the plurality of senses supported by biblical metaphors and figuration. Although biblical words in a given grammatical-historical context typically have one sense, when these words are providentially ordered in relation to figural signs, they take on extended senses by which they become capable of supporting many senses (*multos sensus*). It is important to stress that the multiple senses inherent in Scripture's literal figures render their theological sense according to the specificity of biblical words, and not apart from them. In this way the multivalent character of the figural sense is affirmed. However, at the same time, the figural sense remains under the grammatical control of the literal sense, allowing for an exegetically bounded and disciplined multivalency, rather than uncontrolled versions of Scripture's literal sense, which identify its polyvalency with postmodern forms of radical indeterminacy. Benjamin Jowett's infamous objection—if a text can mean more than one thing, it can mean anything[151]—makes sense only in a world where biblical meaning is completely defined by its relationship to original historical context, but not in a world where authorial intention and historical context are part of a larger providential drama by which Scripture's theological sense is rendered.

Jowett's approach would have undoubtedly struck someone like Augustine as a beggarly view of the Bible's character as a vehicle for the triune God's self-disclosure. Augustine does not approach the task of interpreting a given biblical text as though its meaning were something he could master by exhausting the historical circumstances of its origin, thereby arriving at a single, precise, mathematically definitive meaning. Instead he seeks to discover the different ways we can legitimately hear and appropriate the Bible's literal sense within the theological context authorized by Scripture.[152] For Augustine as well as Aquinas after him, under one literal sense (*sub una littera*) the Bible is capable of embracing many senses (*multos sensus*) because of the text's link to a divinely constructed providential history that mediates an inexhaustibly rich theological reality, the reality of the triune God. In like fashion, in his *Literal Commentary on Job* Aquinas argues that the meaning of Scripture's literal sense is what is intended by the inspired *words* the Holy Spirit gave

151. Benjamin Jowett, "On the Interpretation of Scripture," in *Essays and Reviews* (London: Parker & Sons, 1860), para. 372, http://www.ccel.org/ccel/temple_f/essays.ix.html: "If words have more than one meaning, they may have any meaning."

152. See Augustine, *The Confessions*, trans. Henry Chadwick (Oxford: Oxford University Press, 1991), bk. 12, chaps. 31–32.

to biblical authors,[153] rather than a direct function of their consciousness or what was "in their heads" when they penned the words of Scripture. Thus it does not occur to Aquinas to use the literal sense as a starting point by which to probe the religious consciousness of biblical authors after the fashion of Schleiermacher, because meaning for him is not an affair of human consciousness but an affair of providence. Within this providence, inspired biblical *words* speak in distinction from, as well as in relation to, Scripture's metaphorical and figural senses.

The providential rationale at work in the linkage of inspired words with figural things is what ultimately accounts for the fact that biblical authors spoke more than they knew. Thus if one wishes to speak of "scientific" exegesis in the case of Augustine and Aquinas, it would be more appropriate to describe their approach to biblical meaning as "a science of the possible," rather than "a science of precision" in the flat sense found in the natural and mathematical sciences of the seventeenth and eighteenth centuries. At the same time, just because a biblical text or passage can mean more than one thing, it does not follow that it can mean anything. This is because the inspired words the Spirit gave to biblical writers limit the range of possible meanings a given biblical text can have. Moreover, the church has always recognized a number of parameters that limit the range of possible meanings for Scripture's literal sense. In addition to the governing voice of the literal sense, Scripture's theological subject matter (*res*), the rule of faith (*regula fidei*), and the Bible's reception history (ecclesial sense) also place constraints upon the reader's ability to control or manipulate biblical meaning.

While these considerations help explain the hermeneutical priority of the literal sense in rendering the Bible's theological meaning, the theological rationale for this priority ultimately derives from the privileged place biblical words occupy in a theological account of biblical language, as we learned in chapter 1 of this book. As a creaturely analogue and figure of the eternal Word, Scripture takes its cue from Genesis 1:1–2:3 (cf. John 1:1–3) by affirming the priority of inspired speech for the interpretation of created things, including the use of metaphorical and figural signs in the providential construction of biblical sense. Yet the redemptive reordering of creation and the history

153. "Now this premise is proposed symbolically and enigmatically, in keeping with the usage of sacred Scripture, which describes spiritual things under the figures of corporeal things. . . . Now although spiritual things are proposed under the figures of corporeal things, nevertheless, the truths intended about spiritual things through sensible figures belong not to the mystical but to the literal sense because *the literal sense is that which is primarily intended by the words*, whether they are used properly or figuratively." Cited in Schreiner, *Where Shall Wisdom Be Found?*, 222n87, emphasis added.

by which Scripture's figural sense is constructed does not reduce creation and redemptive providence to a mere theater or occasion for the transfer of theological meaning through biblical language. While Scripture's figural sense has a relative rather than independent integrity from biblical language, it cannot be dispensed with by wholly absorbing it into the literal sense. As argued earlier, to do so not only falls into the error of instrumentalizing the role of creation and history within God's redemptive purpose but also initiates a movement toward the erasure of the figural sense in biblical sense-making.

With that erasure comes a downsized version of redemptive providence that centers the construction and transfer of Scripture's theological meaning in a biblical poetics modeled upon the communion of two authorial consciousnesses, one divine and the other human. In this way biblical meaning becomes an affair of consciousness rather than an affair of providence.[154] Here, biblical sense-making is reduced to a conversation between two authors, and the contribution of figural meaning to the construction of biblical sense is wiped out. To combat this, one can prop up the significance of figural signs for Scripture's theological meaning, shifting the center of gravity in biblical poetics away from the literal to the figural sense. But the danger on this route lies in adopting a form of textual occasionalism that undercuts the distinctive contribution biblical words make to theological sense-making, in addition to effectively denying their governing authority over the meaning of Scripture's metaphorical and figural senses. In sum, whether we speak of the way biblical language renders theological meaning in relation to inspired human words (authorial discourse) or in relation to a network of figurally ordered things (figural discourse), the crucial point to grasp is that both modes are integral to the redemptive providence by which biblical language transfers theological meaning to its readers.

---

154. See, for example, E. D. Hirsch Jr., *Validity in Interpretation* (New Haven: Yale University Press, 1967), 48. While Hirsch's own account of meaning as "an affair of consciousness" is not located within a theological model of divine and human authorship, the general premise behind his approach is alive and well in this two-author model for understanding biblical poetics. In questioning the sufficiency of this model, the point is not to deny that it remains theologically meaningful to speak of God as the "author" of Scripture. Rather, the debate turns on how the word *author* is to be interpreted in this description, as well as the question whether it erases figural signification by modeling divine authorship too closely upon human authorship. Understanding divine authorship on strict analogy with human modes of authorship effectively reduces the construction of biblical sense to the transfer of meaning from one authorial intention to another. The problems associated with this come to fruition in the model for biblical poetics offered by *sensus plenior*. See the discussion in Robert Bruce Robinson, *Roman Catholic Exegesis since "Divino Afflante Spiritu": Hermeneutical Implications* (Atlanta: Scholars Press, 1988), chap. 2.

▪▪ Part 3 ▪▪
Assessment

4

Figural Reading and Modernity

Sharply distinguishing Scripture's literal-metaphorical sense from its allegorical sense threatens to evacuate the metaphors and figures of biblical poetry of theological significance. As we have seen, the Reformation moved in an opposite direction, seeking to directly reunite Scripture's literal sense with its theological sense without the need to speak of extended senses,[1] whether figural or allegorical. Here the concern is not with making proper distinctions but with making too many distinctions. While thirteenth-century concerns to reform the abuse of Scripture's literal sense called for the making of proper distinctions between metaphor and theological allegory, in the sixteenth century these same concerns called for minimizing distinctions in the name of preventing the dissolution of the literal sense. In so doing the question needs to be raised whether the Reformers fell into "the Protestant error" of erasing the contribution figural signs make to biblical poetics, unwittingly contributing to the early modern eclipse of providence in the construction of biblical sense. The answer will be a qualified no rather than an unqualified yes, because Protestant reticence to speak of Scripture's figural or allegorical sense undoubtedly led to new imbalances.[2] This holds true regardless of whether one argues these imbalances were unintended side effects or the end result of sixteenth-century criticisms of the *Quadriga*. Following that I will turn to a critical assessment of interpretive models for construing the Old Testament's

1. Christopher Ocker's study of biblical poetics prior to the Reformation suggests that this move was already afoot in Aquinas. See Christopher Ocker, *Biblical Poetics before Humanism and Reformation* (Cambridge: Cambridge University Press, 2002), 38–43; cf. 6–7.

2. See Thomas H. Luxon, *Literal Figures: Puritan Allegory and the Reformation Crisis in Representation* (Chicago: University of Chicago Press, 1995). Among other things, Luxon's book suggests that Protestant attempts to purge allegory from biblical interpretation were ultimately unsuccessful, causing Puritan thinkers like John Bunyan to compensate for its loss by writing books such as *The Pilgrim's Progress* and *Holy War*.

literal sense that have arisen in the wake of modernity, for example, *sensus plenior*, christotelism, and *Wirkungsgeschichte*. Because these models offer alternative frameworks or rules for interpreting the Old Testament's christological witness, we will need to engage the underlying assumptions upon which they are built, especially the way in which those assumptions reconfigure our understanding of the Old Testament's christological sense.

Reforming the Literal Sense: The Reformation and Modern Hermeneutics

Some have read the Reformation as a radical break with late medieval hermeneutics, viewing it as the foundation upon which modern readings of the literal sense have been built. The work of Heiko Oberman and his students has shown that the Reformation's relation to medieval hermeneutics is far more nuanced and complicated than this revolutionary reading suggests.[3] The Reformation shares more continuity with medieval hermeneutics than previously thought. The Reformers did not jettison the theological instincts at work in the *Quadriga*'s construal of the literal sense for the sake of starting over on a wholly new foundation. It is more helpful to think of magisterial Reformers like Luther and Calvin as reformers of the medieval *Quadriga*, rather than as revolutionaries in the modern political sense of the term. At the same time there are also genuine discontinuities between Reformation commentators and their medieval forebears, and thus it remains meaningful to speak of Reformation hermeneutics in distinction from medieval hermeneutics.[4] That being said, the nature of these discontinuities does not fully support the claim that the Reformation laid the foundation for a new understanding of the literal sense *as* the historical sense *tout court*.[5] Here it is helpful once again to cite the remarks of Brevard Childs: "Because of the similar emphasis on the literal sense between the Reformers and the new advocates of the historical critical method, it has been customary for textbooks to see a line of direct continuity between these two periods, indeed, to find in the Reformers a warrant for critical exegesis. If one tests this theory

3. Heiko Oberman, *The Harvest of Medieval Theology: Gabriel Biel and Late Medieval Nominalism* (Durham: Labyrinth, 1983); cf. Richard A. Muller and John L. Thompson, eds., *Biblical Interpretation in the Era of the Reformation: Essays Presented to David C. Steinmetz in Honor of His Sixtieth Birthday* (Grand Rapids: Eerdmans, 1996).

4. See James S. Preus, *From Shadow to Promise: Old Testament Interpretation from Augustine to the Young Luther* (Cambridge, MA: Harvard University Press, 1969), 1–6, 267–71.

5. For example, Philip Schaff prefers to construe Calvin as a forerunner of modern biblical hermeneutics who recovered the importance of Scripture's historical sense, rather than a catholic reader of Scripture with continuing debts to patristic and medieval hermeneutics. See Philip Schaff, "Calvin as a Commentator," *Presbyterian and Reformed Review* 3, no. 11 (1892): 462–69.

on the problem of *sensus literalis*, the appeal to an easy historical and theo-logical continuity runs into major obstacles. In fact, the discontinuities are far more significant."[6] With these comments in view it is more accurate to suggest that the Reformation was a recovery, continuation, and expansion of the theological instincts by which the early church construed the literal sense, though the Reformation adopted a more economical approach. We may therefore speak of the Reformation's approach to biblical hermeneutics as *reformed* Catholicism.

The magisterial Reformers did not depart from the church's traditional conviction that Scripture's literal sense admits of figural or extended senses. Rather, like others before them, they were concerned with the breakdown of the governing influence of the literal sense on its figural senses, a problem that had reached a critical point in certain forms of medieval exegesis.[7] For these reasons it is misleading to portray Luther and Calvin as proto-modern revo-lutionaries who redefined the literal sense as the historical sense, anticipat-ing later figures like J. P. Gabler and the historicized approach to the literal sense later found in modern historical-critical exegesis.[8] As we learned in chapter 2 of this book, Luther's and Calvin's reforms did not replace Scrip-ture's allegorical or figural senses; instead, they sought to *expand* the literal sense by redefining its scope in such a way as to subsume its extended senses within it. In this they were anticipated by figures in late thirteenth-century scholasticism such as Nicholas of Lyre. Lyre's attempts to expand the scope of Scripture's literal sense testify "to the new prestige and scope which the

6. Brevard S. Childs, "The *Sensus Literalis* of Scripture: An Ancient and Modern Problem," in *Beiträge zur alttestamentlichen Theologie: Festschrift für Walther Zimmerli Zum 70. Geburtstag*, ed. Herbert Donner, Robert Hanhart, and Rudolf Smend (Göttingen: Vandenhoeck & Ruprecht, 1977), 88. Similarly, Richard Muller notes that while the Reformation moved away from the medieval *Quadriga*, preferring a "more philological approach," this concentration on the letter "must not be understood as a sudden shifting of gears into a modern, historical-critical mode of interpretation. The 'literal sense' of the text was still understood by the Reformation exegete as the meaning given by the grammatical understanding of the narrative: in other words, the yield of the *sensus literalis* remained nearly identical to the *historia* of the old fourfold model and was not at all understood as a meaning to be critically reconstructed by the exegete." Richard A. Muller, *Post-Reformation Reformed Dogmatics: The Rise and Development of Reformed Or-thodoxy, ca. 1520 to ca. 1725*, 2nd ed. (Grand Rapids: Baker Academic, 2003), 2:443.

7. Luther's preference for "promise" rather than "figura" derives from the fact that in late medieval hermeneutics, "figura" had simply become a cipher for the historical era of the New Testament and the post-apostolic ecclesial tradition that followed it. As such, it was incapable of capturing the dynamic of Christ's presence within the history of Israel, prior to the apostles and the New Testament era. See Preus, *From Shadow to Promise*, 144–211.

8. The modern approach to the literal sense is called "historical-critical" because the literal sense's historical dimension, as reconstructed by the modern exegete, functions as a critical control on the meaning of the literal sense.

literal sense came to enjoy, within thirteenth-century schools of theology and beyond."[9] Luther and Calvin adopted their own strategies for expanding the scope of the literal sense, the result being that the literal sense "invaded and occupied territory previously governed by allegory, a major redrawing of boundary-lines being the consequence."[10] However, these reforms did not render Scripture's allegorical sense redundant, although Luther and Calvin did succeed in relocating much of its business under new management.[11] At the same time, the new boss promoted by the Reformation was really the old boss but with an even tighter grip on her employees.

Because Scripture discloses a theological subject matter—namely, the tri-une God speaking in Christ—for Luther and Calvin the literal sense cannot be identified with its historical sense *simpliciter* after the fashion of modern historicism, nor with human authorial intention per se. The literal sense is capable of embracing Scripture not only in its grammatical or primary sense but also in its figural or allegorical sense. These extended senses are a hermeneutical consequence of the Bible's inseparable relation to *one* theological subject matter, and their meaning is governed by the same control we find expressed in the hermeneutical theories of the early church and later codified in the brilliant synthesis provided by Aquinas's *Summa Theologiae*. In the exegesis of biblical books, especially the Old Testament, it was not enough for Luther and Calvin to discover a text's grammatical sense and leave matters at that, nor to belabor for apologetic purposes the comparative differences between Israel's witness and the religious views of its neighbors. Rather, they sought to expound the mysteries of Christ and his gospel in the Old Testament's literal sense, not by insisting that its witness be correlated with the New Testament but by struggling to come to terms with the Old Testament's own way of disclosing Christ. The fact that they were not always successful in their efforts or failed to consistently live up to this exegetical ideal does not undercut this claim. It merely demonstrates their limitations in fully working out a christo-trinitarian hermeneutic on terms established by the Old Testament's literal sense.

If Luther and Calvin observe a distinction between the literal and theological senses of Scripture, it is *not* because they regard this distinction as a marker for the notion of historical or reflective distance between the words of

9. See Alastair Minnis, *Medieval Theory of Authorship: Scholastic Literary Attitudes in the Later Middle Ages*, 2nd ed. (Philadelphia: University of Pennsylvania Press, 2010), ix. Rather than follow the fourfold division of biblical sense into a literal sense with three extended senses, Nicholas of Lyre preferred to speak of a "double literal sense."

10. See Minnis, *Medieval Theory of Authorship*, xi.

11. See Minnis, *Medieval Theory of Authorship*, xi.

Scripture and the theological reality of which it speaks. To observe that biblical texts are not the LORD himself registers an ontological difference between Scripture and its theological *res*. But this difference should not be conflated with the modern conception that historical distance characterizes the relation between Scripture's readers and its theological referent. In historical-critical modes for reading Scripture, overcoming the reality of historical distance mandates the need for historical reconstruction in order that readers of Scripture may be reunited with its theological sense.[12] Once the distinction between the Bible's literal and theological sense is construed in this way, modernity's historical reconstruction projects are no longer merely helpful or not, as the case may be, but *required* in order to gain access to Scripture's theological meaning. Closing the historical gap between Scripture's literal and theological senses becomes a matter of one's own efforts, and thus by extension a modern variation on the Pelagian theme of salvation by works—in this case one's historical works. For the magisterial Reformers, this task is accomplished by the triune God, who speaks in Scripture by the Spirit. Historical study and reconstruction do not function as substitutes for this theological rationale but remain fully within its parameters.

As we move toward a discussion of modern efforts to reform the literal sense, it is important to stress that the concern for the literal-historical sense and its governing role in biblical interpretation was never *entirely* lost in premodern exegesis, including the Reformation, though it clearly experienced changing fortunes. For the church of premodernity, the historical dimension inherent in the primacy of the literal sense was not a mere placeholder for a general concept of history, to be filled in according to the assumptions its readers make about biblical history and its character. Biblical history was not a concept one could generalize, nor a limiting concept whose content is to be supplied by filling in the blanks on the basis of readerly assumptions. It is a particular concept native to Scripture's own witness to the providential character of history. It is a providentially constructed history (*historia*) by which the words of Scripture render theological, heavenly, and redemptive realities in creaturely form (*verba*), either through Scripture's literal sense or through its literal sense in conjunction with its figural sense. For Augustine

---

12. On the importance of distinguishing moral from historical distance in biblical interpretation, see R. R. Reno, *In the Ruins of the Church: Sustaining Faith in an Age of Diminished Christianity* (Grand Rapids: Brazos, 2002), chap. 10; cf. also John J. O'Keefe and R. R. Reno, *Sanctified Vision: An Introduction to Early Christian Interpretation of the Bible* (Baltimore: Johns Hopkins University Press, 2005), 13, 27–28, 30, 116. Luther and Calvin thus would have had no problem affirming, along with O'Keefe and Reno, that "the text is the *res*," since their approach to the *text-res* distinction in biblical hermeneutics does not conflate ontological difference with the modern conception of historical or reflective distance.

and Aquinas, Scripture's literal sense is historical because it serves to disclose *God's* historical performances in time—that is, God's providential ways in history—in contrast with modern approaches to Scripture's literal sense that usually identify its historical sense with a historically reconstructed sense. This attenuated way of construing Scripture's historical sense would have made little or no sense to a premodern church that, much like Aquinas, regarded reflection on the literal sense as a meditation on providence. In the church of modernity, whether liberal or evangelical, readers of Scripture typically invoke a concept of history in which providence has already been banished, either because of its theological connotations or because of a narrowly conceived account of biblical poetics that *identifies* the brokering of Scripture's theological sense with inspired human authorship. Such approaches form a significant contrast with the understanding of history at work in premodern accounts of the literal sense, as well as that of the biblical prophets and apostles.

The Reformation, Occasionalism, and the Birth of Modernity

Some historians trace the roots of modernity back to the sixteenth-century Reformation. Others go back even further to the collapse of the relation between nature and grace found in Aquinas, whose account of double signification was a microcosm of the hermeneutical assumptions undergirding that relation. On this reading of modernity the fall from Aquinas gave birth to fourteenth-century nominalism and the early Renaissance period, the womb from which both the Reformation and modernity were birthed. This interpretation reflects a familiar version of Roman Catholic historiography vis-à-vis the Protestant Reformation, which tends to view thirteenth-century scholasticism as a golden age that the fourteenth century fell from by collapsing figural or natural signification into verbal signification, all in the name of unifying the literal sense. The ironic and unintended result was a form of nominalism in which the world of nature and its figural signs took on a life of their own apart from the theological frame of reference provided by biblical language. This dissolution of the link between biblical words and the natural world led to the de-sacramentalization and inevitable aggrandizement of nature. In turn, this gave birth to the rise of voluntarism, a theological state of affairs in which the real presence of the spiritual now depends upon human agency. Because the world of grace is now wholly extrinsic to nature, its presence—and by extension the presence of God himself—must be summoned into the realm of nature through acts of human volition.[13] On this reading the Reformation

---

13. This breakdown also has implications for the doctrine of the real presence in eucharistic communion. The thirteenth-century account of the relation between nature and grace made

was essentially a reactionary movement that compensated for this nominal-ist fracture in double signification by aggrandizing the theological world of grace, effectively wiping out creaturely causality and any meaningful place for secondary causation and human agency. Hence the Reformation belongs to a theological world in which grace no longer makes use of intrinsic and creaturely means to renew the realm of nature but reduces it to a mere theater in which God strides about,[14] externally overwhelming it in a manner akin to the mechanistic accounts of causation one later finds in seventeenth-century physics and natural science.[15]

That this does not represent a nuanced reading of the Reformation doc-trine of *concursus* and creaturely causality can be illustrated from the Ref-ormation's confessional documents, as well as the theological battles that took place over the meaning of secondary causality in post-Reformation scholasticism. While it is often argued that the doctrines of God's sov-ereignty and providence that emerged in the sixteenth century undercut the integrity of creaturely agency and means, there are good reasons for claiming that this is not actually the case. The sovereignty of God is not only the enabling condition for the biblical doctrine of providence, upon which biblical figuration rests, but also the basis for a meaningful account of creaturely causality and its integrity. For if God is not fully sovereign but needs creation and history in order to actualize or realize himself in time, then creaturely agency is but a means to another end, with no integrity of its own within the sovereign purposes of God. As Colin Gunton has rightly suggested, conceiving of God in this way is fatal for the integrity of both history and creaturely agency:

---

possible sacramental access to God in the spiritual realm. This door, having been closed by the breakup of nature and grace, acts of volition and human will became the aesthetic means for reuniting the world of the material with the spiritual. The new aesthetic voluntarism constructed for uniting the spiritual with the material thus led to a view of the real presence in the sacra-ments that depends not upon the Spirit's use of the creaturely agency of priestly consecration but upon its reception by human agents (receptionism).

14. For a sophisticated but controversial attempt to locate Calvin's account of grace and creaturely causality within this nominalist and voluntarist framework, see William G. Witt, "Creation, Redemption, and Grace in the Theology of Jacob Arminius" (PhD diss., University of Notre Dame, 1993). For the differences between Calvin and occasionalist accounts of human agency, see the nuanced discussions in Paul Helm, *John Calvin's Ideas* (Oxford: Oxford Uni-versity Press, 2004); Paul Helm, *Calvin at the Centre* (Oxford: Oxford University Press, 2010). The latter book is especially helpful for distinguishing Calvin's view of creaturely causality from the various forms of occasionalism later fostered by the problematic and unstable nature of anthropological dualism in Descartes.

15. For a classic account of this reading of the Reformation and modernity, see the English translation of part 1 of Henri de Lubac's *Surnaturel* in *Augustinianism and Modern Theology*, trans. Lancelot Sheppard (New York: Crossroad, 2000).

Because [Christian teaching] holds that God is already, "in advance" of creation, a communion of persons existing in loving relations, it becomes possible
to say that he does not need the world, and so is able to will the existence of
something else simply for its own sake. Creation is the outcome of God's love
indeed, but of his unconstrained love. It is therefore not a necessary outcome
of what God is, but is contingent. This is important, because it enables us to
say that the world is given value as a realm of being in its own right. It is in the
words of Genesis "very good," not only partly good or as a means to an end,
but simply as and for what it is: the created order.[16]

This upholds the particularity and integrity of history rather than abol-
ishing it, for creation exists not for the sake of realizing an unrealized possibility within God but for its own sake *within* the sovereign purpose of
God. History and creaturely volition thus have a distinct integrity within
the providence and purpose of God.[17] The alternative is to subsume the
medium of creation into a problematic form of occasionalism in which creation has no voice of its own[18] but is simply a passive medium upon which
the voice of God is imposed, after the manner of a divine ventriloquist.[19] In
the realm of biblical hermeneutics this inevitably leads to a form of textual
occasionalism whereby the human authors of Scripture become little more
than plucked instruments or a merely passive occasion for the rendering of
Scripture's theological sense.

Hopefully enough has been said to raise a question mark over historiog-
raphies that attempt to construct a straight line from fourteenth-century

16. Colin Gunton, *The Triune Creator: A Historical and Systematic Study* (Edinburgh:
Edinburgh University Press, 1998), 9–10.

17. It is for this reason that *The Westminster Confession of Faith* III.1 states that "the liberty
or contingency of second causes" involved in creaturely integrity is not rendered meaningless
by God's sovereignty but rather *established* by it. While this is doubtless paradoxical and even
mysterious, it does capture the logic of Gunton's statement.

18. For a modified account of occasionalism that retains a place for creaturely agency, while
at the same time arguing for the elimination of a *tertium quid*, or "third thing," standing between Creator and creature, see Ephraim Radner, *Time and the Word: Figural Reading of the
Christian Scriptures* (Grand Rapids: Eerdmans, 2016), 87–91, 98–99; cf. 63n31.

19. It was Descartes, not the magisterial Reformers, who erased the reality and integrity of
creaturely causality in history. For a discussion of the way in which his mechanistic account of
causality effectively erased the reality of purposive causation and cleared the way for occasionalism, see Helm, *Calvin at the Centre*, 43–44, esp. 44: "Such mechanism endangered the alliance
of Aristotle and Scripture, because at one stroke it eliminated internal principles of causation,
internal forces, in favour of accounting for movement and change by wholly external forces upon
inert matter." Cartesian accounts of causality are part of the larger story by which mechanical
or external causes replaced teleological or internal causes in the explanation of movement. See
Frederick Beiser, "The Enlightenment and Idealism," in *The Cambridge Companion to German
Idealism*, ed. Karl Ameriks (Cambridge: Cambridge University Press, 2000), 19.

nominalism through the Reformation into modernity. At the same time, it needs to be said that the heavy emphasis on verbal signification in the Reformation's radical and sectarian wings did tend toward a Protestant poetics that threatened to collapse Scripture's figural senses into a more narrowly conceived and characteristically modern account of the literal sense.[20] Moreover, the efforts of the magisterial Reformers to expand the scope of the literal sense by subsuming its figural senses under the single umbrella of the grammatical-historical sense has at least a formal resemblance to the reduction of figural signs to biblical words. For these reasons an even-handed approach to the Reformation also recognizes it to be a period of transition into the era of modernity, which, despite the best instincts and practices of the magisterial Reformers, led to new imbalances in biblical interpretation.

Modernity is not a normative science, of course. It does not lie at the summit of a historical path running from the benighted past of the early church down to the present, as though it could be properly assessed by invoking a Whig historiography that assumes the primacy of the present for measuring the worth of the past.[21] Modernity is neither a golden age nor a dark age; it is one challenging period among others in the history of God's providential dealings with the post-biblical church. We may therefore learn some things from the reading practices of church history without taking them as the norm for what it means to read the Bible literally and placing upon them a burden they simply cannot bear. The trouble is that there are a number of serious deficiencies in contemporary understandings of the literal sense that have rendered problematic the unity of Scripture. These deficiencies make it difficult if not impossible for moderns to understand the Christian character of the Old Testament within an account of biblical hermeneutics as a two-testament enterprise. The best way to get at these deficiencies and the problems they raise is to spend some time tracking the way in which the church's approach to biblical interpretation changed with the birth of modernity, once again in the name of reforming the literal sense.

---

20. For historical examples drawn from the world of post-Reformation radicalism, see Luxon, *Literal Figures*, 1–33.

21. See Herbert Butterfield, *The Whig Interpretation of History* (New York: Norton, 1965); cf. also the modern myth of progress undergirding Immanuel Kant's eighteenth-century essay "Was ist Aufklärung?" ("What Is Enlightenment?"). A discussion of Butterfield's continuing importance for historiography may be found in Richard A. Muller's article "Reflections on Persistent Whiggism and Its Antidotes in the Study of Sixteenth-and-Seventeenth-Century Intellectual History," in *Seeing Things Their Way: Intellectual History and the Return of Religion*, ed. Alister Chapman, John Coffey, and Brad S. Gregory (Notre Dame, IN: University of Notre Dame Press, 2009), 134–53.

Reforming the Literal Sense: The Literal Sense as Authorial Consciousness

To understand the eclipse of the biblical doctrine of providence that took place in the eighteenth-century Enlightenment, we must begin with the seventeenth century, because it is during this period that the literal sense and the reality of providence begin to go their separate ways. While Deism's contributions to revisionary accounts of Christianity and providence in these centuries are well documented, comparatively less attention has been devoted to the impact changing views of anthropology had on the literal sense, especially the implications for our understanding of the place and role of human authorship in biblical interpretation. The recalibration of the literal sense that took place in eighteenth-century modernity was anticipated in important ways by the rise of a new anthropology in the philosophical world of the previous century, which facilitated the move from providence to human consciousness as the primary locus for the construction of meaning (poetics). This paved the way for modern approaches to the literal sense as an authorial sense situated within the larger framework of a reconfigured two-author model for biblical sense-making.

Seventeenth-century approaches to poetics are closely tied to a particular anthropology or way of constructing the human self. These approaches later gained popularity in the eighteenth and nineteenth centuries through the work of philosophers such as René Descartes and John Locke, and elements later became manifest in Schleiermacher's approach to biblical hermeneutics. At the outset it is important to recognize that the anthropology, or doctrine of humanity, we work with directly impacts our understanding of authorial sense in Scripture, because authors are human selves or persons. The famous maxim of Descartes, *Cogito ergo sum*, "I think, therefore I am," epitomized the anthropological judgment that an individual's essential self belongs to the realm of the ideal. "I am a thinking thing," says Descartes.[22] This is the essence of what it means to be a person or self—or in more formal terms, that which a self is and apart from which it cannot be. The thinking self, rather than the bodily, phenomenal, or outward self, is the *real* self for Descartes, an assumption more or less common to all idealist anthropologies of the self that were to follow. What are people? People are ideas with feet.

A little further down the road after Descartes, Locke expanded this notion of the self to include the category of consciousness. In the second edition of *An Essay Concerning Human Understanding* (1695), Locke defines the self as

---

22. See René Descartes, "Meditations on First Philosophy," in *The Philosophy of the 16th and 17th Centuries*, ed. Richard Popkin (New York: Free Press, 1966), 136, 141.

"that *conscious* thinking thing . . . which is sensible, or conscious of pleasure and pain, capable of happiness or misery, and so is concerned for itself, as far as that consciousness extends."[23] To be sure, Locke is prepared to admit that "the body too goes to the making [of] the man."[24] But for both Locke and Descartes before him, the body remains epiphenomenal, secondary, or incidental to our real or essential self. The influence of Descartes on Locke's anthropology is especially evident in his account of the self as "that conscious thinking thing," which more or less echoes Descartes notion of the self as "a thinking thing." However, Locke's anthropology makes explicit something that remains implicit in Cartesian anthropology—namely, the notion of the self *as* consciousness.[25] What is the self? Descartes answers, "I am a *thinking* thing"; Locke further answers, "I am a *conscious* thinking thing." Locke's *real* self is basically a self-aware or self-reflective *consciousness* fixed within a body. Thus while Locke is regularly identified with empiricism, his anthropology fully shares in the assumption, common to all idealist anthropologies of the self, that our inner or conscious self is the real self.

What difference, if any, does this view of the self or anthropology make for our understanding of the relationship between biblical authors and the Bible's literal sense? Again, it is important to keep in mind that biblical authors *are* selves. It follows that our anthropology or view of the self will have an impact on our view of biblical authors. What are people for Locke? People are *conscious* ideas with feet. If this be true of people, then by extension it is also true of biblical authors. Once this idealist anthropology begins to gain traction in the world of biblical hermeneutics, a transformation in the way biblical authors are conceived takes place, and with that also comes a change in the way the construction of biblical sense is understood. The contribution to biblical sense made by biblical authors is no longer understood within the

---

23. See John Locke, *An Essay Concerning Human Understanding*, ed. R. Woolhouse (London: Penguin, 1997), 307, emphasis added.

24. Locke, *Essay Concerning Human Understanding*, 306.

25. See the discussion of Locke's anthropology in Christopher Fox, *Locke and the Scriblerians: Identity and Consciousness in Early Eighteenth-Century Britain* (Berkeley: University of California Press, 1988). Fox notes that an anthropology centered upon consciousness also created theological anxiety in Locke's day because it destabilizes the idea of personal identity as that which endures through time, which the traditional category of substance had formerly supplied for the concept of personal identity. How could persons be properly or justly judged in the next life if they were not the same persons? Consciousness as an anthropological description of the self undercut the notion that people have "essences" or "natures" that remain the same through time, rendering problematic the concept of eschatological or final judgment. On the influence of Locke's theory of personal identity in modern cinema, see Basil Smith, "John Locke, Personal Identity, and Memento," in *The Philosophy of Neo-Noir*, ed. Mark T. Conard (Lexington: University Press of Kentucky, 2009), 35–46.

framework of providence. It is conceived of within the framework of human consciousness and the model it provides for construing the authorial dimension inherent in Scripture's literal sense. The construction of meaning, as well as its reception, is now "an affair of consciousness."[26] Earlier struggles to properly relate the literal sense to Scripture's figural senses now take a back seat, and the new driver who takes the wheel motors off in a different direction. The issues for biblical interpretation no longer focus on finding ways to tighten up the relation between Scripture's literal and figural senses, strengthening the controls on figural meaning provided by the literal sense. Questions pertaining to double signification and the proper role of the literal sense within that account presupposed a providential framework for the construction of biblical sense. But the framework in which those questions made sense has now been pushed off center stage, and a new framework centered upon a particular anthropology stands in its place. The issues for biblical interpretation now center upon human inwardness and its relation to the literal sense.

On this model for understanding authorial sense, the *real* author is the "thinking thing" or human consciousness *behind* the literal sense. The text itself, being the outward or secondary expression of the author's real self, now functions as an *instrumental* means to the end of accessing the author's real self—or in Lockean terms, the authorial consciousness housed in the text. The impact of this model upon biblical interpretation may be seen in the way it shifts the proper locus for biblical meaning from the inspired words of the text to the *conscious* intentions of its authors. Biblical meaning is now a function of what its inspired authors were aware of when they penned the words of Scripture, rather than the inspired words of the biblical text per se. This contrasts with earlier accounts of authorial sense in biblical interpretation. These accounts did not make a sharp distinction between authorial intention and the inspired words of Scripture but regarded them as integrated realities.[27] Questions pertaining to the meaning of Scripture's authorial sense were not clearly distinguished, let alone separated from, questions about "the way the words run" in the biblical text. With the rise of a new anthropology rooted in human consciousness, what it means to speak of authorial intention is no longer a function of biblical words per se but of what was in the heads of biblical authors when they wrote—or, to borrow language from Descartes,

---

26. The phrase is that of E. D. Hirsch, whose account of the importance of authorial intention for the interpretation of texts is rooted in an idealist anthropology of the self. See E. D. Hirsch Jr., *Validity in Interpretation* (New Haven: Yale University Press, 1967), 48.

27. For an example of an integrated account of authorial intention and biblical words, recall our earlier reference to Aquinas's *Literal Commentary on Job*.

the "clear and distinct ideas" present to their consciousness.[28] The new account of authorial sense fostered by this Cartesian intentionality replaces an account of biblical authorship rooted in the framework of providence with an account that takes its bearings from another frame of reference, one more narrowly focused on the relation between authorial consciousness and the literal sense. The role of inwardness and subjectivity in the construction of biblical sense is no longer defined by its integration into a larger account of providence but has an independent integrity of its own. As a result, the focus of biblical interpretation no longer centers upon the text but upon the authorial *subject* who contributed to the production of the text, because the theological sense of Scripture is now closely linked with the conscious intentions of that subject.

As the heir apparent of this tradition, the early nineteenth-century theologian Schleiermacher worked out an account of biblical interpretation comprised of two aspects. For our purposes we can refer to these as grammatical and psychological exegesis.[29] In grammatical exegesis the biblical interpreter seeks to understand all that is properly involved in understanding the historical, social, and cultural dimensions of biblical language. On the basis of this understanding the interpreter then engages in psychological or "divinatory" exegesis that seeks to penetrate behind the words of the text to the religious consciousness that produced those words. Divinatory exegesis thus enables the interpreter to recover the author's spirit or psyche in its pre-linguistic or unmediated form. The move from biblical text to authorial consciousness made possible by divinatory exegesis is crucial for Schleiermacher, because the goal of exegesis is not simply to increase one's historical knowledge of biblical texts. To be sure, Schleiermacher shares the modern conviction that historical reconstruction is not only helpful but also essential to the task of understanding biblical language. However, the goal of this reconstruction is not simply to supply us with historical information about the text. Rather, it is to provide an instrumental means to the end of communing with its human author or, more specifically, with the religious consciousness of that author. This goal is secured by psychological or divinatory exegesis, whose express purpose is to facilitate the communion of spirits between biblical author and interpreter. In the shared consciousness between biblical author and

28. See Descartes, "Meditations on First Philosophy," in Popkin, *Philosophy of the 16th and 17th Centuries*, 141–42, where he takes it to be a general rule "that all that is very clearly and distinctly apprehended (conceived) is true."

29. See Friedrich Schleiermacher, "The Hermeneutics: Outline of the 1819 Lectures," in *The Hermeneutic Tradition: From Ast to Ricoeur*, ed. Gayle Ormiston and Alan Schrift (Albany, NY: SUNY Press, 1990), 85–100.

interpreter fostered by this exegesis, differences between individuals occupying different bodies and locations in time are overcome and the interpreter's ability to transform oneself into another is realized.[30]

Stated in more positive terms, Schleiermacher's goal was to use Scripture as a means of listening to a friend rather than treating it as an object of inquiry in the scientific sense.[31] That he succeeded in winning many followers on this score is evident from the later declaration of Benjamin Jowett that "the goal of interpretation is to get rid of interpretation and leave us alone in the company of the author."[32] That being said, Schleiermacher's approach to Scripture's literal sense reflects a basic problem with the hermeneutics of nineteenth-century Romanticism and its notion of the artistic genius.[33] The biblical text itself is simply an external medium or artistic production that houses this artistic genius. Indeed, a literary text in Romantic hermeneutics is essentially the exfoliation of spontaneous genius. It represents a unique consciousness that has been gifted to the artist's psyche by means of the revelatory intrusion of noumenal realities into the world of phenomena. Thus in the case of the inspired authorial genius at work in Scripture, one must penetrate behind the artistic medium of the biblical text to commune directly with the author's consciousness, for it is this consciousness that connects us with God's consciousness. Grammatical exegesis must therefore lead us to divinatory interpretation, so we can penetrate beyond the inspired words of the biblical text to the authorial genius behind it.[34] In the grammar of the text,

---

30. See Schleiermacher, "Outline of the 1819 Lectures" in Ormiston and Schrift, *Hermeneutic Tradition*, 98; cf. also Hans-Georg Gadamer, *Truth and Method*, 2nd rev. ed., trans. J. Weinsheimer and D. Marshall (London: Continuum, 2006), 188.

31. For this reason, Anthony Thiselton argues that "to reduce Schleiermacher's system to a mere genetic historical reconstruction does violence to the subtlety and complexity of his carefully nuanced and dialectical work." Anthony C. Thiselton, "'Behind' and 'In Front of' the Text: Language, Reference, and Indeterminacy," in *After Pentecost: Language and Biblical Interpretation*, ed. Craig Bartholomew, Colin Greene, and Karl Möller, Scripture and Hermeneutics 2 (Grand Rapids: Zondervan, 2001), 98.

32. Benjamin Jowett, "On the Interpretation of Scripture," in *Essays and Reviews* (London: Parker & Sons, 1860), para. 384, http://www.ccel.org/ccel/temple_f/essays.ix.html.

33. This idea finds its way into Romanticism through Kant's discussion of genius in his *Critique of Judgment* (1790). In part 1 of the *Critique of Judgment*, he writes, "Genius is a talent for producing something for which no determinate rule can be given, not a predisposition consisting of a skill for something that can be learned by following some rule or other." For Kant, genius does not manifest itself in a skilled use of previously existing materials or tradition. Authentic genius does not look to the past for models or rules, because it is an intrusion of the noumenal into the phenomenal that brings its own rules with it.

34. Gadamer rightly notes that for Schleiermacher, interpreting a text is "ultimately a divinatory process, a placing of oneself within the framework of the author, an apprehension of the 'inner origin' of the composition of a work, a recreation of the creative act. . . . The structure of thought we are trying to understand as an utterance or as a text is not to be understood in

historical distance is already present because of the historically conditioned character of biblical language. For this reason, when one reads a biblical text on its grammatical level, the distinction between the consciousness of a biblical author and that of the reader remains fixed. Stated differently, grammatical exegesis concerns itself with what is historically alien rather than familiar to the communion of spirits. This is why grammatical exegesis per se will always remain inadequate for the purposes of facilitating communion between the biblical author and his interpreters, and also why the interpretive move facilitated by divinatory exegesis remains critical for Schleiermacher. Divinatory exegesis puts us in touch with the consciousness of the author, and *that* consciousness puts us in touch with God's consciousness.

In retrospect it is not difficult to see that Schleiermacher's divinatory exegesis participates in the familiar Romantic quest to wipe out mediation by entering into a pure communion of spirits, where the hermeneutical struggles fostered by modern concepts of historical distance no longer apply. His argument that the ultimate goal of exegesis is to facilitate communion with a friend also has a certain Augustinian flavor to it, although for Augustine the immediate friend in view would be the triune God rather than the divinely infused consciousness of a biblical author. Nevertheless, the hermeneutical price to be paid is too steep, inevitably bringing with it much of the problematic baggage one finds in the tradition of Romantic hermeneutics. Schleiermacher's quest to commune with the "original" authorial consciousness that produced the text tends to isolate biblical authorship from its relation to the larger providential drama at work in the construction of biblical meaning. This results in a one-sided, obsessive focus upon the importance of original authorial intention for the meaning of Scripture's literal sense. At the end of the day Schleiermacher's approach shifts our focus from the literal sense of a text to the particular human consciousness that produced it. To be sure, biblical narratives remain important for Schleiermacher, but their continuing importance is a means to another end—namely, that of gaining access to the religious consciousness behind them. Scripture's literal sense is reduced to the outer form or projection of a deeper-lying religious consciousness. Access to this consciousness is the objective that biblical interpreters now seek to achieve. This has the unfortunate effect of construing biblical narrative

---

terms of its subject matter but as an aesthetic construct, a work of art or 'artistic thought.' If we keep this in mind we will understand why what is at issue is not a relation to the subject matter (Schleiermacher's 'being')" (Gadamer, *Truth and Method*, 187); for an alternative reading, see Hans Frei, *The Eclipse of Biblical Narrative: A Study in Eighteenth and Nineteenth Century Hermeneutics* (New Haven: Yale University Press, 1974), 299–300, who claims that Gadamer exaggerates the character and role of divinatory exegesis in Schleiermacher.

as a form of linguistically mediated subjectivity whose primary purpose is to disclose a particular consciousness, rather than conceiving of canonical Scripture as a witness to God's redemptive providence in time.

Conclusion

What role now remains for the words of Scripture? Barth famously referred to Schleiermacher's hermeneutics as "consciousness theology," and at this juncture it is perhaps not too difficult to understand why that shorthand applies. Among the liabilities fostered by Schleiermacher's interpretive focus upon authorial consciousness is the instrumentalization of the literal sense. Scripture now functions as a set of clues for recovering the biblical author's inspired consciousness, thought to reside somewhere behind the text in the independent realm of *Geist* (Spirit) where historical issues no longer vex or trouble the reader. The end result is to instrumentalize the role of the biblical text in meaning-making, reducing it to a husk one must penetrate through or behind in order to get to the inspired genius of the author.

The implications of this anthropology of consciousness for the practice of biblical interpretation are substantial. The construction of the authorial self that underwrites the hermeneutics of Descartes, Locke, and Schleiermacher substitutes a particular version of authorial intentionality for the providential intentionality at work in Scripture's formation history. This substitution carries with it the implicit genre judgment that Scripture is a *source* or set of historical clues instrumentally useful for communing with biblical authors, rather than being a theological *witness*.[35] The Bible's literal sense becomes something like a stage upon which an author-actor delivered an original performance, now a part of history and moored in the past. The task of biblical interpretation is to summon that author back to the stage for a command performance by re-creating the stage through historical reconstruction. Prayer and the Holy Spirit then take care of the rest by blessing our historical labors with success. The false move underwriting this account traces back to the original fracture between biblical authors and the literal sense fostered by the anthropology of consciousness. A providential account of authorial intention resists the disintegration of the relation between literal and authorial sense,

---

35. The importance of understanding biblical language in terms of its theological referent or subject matter, and not merely as *performance* (cf. speech-act theory), lies at the heart of the distinction between Bible as *source* and Bible as *witness*. It also reminds us that when theologically and properly formed, subject matter explanations (*Sacherklärung*) remain crucial for a biblical account of language, their historicist and rationalist abuses notwithstanding. For examples of such abuses, see Frei, *Eclipse of Biblical Narrative*, 86–104.

insisting that what we mean by authorial sense must remain tied to the inspired words the Spirit gave to biblical authors. The operative assumption here is that Scripture's inspired words say more than conscious authorial intentions, because of the relation between those *words* and God's providential ordering of *things*. Thus while Scripture's inspired words include the conscious intentions of biblical authors, in lieu of their linkage with providentially ordered things, their meaning is never simply reducible to nor strictly identifiable with what a given human author was conscious of intending.

In practical terms this means that the focus of biblical interpretation is not a matter of getting into the heads of biblical authors, probing the precise limits of their consciousness by asking the question "Just how much were they conscious of when they wrote these words?" Instead exegesis begins with the recognition that because the Holy Spirit inspired the words of the biblical text, the best way to gain access to the meaning of its history is to give careful attention to the canonical profile and figural shape of its words. The use of modern historical tools and methods can be a great blessing for the pursuit of this goal, provided we use them to better understand Scripture's own way of ordering its history rather than using them on the basis of false assumptions about its literal sense or to reconstruct an alternative history. The problem is that these alternative histories inevitably fail to do the work or achieve the goals they set out to accomplish, which is perhaps not surprising at the end of the day. That story and its inevitable outcome have already been told in Isaiah 40–66. Any "history" that claims to be God's history must recognize that God alone orders the end from the beginning, the former and latter things by which both prophecy and gospel do their sense-making. Accounts of the literal sense based upon anything less than the providential intentionality inherent in that history are bound to fail, simply because these alternative histories cannot carry the theological freight of biblical history.

An illustrative example of this may be found in the anthropology of consciousness and its impact upon our understanding of the rule of faith. The *conscious* intention of biblical authors now draws the circle within which biblical sense-making is delimited, linking Scripture's words with their theological subject matter in a way that reconfigures the parameters of biblical poetics. In so doing it offers a new rule for reading Scripture that truncates the scope of its redemptive providence. By shifting the locus for the production of biblical meaning from a biblically robust account of providence to *one* dimension of that providence, biblical sense becomes a function of authorial consciousness, rather than the inspired words of the text. Authorial sense is no longer a native resident living within the literal sense but a resident alien whose relation to the literal sense is merely incidental. The Bible's literal sense now functions as a container housing the authorial sense, a container that must be transcended in order to get in touch with Scripture's theological sense. There is a certain irony in these observations, because accounts of the literal sense that prop up the importance of authorial intention for biblical interpretation typically do so in the name of establishing controls upon biblical meaning. In many such accounts authorial intention gets too closely identified with the conscious intentions of biblical authors, resulting in an abridged version of providential poetics that serves to loosen rather than tighten the relation between Scripture's literal and figural-theological sense. More disturbing is the way in which this move impacts our understanding of the Old Testament's christological sense, as well as kindred issues surrounding the New Testament's use of the Old Testament.

The Old Testament's christological sense is not grounded in the conscious intentions of biblical authors but in the inspired words they penned. The Old Testament authors speak more than they know because in their literal and figural senses those words are integral to a Christ-shaped providential economy that includes, but is not limited to, what the authors were consciously aware of. Old Testament saints who trusted in the inspired words of Moses and the prophets enjoyed the benefits of Christ's redemption, not because of the "fit" between what was in their heads and the Old Testament's christological sense but because of the objectively real link between Christ and the text's words—a link that is providentially constructed and not simply a function of authorial subjectivity or the conscious authorial intentions of those who wrote Scripture's words.[36] When we shift the center of gravity in biblical poetics from the objective realm of providence to human inwardness and subjectivity, the Old Testament's ability to refer to and disclose its christological sense becomes a reality that originates inside a human agent or, in more modern terms, the knowing self, rather than the eternal life of the Trinity and the redemptive providence by which christological mysteries are disclosed. This is a characteristically modern move, native to the philosophical tradition running from Descartes to Kant. However, it finds no resonance in Scripture's own account of the providential and figural nature of the relation between God and creatures.

36. This is not to make the additional claim that neither Moses nor the prophets consciously spoke of a coming Messiah. Indeed, the level of christological awareness in the words of Moses and the prophets would probably outstrip the level of awareness possessed by a nominal churchgoer in our day. The point is that the christological sense and function of the words of Moses and the prophets did not depend on their ability to understand all the historical details that accompany his first advent or his work of redemption. Moreover, enjoying a thing is not necessarily the same thing as being able to articulate or state in words what you are enjoying. Cf. the discussion in Frei, *Eclipse of Biblical Narrative*, 35–36.

This approach to the Old Testament's christological sense is bound to frustrate modern-day gnostics who identify salvation with knowledge in the subjective sense. But "faith is the substance of things hoped for, the evidence of things not seen" (Heb. 11:1 KJV). Although faith produces knowledge and cannot be separated from knowledge, it is neither reducible to nor directly identifiable with what we know or are aware of. The world of theological realism in which the Bible's literal sense is rooted resists this modern move, working with a different account of how Scripture's inspired words both refer to and mediate Christ. What enables the Old Testament's literal sense to render its christological sense is not the Old Testament's relation to the New Testament, nor even the fit between what is "in" the consciousness of its human authors and the historical figure of Christ himself. Rather, it is what the Old Testament's words are externally connected with that enables them to render their christological sense. That external connection exists because the triune LORD of history has entered into causal relations with us through his self-disclosure in the redemptive providence witnessed to in Scripture.[37] The ability of biblical words to refer to and mediate Christ depends upon the inspired words the Spirit gave to its authors *and* the providential linkage of those words with christo-trinitarian realities. In this way Scripture's christological meaning remains an affair of providence rather than an affair of human consciousness.

Reforming the Literal Sense: The Literal Sense as Historical Sense

Earlier we noted that while the literal sense may be variously construed as the verbal sense, the authorial sense, or the historical sense, these three

37. This account of biblical reference has been influenced by the causal theory of reference in Saul Kripke, *Naming and Necessity* (London: Basil Blackwell, 1980); cf. also the helpful discussion of Kripke's work in Janet Soskice, *Metaphor and Religious Language* (Oxford: Clarendon, 1985), 119–41. Kripke argues that it is our external connection with historical traditions that makes reference work. This contrasts with the descriptive theory of reference in Frege and Russell, who argue that what makes reference work is the proper fit between what is in our heads and what we are referring to. On the latter account, reference cannot work unless a correct description is present in the head of the one doing the referring. Kripke argued against the adequacy of this account, pointing out that reference still works even when an improper description is in view. Thus if I refer to Jerry Lee Lewis as the inventor of rock 'n' roll, I can still be referring to Lewis even though the description is mistaken and Little Richard is the inventor of rock 'n' roll. For a helpful discussion of Kripke's views from which the latter example is taken, see Colin McGinn, *The Making of a Philosopher* (New York: Harper Perennial, 2003). The implications of Kripke's theory for biblical hermeneutics finds an interesting anticipation in rabbinic accounts of an unbroken chain of oral tradition going back through the elders to Joshua and Moses. See Michael Fishbane, "The Teacher and the Hermeneutical Task: A Reinterpretation of Medieval Exegesis," *JAAR* 43, no. 4 (1975): 709–10.

descriptions belong together. We have also seen how one approach to the literal sense, arising from a non-biblical view of selfhood, loosened the relation between the Bible's literal and authorial sense, leading to a defective understanding of the Old Testament's christological sense. We now turn to another modern approach more explicitly aimed at reforming the Bible's literal sense. Here we are not concerned with the dualism involved in treating Scripture's authorial sense and its literal sense as separable categories, breaking down the dialectical relation between them.[38] Rather, our concern will be with the conflation of the literal sense with the historical sense, a project motivated by the goal of establishing an objective control on the meaning of biblical words and closely associated with the scientific spirit of eighteenth-century modernity. Accordingly, modern exegesis sought to transform the church's approach to the literal sense into an objective science free of the confessional bias found in theological exegesis. This quest for a "Bible without dogma" produced a modern version of biblical interpretation commonly styled "scientific exegesis." In many ways J. P. Gabler's 1787 Altdorf address establishes the historical agenda and priorities involved in the practice of this exegesis.[39]

Many scientific projects of this sort were up and running in the late eighteenth century in other disciplines as well—for instance, the discipline of philosophy. Kant hoped to develop a method in philosophy that would place philosophy on "the secure path of a science,"[40] putting an end to philosophical speculation impeding the progress of philosophy. In like fashion Gabler hoped to develop a scientific method for biblical exegesis that would put an end to the speculative excesses in confessional exegesis, which he regarded as the source of "fatal discords" and numerous sects in the church's history. Rather than contributing to further division in the church, he hoped to promote its unity by developing an approach to Scripture's literal sense aimed at reestablishing catholic consensus on its meaning. His operating assumption was that the frame of reference provided by the church's creeds and confessions for reading Scripture had failed to establish such a consensus due to its lack of an objective or critical control by which to adjudicate conflicting

38. Drawing upon the work of Gilbert Ryle, Frei rightly observes that "the author's intention is not a separable mental entity or action from the consecutive activity of working out his writing. An intention is an implicit action, an action an explicit intention; in the words of Gilbert Ryle, 'to perform intelligently is to do one thing and not two things.'" Frei, *Eclipse of Biblical Narrative*, 281; cf. viii.

39. For an English translation of Gabler's 1787 address, see J. Sandys-Wunsch and L. Eldredge, "J. P. Gabler and the Distinction between Biblical and Dogmatic Theology: Translation, Commentary, and Discussion of His Originality," *SJT* 33, no. 2 (1980): 133–58.

40. Immanuel Kant, *Critique of Pure Reason*, trans. Norman K. Smith (London: Macmillan, 1958), 17.

readings of Scripture's literal sense. Overcoming the ecclesial divisions fostered by sectarian and pietistic readings of Scripture called for a new frame of reference for biblical interpretation in order to restore church unity. However, the basis for this unity could no longer be grounded in the catholicity derived from reading Scripture in the framework provided by traditional creeds such as the Nicene Creed. On Gabler's view, it was clear the Nicene project had failed. Healing the church's ecclesial rifts called for a new frame of reference for reading Scripture, a standpoint provided by objective and *historical* reason. By applying this form of reason to biblical interpretation, Gabler hoped to reconstitute and reorder the divided church of his day.

In order to clearly distinguish the literal sense from the interpretive framework provided by the church's theological creeds and confessions, Gabler redefined the meaning of Scripture's literal sense along more restricted lines. In so doing he established a firm boundary between the literal and theological sense of Scripture. According to the version of biblical interpretation he promoted, the true character and pedigree of Scripture's literal sense is historical—that is, of historical origin (*e genere historico*). From this it follows that biblical interpretation proper is chiefly a historical enterprise that primarily concerns itself with study of the historical, social, and cultural backgrounds of the inspired authors who wrote Scripture—in short, with their original historical context.[41] In making this move, it remains unclear whether Gabler intended to subordinate the literal sense to its historically reconstructed sense. In all likelihood he regarded the study of its historical circumstances as the best way to gain a purchase on the meaning of Scripture's literal sense, offering an objective means for accessing the intentions of biblical authors not otherwise available in confessional exegesis. Whatever Gabler's intentions, the effect was to generate a culture of biblical reading styled "scientific exegesis." On this account, accessing the meaning of Scripture's literal sense came to be identified with exposing its historical background and recovering its original historical context.

It is important to recognize that "history" in Gablerian scientific exegesis is no longer co-extensive with God's providential ordering of things.

41. Gabler himself speaks of a "truly biblical theology." It is clear, however, that he regards this as biblical interpretation in the proper sense, and in any case, his use of the phrase "biblical theology" is at best problematic, because the sense in which he is using it assigns a non-traditional, historicized sense to what it means to speak of "theology." For Gabler's own language, see Sandys-Wunsch and Eldredge, "J. P. Gabler and the Distinction between Biblical and Dogmatic Theology," 137: "There is a truly biblical theology, of historical origin, conveying what the holy writers felt about divine matters; on the other hand there is a dogmatic theology of didactic origin, teaching what each theologian philosophises rationally about divine things, according to the measure of his ability or of the times, age, place, sect, school, and other similar factors."

Scripture's historical dimension is now a much more modest affair, because its literal-historical sense is now identified in a stricter sense with what biblical authors intended in their original historical contexts or with what Christopher Seitz styles an "authors-in-times" model for adjudicating the meaning of the Bible's literal sense.[42] Here the providential locus for biblical meaning has not been shifted to authorial consciousness (*authors*-in-times) but to an original historical context for accessing that consciousness (authors-in-*times*). The difference is subtle but nonetheless real. Whether one psychologizes the literal sense or historicizes it, in either case the focus of biblical interpretation—and by extension that of biblical inspiration—becomes something other than Scripture's literal sense. That "other" is not the triune God of Scripture but the text's historical sense. Biblical interpretation proper now concerns something behind or tangential to "the way the words run" in Scripture, rather than the words of the text per se. As we observed in the case of psychologizing approaches to the literal sense, this move leads to the dissolution of the integral relation between the Bible's literal sense and its figural-providential way of configuring history. The provision of another setting or framework for accessing Scripture's historical sense then becomes necessary, because our access to the text's meaning always presupposes a context or accompanying frame of reference. That new setting or rule for reading Scripture's history now becomes the frame of reference provided by the original historical context, the latter of which is typically supplied by the reconstructive efforts of professionally trained biblical scholars. What it means to speak of history in reference to the Bible now emerges in a new frame, though in a more beggarly form. When compared to the historical vision inherent in the witness of Scripture's literal sense to redemptive providence, this new frame that scientific exegesis offered proved to be a downsized version at best.

This provides an instructive point of contrast with the approach to the literal sense found in the magisterial Reformers. Although modern proponents of scientific exegesis often claim the Reformation as the proper forerunner to historical-critical readings of Scripture, this claim is misguided. Gabler's pursuit of a Bible without dogma is predicated on the assumption that one can gain access to the meaning of biblical words on the level of original historical context *without* the need to situate those words in a theological frame of reference in order to make sense of them. Original historical context as Gabler understood it is not a theologically conditioned category,

42. Christopher R. Seitz, *Prophecy and Hermeneutics: Toward a New Introduction to the Prophets* (Grand Rapids: Baker Academic, 2007), 34–38.

capable of being comprehended within a *providential* history. Providence is an interpretive category at once both historical and theological, with a foot in both worlds, as it were. In order to provide a truly objective and non-confessional control upon the meaning of Scripture's literal sense, the category of providence would have to be avoided, because in Gabler's view theological frames of reference *obscure* rather than *clarify* the literal sense of Scripture.[43] If we are to reform the abuses of the literal sense and restore catholicity in the church, we must make a new beginning for biblical exegesis by *starting over* on a non-theological, historical foundation. Gabler's program for reform thus reflects one of the foundation myths at work in modernity's self-image and historiography—namely, that modernity is the great new beginning. It also reflects the logic of revolution rather than reformation.

Of course, Gabler's reduction of Scripture's history to something moderns call original historical context did not succeed in providing a non-theologically biased or non-confessional approach to the literal sense. This is simply because history still had to be understood according to a particular framework and set of theological assumptions about God and the nature of Scripture's literal sense. This points to yet another irony in the history of various efforts to reform the literal sense. But it also clearly distinguishes Reformers like Luther and Calvin from Gabler's version of scientific exegesis. By means of theological categories such as promise and providence, Luther and Calvin sought to secure a place for Scripture's theological sense *within* the literal sense. To do this, they expanded the scope of the literal sense to *include* the senses formerly known as the figural or allegorical senses. Gabler moves in a decidedly different direction. Rather than expanding the scope of the literal sense to include its theological sense, Gabler sought to reduce the scope of Scripture's literal sense to its original historical sense. Thus Gabler rather than Luther and Calvin should be numbered among those who helped usher in a modern revolution in the church's understanding of Scripture's literal sense.

What we learn from Gabler's program for reforming the literal sense takes us back to a point made earlier on in our historical voyage through the sea of changes that have impacted the meaning of Scripture's literal sense

---

43. On this score, compare the remarks of R. R. Reno: "If self-consciousness about the role of history in shaping human consciousness makes modern historical-critical study *critical*, then what makes modern study of the Bible modern is the consensus that classical Christian doctrine distorts interpretive understanding. . . . The disciplines of close philological analysis 'would enable us to separate the elements of doctrine and tradition with which the meaning of Scripture is encumbered in our own day.' The lens of understanding must be wiped clear of the hazy and distorting film of doctrine." See Reno's editorial introduction to Peter J. Leithart, *1 & 2 Kings*, BTC (Grand Rapids: Brazos, 2006), 8.

through time. While the church has variously construed the literal sense in terms of its verbal, authorial, and historical senses, these three senses were taken to be integral aspects of one reality, rather than separable components within a larger whole or, for that matter, independent occupants of a larger boarding house called the literal sense that just happen to be renting rooms next to one another. Once Scripture's historical sense is detached from its proper home within a larger providential composition, its integral relation to the literal sense becomes tenuous, and the need to approach its history in a frame of reference other than the literal sense is then mandated. In the end, Gabler's provision of a reconstructed historical setting for the Old Testament's original voice displaces its literal sense, just as consciousness did in the seventeenth century. Without an account of providence to hold together biblical words with theological realities, Gabler ended up historicizing Scripture's authorial sense, with the primary locus for the meaning of literal sense now being something called "original historical context" rather than God's providential ordering of things. To be sure, the authorial sense inherent in the literal sense remains important for Gabler, just as it did for Schleiermacher after him. But accessing that sense is now a function of the speculative reconstruction of its original historical context. Access to the Old Testament's original sense is now a matter of getting outside the frame of reference brokered by its literal sense, while at the same time entering into another frame of access or "rule for reading" provided by historical reconstruction. Scripture's original authorial sense remains accessible but only on terms established by the historicized account of authorial intention native to this new frame of reference.

The problem for Gabler is that the ability of Scripture's historical sense to function as an independent or fully objective control on the literal sense is limited *from the outset* by the dialectical nature of its relationship with the literal sense. The term *dialectic* may be used in a number of ways. In its most basic sense it simply refers to a discourse or conversation between two different though not necessarily incompatible points of view. The point of dialectic is not to wholly resolve the tension between differing points of view by collapsing the distinction between them but to accept that tension as basic to the very possibility of communication between the perspectives in question. The perspective on the Bible offered by its historical sense is intrinsically related to the perspective offered by its literal and figural senses, a stubborn fact that Gabler's version of scientific exegesis overrides from the outset. Approaching Scripture's literal sense from the critical vantage point of the historical sense, where historical sense means non-providential or non-theological sense, can be accomplished only by supposing from the outset that Scripture's historical and literal sense are separable components, fully capable of being cleanly distinguished and neatly divided from one another. But the inspired human activity that produced the literal sense cannot be separated into historical and textual components in the name of providing a scientific control on its meaning, for in the providential economy by which biblical meaning was constructed, Scripture's historical and literal senses are distinguishable only in their relatedness. Separating them like Gabler does results in the same version of unstable hermeneutical dualism found in the anthropology of consciousness, whereby Scripture's authorial sense assumes a life of its own. The effect of this program for reforming the literal sense is to shift the locus for biblical meaning once again from the inspired words of Scripture to an external and separable frame of reference—in this case the frame provided by the reconstruction of original historical context, rather than authorial consciousness per se.

The dialectical nature of the relationships between Scripture's verbal, historical, and authorial senses is essential to the transfer of meaning between biblical author and reader. Moreover, since the transfer of biblical meaning always presupposes a context, breaking down the literal sense into separable components *necessitates* the provision of a new frame of reference for Scripture's original or historical sense. This fracture is already operative wherever we find the argument that our primary access to the inspired intentions of biblical authors derives from a reconstruction of their original historical context, rather than the words of Scripture and the theological rule for reading those words authorized by Scripture itself. The approach to biblical interpretation Gabler helped pioneer soon found expression in Protestant circles committed to honoring biblical authority under the banner of *sola Scriptura*. The irony is that historicized accounts of the authorial sense end up privileging a reconstruction of the literal sense over Scripture's own provision of a setting for its words. This move also reflects a crucial assumption in Gabler's program, often left unstated, that Scripture is incapable of providing controls on biblical meaning through its own literal sense and relation to the triune LORD who authored the text. This loss of confidence in the Bible's ability to broker its intentions to future readers typically provides the mandate for historical-critical approaches to biblical interpretation. Whatever else its faults, premodern biblical interpretation resisted the equation of Scripture's literal sense with either the conscious intentions of biblical authors *or* the text's original historical context. This allowed the internal relations between the authorial, historical, and verbal senses to remain intact, preventing them from emerging as objects of interest in their own right.

Deforming the Literal Sense: *Sensus Plenior*, Christotelism, and *Wirkungsgeschichte*

Whether we speak of the communication of Scripture's theological sense through its literal sense or through its literal sense in conjunction with its figural sense, in both cases providence functioned as the historical glue holding together these senses, by which the transfer of meaning was made possible. However, the pressures exerted upon biblical interpretation by the rise of idealist anthropologies and historical reason led to the eclipse of providence in biblical poetics, while cultural pressures fostered by Deism helped secure its further demise. In the wake of these pressures an attenuated version of the Old Testament's original sense arose, detached from its native setting in a larger providential composition and transposed into smaller frames of reference provided by "original" authorial intention and "original" historical context. Both proved to be insufficient bases for supporting the union of the Old Testament's original voice with its theological sense, because the connecting link that providence formerly supplied between the Old Testament's original context and its theological sense was replaced by historicized accounts of original intention and original context. What was formerly meant by these realities was broken loose from their integral relation to providence and became identified, via the anthropology of consciousness, with the problematic notion of *conscious* intention.

Idealist anthropologies identify the intentions of biblical authors with the "clear and distinct" ideas present to authorial consciousness within an original historical context. The difficulty is that one cannot say that Old Testament authors consciously intended to speak of Jesus Christ or had a clear and distinct idea of him, because the historical and material means for integrating these ideas and intentions with the Word-not-yet-made-flesh no longer exist once the doctrine of providence has been ushered off the stage of Israel's history. Old Testament authors no longer speak more than they know, and for this reason the Old Testament's christological sense must now be clearly distinguished from its literal or original sense proper. The impact of this upon biblical interpretation is significant, because the hermeneutical problems involved in uniting Scripture's literal and theological senses also translate into problems for its christological sense. These problems have an especially virulent impact on the character of the Old Testament's christological witness, because on this approach, christology is a theological category, while the Old Testament's original sense is a historical category. In the wake of this bifurcation, Scripture no longer has a single subject matter testified to in both testaments, albeit under two different historical economies. Instead, Scripture now has two subject matters, one "original" and "historical" in nature, and the other "theological." This brings our discussion around full circle to Luther's perceptive criticism of the problems with Emser's "twofold Bible."[44]

This interpretive move undercuts the theological significance of the original sense in Israel's scriptures, and since the christological sense is a particular species of theological meaning, the move also spells doom for the Old Testament's christological witness. Having been banished from the Old Testament's original sense, the Old Testament's christological sense becomes the function of a future historical context or material effect lying beyond its own historical horizon, at least if human creatures are to know that sense, since there can be no access to Scripture's theological meaning apart from its mediation through a particular historical economy. The future historical context provided by the Old Testament's material or textual effect upon subsequent history, which authorial intention and original historical context failed to supply, now provides the material means for accessing its theological sense. This should not come as a surprise, since the interpretive categories of conscious intention and original historical context cannot bear the weight of the Old Testament's christological sense, especially after their meaning has been thinned out by means of their relocation and exile from their native home in the doctrine of providence. Since exegetical focus upon authorial intention and original historical context cannot unite the Old Testament's literal sense with its christological sense, it therefore becomes necessary to relocate the Old Testament's christological sense in a historical or material means of access other than its own literal sense. In sum, whether we psychologize or historicize the literal sense in the hope of establishing a non-confessional basis for Scripture's interpretation, the christological sense loses its original home in the Old Testament, finding only eschatological instead of original expression in the witness of Israel's scriptures.

Sensus Plenior

It is within the framework of this hermeneutical problematic that the later notion of *sensus plenior* comes to the fore, offering yet another model for reuniting the Old Testament's literal and theological sense. Although the term appears to have originated in Roman Catholic circles,[45] it eventually

---

44. Martin Luther, *Answer to the Hyperchristian, Hyperspiritual, and Hyperlearned Book by Goat Emser in Leipzig—Including Some Thoughts Regarding His Companion, the Fool Murner*, in *Luther's Works*, vol. 39, *Church and Ministry I*, trans. Eric and Ruth Gritsch (Philadelphia: Fortress, 1970), 179.

45. According to Robert Bruce Robinson, the term *sensus plenior* was first coined in 1925 by the Roman Catholic scholar Andrés Fernández. See Robert Bruce Robinson, *Roman Catholic*

came to exert an influence on Protestant biblical interpretation as well.[46] Once the providential link integrating biblical words with their theological subject matter was replaced by authorial intention and original historical context, it was but a short step to Ray Brown's famous construal of the *sensus plenior* as "that *additional*, deeper meaning, intended by God but not *clearly* intended by the human author, which is seen to exist in the words of a biblical text (or group of texts or even a whole book) *when* they are studied in the light of *further* revelation or development in the understanding of revelation."[47] It is important to appreciate the fact that *sensus plenior* was constructed in the context of a specifically modern concern to account for the hermeneutical mechanism whereby the apostles were able to discover christological meanings in the Old Testament's literal sense not clearly intended by Old Testament authors. To illustrate the relation between the literal and theological senses inherent in this approach, it is helpful to draw an analogy between the Old Testament's literal sense and a two-story house. In this house two occupants live, one on the ground floor, and the other on the upper floor. The problem is that the house lacks a set of stairs for connecting the ground floor with its upper floor. Consequently no real communion or commerce between its two occupants is possible as long as they remain within the house the Old Testament built. Later on another house is constructed, which we will call the New Testament's literal sense. It is this later house that finally provides the "staircase" linking the Old Testament's upper and lower floors, so that access to the occupant residing in its upstairs guest room finally becomes possible.

This account of Scripture's literal sense problematizes the relation between the Old Testament's original sense and its christological sense. In order to ensure that this sense is not completely evacuated from the Old Testament's original sense, it must be kicked upstairs, as it were, into the hidden realm of divine authorship and intention.[48] The difficulty is that there is no material

---

Exegesis Since Divino Afflante Spiritu: *Hermeneutical Implications* (Atlanta: Scholars Press, 1988), 29.

46. See Douglas J. Moo, "The Problem of *Sensus Plenior*," in *Hermeneutics, Authority, and Canon*, ed. D. A. Carson and John D. Woodbridge (Grand Rapids: Zondervan Academic, 1986), 175–211; cf. also Peter Enns, "Fuller Meaning, Single Goal: A Christotelic Approach to the New Testament Use of the Old in Its First-Century Interpretive Environment," in *Three Views on the New Testament Use of the Old Testament*, ed. Kenneth Berding and Jonathan Lunde (Grand Rapids: Zondervan, 2008), 167–217, esp. 213–15. As suggested by the words "fuller meaning" in the title of his essay, Enns's account of christotelism shares a number of affinities with *sensus plenior* (see his comments on pp. 204–9).

47. Ray Brown, *The* Sensus Plenior *of Sacred Scripture* (Baltimore: St. Mary's University Press, 1955), 92, emphasis added.

48. In his critique of R. Brown's account of *sensus plenior*, Robinson notes the problems involved in the idea of a theological meaning located in the literal sense by God that is not also

means for accessing the christological intentions of the divine author residing upstairs. This is because the historically integrative staircase provided by the doctrine of providence no longer exists, making it impossible to restore communion with the christological witness of the author living and writing in the guest room upstairs. Moreover, on the hermeneutical terms set by this historicized account of authorial intention, which *sensus plenior* inherits from Descartes and Gabler, it cannot be said that the guest residing upstairs has been *clearly* invited to stay by the resident living on the ground floor. Thus the possibility of meeting that guest, let alone communing with him, must be deferred to a later historical context. No material means exists for gaining access to this divine author and the christological story he is writing, because his relation to the Old Testament's original sense is primarily eschatological in character, properly belonging to a telos outside the Old Testament rather than to a telos within its own original canonical form. The literal and figural means the biblical doctrine of providence once provided for securing this access must now be deferred until the later construction project associated with the New Testament has been completed.

The familiar tendency toward instrumentalizing the literal sense, a tendency inherent in both Cartesian and Gablerian intentionality, now resurfaces with a vengeance. Because the Old Testament's christological sense primarily belongs to its eschatological rather than its original sense, the latter of which is at best an inchoate and confused witness to Christ, the text's original sense is in need of retrospective sorting by the New Testament. Indeed, it is the primary function of the New Testament to perform this clarifying and perhaps even critically corrective task. In this way the Old Testament's witness to Christ is reduced to a form of textual occasionalism wherein the Old Testament ceases to be a christological witness in its own right and becomes instead the mere occasion for the later unfolding of the christological witness of the New Testament. The New Testament's theological purpose and function is also transformed. Instead of Israel's scriptures being used to clarify and identify the nature of Christ's person and work, the theological purpose

located in the agency of inspired human intentions: "The theory of the *sensus plenior* holds that a determinate mental entity is created by God's consciousness. That entity must be transmitted to the text, which is produced concretely by a human author, acting under inspiration. The *sensus plenior* meaning must pass in some fashion through the consciousness of the human author and some account must be given of the mechanism by which this takes place if there is not to be a damaging lacuna in the theory" (Robinson, *Roman Catholic Exegesis*, 36). The "damaging lacuna" that Robinson speaks of directly raises the question of how, given the way *sensus plenior* loosens the relation between the Old Testament's christological sense and its literal sense, one gains hermeneutical access to its christological sense from within its own horizon.

of the apostolic witness becomes that of clarifying and/or correcting the Old Testament's witness.

The attempt to reunite the Old Testament's literal and christological sense by means of the hermeneutical model provided by *sensus plenior* occurs in the wake of the significant changes in the church's traditional understanding of the Bible's literal sense, a transformation which idealist anthropologies and historical reason helped create. It is an interpretive category native to the Cartesian and Gablerian forms of authorial intentionality that sought to reestablish biblical interpretation on a non-confessional, non-providential basis. It takes as its starting point an abridged version of biblical providence, framed within a two-author model for biblical poetics and rooted in "clear and distinct" ideas present to human consciousness within a given historical context. However, one cannot say that Old Testament authors *clearly* intended to speak of Christ. Thus in order to preserve at least a formal relation with the Old Testament's literal sense, one must push its christological sense to the upper floor of a two-story house called literal sense, and it cannot come back downstairs again until the New Testament's historical context provides the material means to make this possible.

In addition to the problems already canvassed, this also has troubling implications for how we understand the interpretative category of biblical authorship, both divine and human. The recalibration of the literal sense that took place in eighteenth-century modernity helped engineer the move from providence to human consciousness as the proper locus for the construction of biblical sense. This in turn paved the way for a different understanding of the church's traditional two-author model for interpreting biblical poetics. The analogy of the two-story house for understanding the relation between literal and theological senses in *sensus plenior* also helps illuminate the particular logic by which this new two-author model came to dominate biblical interpretation after Descartes and Gabler. For if it is not the providential linkage of words and things that accounts for our ability to access the christological sense residing in the house the Old Testament built, then by what mechanism or model shall we account for that access?

According to the logic of *sensus plenior*, the christological or surplus meaning residing in the Old Testament's literal sense is now the function of a two-author model (*sans* providence) for relating its literal and christological sense. In this way the Cartesian-Gablerian account of authorial intention and original historical context in *sensus plenior* naturally leads to the reconstruction of the two-author model implied by the church's traditional account. This is because the transfer of theological meaning once made possible by the providential integration of Scripture's literal and theological sense has been replaced by a new model centered upon a non-providential account of the relation between divine and human authorship. This way of construing the relation between divine and human authorship lacks a material means for accomplishing the transfer of theological meaning between these authors, because the historical and material means that formerly achieved such integration is now absent. As a result, the construction of biblical sense is now modeled upon a reconfigured account of divine and human authorship in which the contribution of providence to the communication of theological meaning has been wiped out. To be sure, the upper room of the Old Testament's literal sense still hosts a divine author engaged in writing a book about Christ, but access to the meaning of that book remains inaccessible within the Old Testament's own literary horizon.

These considerations expose the limitations inherent in Cartesian and Gablerian accounts of intentionality for a christologically robust account of the Old Testament's literal sense. They also uncover the modern reconstruction of the relation between divine and human authorship at work in *sensus plenior*. While this reconstruction bears a formal resemblance to the church's traditional account of this relation, it operates with a decidedly different logic that is bereft of providence and fully captive to "the agony of authorship" troubling biblical interpretation in our day.[49] In place of the church's traditional account there now stands a two-author model that cannot provide the needed integration to reunite the Old Testament's christological sense with its literal sense in more than a formal way. The roots of this problem once again take us back to Aquinas and the hermeneutical issues involved in properly grasping Aquinas's account of double signification. In what sense may we properly call God an *author*? God does not write but inspires human agents to write—agents who then attach inspired words to particular things. In Thomistic scholarship, this is typically described as first-order or verbal signification. In addition, God also generates meaning by creating figural relations between signs or things and then linking their meaning to inspired words through his providential ordering of time. Although this kind of sense-making is often referred to as second-order or natural signification, the word *second* can be misleading, because on Aquinas's account of things, second-order signification forms the enabling condition for the possibility of meaningful verbal signification. In short, the figural relations between things established by God's providence undergird the efficacy of verbal signification.

49. I am indebted to Christopher Seitz for suggesting this phrase to me while responding to Tremper Longman III during a conference on the book of Ecclesiastes.

The point to stress is that this second kind of meaning-making is fundamentally different from the first because it doesn't involve the inspired writing or consciousness of human authors but the divine ordering of history. This is not a matter of "authorship" in the ordinary sense of the term but that which makes inspired human authorship possible in the first instance. Aquinas was right to highlight the uniqueness of this aspect of biblical poetics, because without it no material linkage between inspired words and theological realities is possible. The problem with *sensus plenior* is that it construes divine authorship on a strict analogy with human authorship.[50] The effect of this is to collapse the meaning and function of divine authorship into the category of human authorship, leaving no place for the historical and material means of integration provided by God's unique ability to order history, linking former and latter things and thus declaring the end from the beginning.

In this way the human agency and intention at work in authorial sense-making became the model for the divine agency and intention at work *in the whole* of biblical sense-making. God became an author producing authorial meanings after the manner and fashion of a human author, assuming the normal role played by human agency in the production of textual sense.[51] This had the effect of reducing the providential construction of biblical meaning to a transfer that takes place between a divine author and his intentions, on the one hand, and a human author and his intentions, on the other. Biblical sense-making effectively becomes a conversation between two authors, one divine and the other human, in which the contribution of God's providential ordering of history to the construction of biblical sense is either erased or radically abridged. In the case of the Old Testament this carries with it the further implication that the text's christological sense stands in abeyance until the historical era of the New Testament arrives. There is simply no way to account for the rise of *sensus plenior* as an interpretive model for uniting the two testaments apart from the decline of providence in the church's account of Scripture's literal sense. By the time *sensus plenior* comes on the scene, the connecting link between the literal and theological senses formerly supplied by providence is now supplied by a historicized account of authorial intention. To be sure, such an account still requires a certain version of providence. However, it not only identifies that providence with a defective account of authorial intention but also fails to account for those instances in the Old Testament where the theological sense is rendered through the figural sense, not apart from but in conjunction with the literal sense. This two-author

50. See Robinson, *Roman Catholic Exegesis*, 29–55; cf. 149–50.
51. Robinson, *Roman Catholic Exegesis*, 149.

model effectively erases the Old Testament's figural sense as a canonical medium for brokering its christological sense. The Old Testament's figural sense is no longer a native resident residing within its literal sense. It is entirely the function of a retrospective reading performed by New Testament authors.[52]

The material transfer of christological meaning was made possible in the Old Testament through the providential union of biblical words and figural-theological realities. Unlike the merely formal relation between literal and theological sense that later emerged in *sensus plenior*, this secured the actual existence of a material link between the Old Testament's christological and literal senses, which idealist anthropologies and non-confessional versions of historical reason then proceeded to push offstage. The problems such presents for gaining access to the Old Testament's christological witness should now be clear. When the Old Testament's christological sense has little more than a purely formal connection with its literal-historical sense, the problem of hermeneutical access to that sense *in Israel's own day* arises as a necessary consequence, deferring that access to a historical context yet to come. The result is a purely eschatologized version of the Old Testament's christological sense that identifies that sense not with the Old Testament's own historical sense and material form but with its future effective history, the latter of which provides the *material* means for accessing its meaning. Understood within the framework of *sensus plenior*, the New Testament establishes both the material *means* necessary for gaining access to the Old Testament's christological sense and a material *control* upon that sense.[53]

Christotelism

Viewed from this vantage point, *sensus plenior* shares a family resemblance with another recent approach to the Old Testament's literal sense styled *christotelism*. Christotelism shares the Cartesian-Gablerian account of authorial intentionality that undergirds the approach of *sensus plenior*

52. For an example of the consequences this assumption has for how we assess Paul's use of figural reading in 1 Corinthians 10, see Richard Hays, *Echoes of Scripture in the Letters of Paul* (New Haven: Yale University Press, 1993), 91; cf. also Richard Hays, *First Corinthians*, IBC (Louisville: Westminster John Knox, 1997), 160. Hays suggests that Paul is drawing a rather "fanciful" analogy between Israel and the church in this passage and that his reading of Israel's wilderness sojourn is an "imaginative act of reading Exodus as metaphor for human experience." Hence "Paul's metaphors should not be pressed" (*Echoes of Scripture*, 91), lest we fall into the error of "supposing that the Old Testament itself interprets these events as sacramental symbols or that Jewish tradition before Paul had conceived of these events as figurative foreshadowings of future realities." *First Corinthians*, 160.

53. Don Collett, "Reading Forward: The Old Testament and Retrospective Stance," *ProEccl* 24, no. 3 (2015): 183.

to the Old Testament's christological sense. Consequently, one cannot gain
access to the text's christological sense on the level of the intended words
and inspired utterances of Old Testament authors. For christotelists, the
solution to this problem is to ground the Old Testament's christological
sense in the theological goals of apostolic exegesis, rather than the inspired
words of Old Testament authors speaking within their own historical frame
of reference. Enriched by the hermeneutical world of the Second Temple
period, the goal of apostolic exegesis was to retrospectively "find" Christ
in Israel's scriptures by exploiting the interpretive methods of the historical
milieu in which they were situated. A rather sharp distinction between the
intended words of Israel's scriptures and apostolic interpretive goals lies at
the heart of christotelism. The Old Testament's literal sense does not bear
witness to Christ on its own semantic level, apart from the theological goals
of apostolic exegesis, but awaits correlation with those goals before it may be
said to be Christian scripture in more than a future sense. The reading that
emerges from this correlation identifies the Old Testament's christological
sense with its reception by the apostolic witness. However, we are not to
imitate the interpretive methods of the apostles but rather to imitate their
christological goals, taking captive Israel's scriptures by seizing them in the
service of their christological convictions.[54]

Advocates of this approach often draw upon analogies between modern
detective novels and the Bible in order to illustrate the way in which the Old
Testament's christological sense depends upon a later knowledge of its end
or telos. Thus christotelists speak of a first reading of the Old Testament
in which the reader is unaware of its ending, much like the experience of
reading a modern detective novel in which the outcome remains unknown.
After this a second reading is performed in which the novel's ending is
known—here, by virtue of the New Testament's witness to that end. The
greater clarity provided by this second reading serves to support the claim
that the Old Testament's literal sense does not render its witness to Christ
on the original level of its intended *words* but renders its witness in terms
of a reader's later knowledge of the text's eschatological goal or telos. If
one asks *how* the Old Testament's inspired words mediate our knowledge
of Christ, the answer ultimately finds its ground in the reader's a posteriori
knowledge of the Old Testament's historical telos, rather than the a priori
and objective relation of those inspired words to Christ, the eternal Logos

---

54. Peter Enns, *Inspiration and Incarnation: Evangelicals and the Problem of the Old
Testament* (Grand Rapids: Baker Academic, 2005), 152–63; cf. also the arguments in Peter
Enns and Dan McCartney, "Matthew and Hosea: A Response to John Sailhamer," *WTJ* 63
(2001): 97–105.

and Archē, who as "the firstborn of all creation" is "before all things" (Col. 1:15, 17).[55]

However, it is only partially true that "stories can only be told by those who know the end,"[56] especially when the storytellers in view are human agents rather than the triune LORD of Scripture. Hirsch's Cartesian dictum that "meaning is an affair of consciousness"[57] undergirds the notion that Old Testament Christology is grounded in the reader's perception of an end, or a retrospective "second reading" of the Old Testament motivated by the reader's grasp of its telos.[58] This turn toward inwardness privileges human cognition and readerly perception as the connecting link between past and present, rather than God's establishment of the end from the beginning, as testified to in Isaiah 40–48 (41:22; 42:9; 43:9, 18; 46:9; 48:3, 6). The effect is to subjectivize Old Testament Christology by making its efficacy depend on an act of human cognition, rather than on God's providential ordering of things. Evangelical modernity bears witness to a wide variety of these "christotelisms," and the problems they raise for a Christian reading of the Old Testament are also anticipated, at least to some extent, in the premodern church.[59]

In the Old Testament's construction of its witness to Christ, rendered at many times and in various ways (cf. Heb. 1:1), the theological function of human perception is not primary but derivative. It rests upon and therefore presupposes God's providential ordering of things in order to operate. Meaning is an affair of providence in the first instance. This means that the reader's perception of an end occurs within a providentially constructed witness that not only precedes that perception in time but also provides a prior context of recognition, grammar, or rule by which to individuate and identify the "end" perceived. On this approach, the reader's perception of a telos is a referential judgment enabled by the theological pressures inherent in the original sense of Israel's scriptures—a sense capable of speaking a word to its own day as well as to a generation to come, because it finds its origin in Christ, the eternal Word and Archē, the Beginning of the LORD's way in creation and the human

55. See the discussion of these verses in Christopher R. Seitz, *Colossians*, BTC (Grand Rapids: Brazos, 2014), 86–101.

56. Peter J. Leithart, *Deep Exegesis: The Mystery of Reading Scripture* (Waco: Baylor University Press, 2009), 41; cf. Don Collett, "The Defenestration of Prague and the Hermeneutics of 'Story': A Response to Peter Leithart," *Reformed Faith & Practice* 3, no. 2 (2018): 32–38. Parts of that interaction have been reproduced here.

57. Hirsch, *Validity in Interpretation*, 48.

58. Francis Watson, "The Old Testament as Christian Scripture: A Response to Professor Seitz," *SJT* 52 (1999): 227–32, esp. 229–30; cf. also N. T. Wright, *The New Testament and the People of God* (Minneapolis: Fortress, 1992), 115.

59. See the discussion in Preus, *From Shadow to Promise*, 9–132.

history that followed (Gen. 1:1–3; Prov. 8:22; John 1:1–3; Col. 1:15–17). Thus history's significance is a matter of not simply what comes at its telos or end[60] but also the ontological pressures at work in its beginning. The archē of the Word is already at work in history before history reaches its telos, and so the story starts before the end, even though our experience of the end makes possible a new understanding of that story. It is this prior, ontological pressure that enables a "reading forward" of the Old Testament,[61] such that the New Testament's use of the Old is not merely a Christian backdraft on the Old Testament[62] but a second "accorded" testimony given to bear witness to the new historical events of Christ's incarnation, death, resurrection, and exaltation (1 Cor. 15:3–4).

Moreover, while it is true that the incarnation as a *historical* event belongs outside the Old Testament's horizon, it does not follow that Israel's scriptures provide no witness to that event. The Old Testament bears witness to the history lying beyond its own literary horizons, including the event of the incarnation, though in a language and semantics appropriate to its own frame of reference rather than the historical frame of the New Testament.[63] In making the Old Testament's christological sense depend upon a second reading of Israel's scriptures conducted from the vantage point of the apostolic

60. This is the defining feature of Whig historiography, which privileges the primacy of the present for interpreting the past—an approach to historiography in which the voice of the past is colonized by the present and ceases to pressure the present on its own terms.

61. See Collett, "Reading Forward," 178–96.

62. See Frei, *Eclipse of Biblical Narrative*. Frei notes that for Calvin, the Old Testament derives its forward motion from its own literal sense and *not* from "the wedding of that forward motion with a separate backward perspective upon it" (36)—that is, from its correlation with a retrospective stance that then exercises a sort of Christian backdraft upon the Old Testament.

63. Following the lead of the early church, Matthew Bates argues that the intratrinitarian conversations disclosed in the Old Testament Psalms anticipate the full range of Scripture's historical economy stretching from creation to consummation, including the incarnation as well. Although from the perspective of the Psalter these events still belong to the future, the conversations between the Father and the Son in the Psalter often treat them as events that have already been accomplished. Here the Old Testament's literal sense functions much like the grammatical category known as the prophetic perfect, wherein a future event is regarded as already fulfilled and in the past. See Matthew Bates, *The Birth of the Trinity: Jesus, God, and Spirit in New Testament and Early Christian Interpretation of the Old Testament* (Oxford: Oxford University Press, 2015). Christine Helmer's earlier work on Luther's reading of the Psalms anticipates Bates's argument, though unlike Bates she does not center that argument in the early church's use of prosopological exegesis. See Christine Helmer, "Luther's Trinitarian Hermeneutic and the Old Testament," *MT* 18, no. 1 (2002): 49–83. For helpful discussions of prosopological exegesis in the early church predating Bates's work, see Michael Fiedrowicz, "General Introduction," in *Expositions of Psalms 1–32*, Works of Saint Augustine III/15, trans. Maria Boulding, O.S.B. (Hyde Park, NY: New City Press, 2000), 50–60; Michael Cameron, *Christ Meets Me Everywhere: Augustine's Early Figurative Exegesis* (Oxford: Oxford University Press, 2012), 165–212.

witness, christotelism falls into the old idealist error of confusing the act of recognition with the thing itself, resulting in a reversal of the proper sequence between the order of being and the order of knowing. Such a reversal was anticipated in modernity's appropriation of the Berkeleyan confession that "to be is to be perceived" (*esse est percipi*).[64] Since such perception is not possible for Old Testament Israel living prior to the incarnation, the New Testament witness to that event is required before the christological sense of the Old Testament can be activated. The Old Testament's christological sense thus becomes something like instant coffee, which must have the hot water of the New Testament's witness poured upon it before it can properly be called coffee.[65] The theological realism in which figural reading is rooted resists this account of the Old Testament's christological sense. That sense is grounded not in a given reader's experience as it moves from a first to a second reading of the Old Testament but in an objectively real link between Christ and the Old Testament words established by God's providential ordering of things.[66] Saving faith in both testaments is a matter not of quantifying the historical information residing in the heads of human beings but of trust in God's word of promise—an observation congruent with Frei's observation that Israel's enjoyment of christological realities under the economy of the Old Testament is not necessarily the same thing as the ability to articulate what they were enjoying.[67]

In spite of these problems, christotelism remains popular in Protestant evangelical circles as an interpretive model for construing the Old Testament's literal sense. At least part of the reason for this popularity stems from the fact that the view often trades upon a subtle conflation of the person of Jesus Christ with the New Testament's literary witness. Properly speaking, the New Testament is not the end or goal of Israel's scriptures but an apostolic and textual *witness* to that goal, which properly speaking is the person and work of Jesus Christ. This conflation of text and person not only collapses the distinction between the New Testament text and its subject matter but also confuses the goal or telos of Israel's scriptures with the New Testament witness per se, rather than the person of Jesus Christ, who stands at the historical center of both testaments. The presence of this confusion in christotelism allows it to

64. This phrase is taken from principle 3 in George Berkeley's *A Treatise Concerning the Principles of Human Knowledge*, ed. Kenneth Winkler (Indianapolis: Hackett, 1982). Since for Berkeley, what it means to speak of the reality of creaturely existence finds its authorizing ground in the sustaining consciousness of God's perception, it remains debatable whether Berkeley himself shares in this reversal.

65. My thanks to Christopher Seitz for suggesting this illustration.

66. Collett, "Reading Forward," 180.

67. Frei, *Eclipse of Biblical Narrative*, 35.

trade on the church's traditional teaching that the person and work of Jesus Christ is the historical goal or telos of Israel's scriptures, while at the same time identifying that goal with the apostolic witness rendered by the New Testament's testimony. The difference between christotelism and the church's traditional belief on this score may be subtle, but it is fraught with damaging consequences for the Old Testament's christological witness. Identifying the Old Testament's christological sense with its New Testament reception undercuts the integrity of its christological witness, which discloses itself in relation to as well as apart from the New Testament. The proper historical telos and fulfillment of the Old Testament is not the New Testament but the person of Jesus Christ, whom the church confesses as the Christ witnessed to in Israel's scriptures (Luke 24:27, 44; John 5:39, 46; 1 Cor. 15:3–4). It is in relation to this telos that the scriptures of Israel do their sense-making, rather than in relation to the New Testament per se.

In the church of modernity, identifying the Old Testament's christological sense with its New Testament reception often functions as an interpretive category for uniting the two testaments. This is in distinction from the church's traditional approach, which avoided the dangers of abstraction by locating the historical center of the testaments in the person and work of Jesus Christ. The interpretive category *Vetus Testamentum in Novo receptum*, or the Old Testament as the New receives it, identifies the christological witness of the Old Testament with the apostolic witness of the New Testament. This approach is so pervasive in our day that it would not be claiming too much to say that it undergirds the majority report with respect to the modern church's understanding of canonical Scripture.[68] In this respect christotelism is not simply an isolated instance of an aberrant approach to the Old Testament's literal sense but another chapter in the story of modernity's attempt to reconfigure Scripture's literal sense.

Confusing the goal of Israel's scriptures with the apostolic witness rendered by the New Testament has damaging consequences for the Old Testament's witness to Christ. It also reconfigures our understanding of Old Testament prophecy. It is insufficient to define the person and work of Christ as merely the telos of Israel's scriptures, because Christ is also the one who is from the beginning (John 1:1–2; Col. 1:15–18), the eternal Archē and archetype who shapes Israel's history from the outset. Because christotelism fails to reckon

---

68. The interpretive category *Vetus Testamentum in Novo receptum* finds expression in continental German Protestantism, as well as in the United States. See Hans Hübner, *Biblische Theologie des Neuen Testaments*, 3 vols. (Göttingen: Vandenhoek & Ruprecht, 1990–95); cf. the critique offered in Christopher R. Seitz, *The Character of Christian Scripture: The Significance of a Two-Testament Bible* (Grand Rapids: Baker Academic, 2011), 53–63, 137–56.

with the person of Jesus Christ as both history's goal and beginning, it falls into the popular error of construing Old Testament prophecy as a long-range missile fired up over the top of Israel's history, landing with the incarnation. Over against this model, the testimony of Moses and the prophets offers what we will call an architectonic model.[69] On this model, Old Testament prophecy bears witness to the way in which Christ the eternal Archē shapes Israel's history "in accordance with" the figural shape of his earthly history—a history yet to come from the perspective of the Old Testament but at the same time already present and prefigured on its own semantic level, both original and eschatological. This shaping does not override the integrity of Israel's history or the original sense of the Old Testament. It does however disclose Christ on the Old Testament's own terms, while at the same time opening a figural window on what is to come in the person and work of Jesus Christ.[70]

Old Testament prophecy speaks a word to the future, not by predicting in the sense that christotelism understands prediction but through the christological significance inherent in the figural shape of Israel's history. It predicts by prefiguring the historical shape of Jesus's earthly ministry in the life of Israel on its own terms, because Christ's person and work are the archē upon which the unique historical shape and witness of both testaments are modeled. Israel's history thus comes first in the order of time, though not in the order of being. This is because the providential ordering of Israel's life is modeled upon an archetypal order and archē rooted in the eternal person and historical work of Jesus Christ.[71] Christotelism ultimately rests upon a defective Christology, *because* it fails to see the way in which the apostolic witness to Christ is exegetically authorized by the distinctive historical shape and teaching of Israel's scriptures. While there is obviously a theological rationale at work in

69. "The prophet is not only a figure of time but he also speaks of times beyond his own time. Indeed, traditionally this is what declares prophecy to be what it is. Prophetic books might be organized according to what is being said at such and such a time by such and such a prophet. But prophets not only speak of times beyond their own frame of reference. What they say *gives rise to time* and accomplishes things through fulfillment and accordance in time." Seitz, *Prophecy and Hermeneutics*, 36–37, emphasis added.

70. For a discussion of the way in which Luther sought to recover the significance of the Old Testament's original sense for its witness to Christ, see Don Collett, "Christ's Work in the Psalms: Luther on Psalm 8 and Scripture's Literal Sense," in *Who Is Jesus Christ for Us Today?— Part II: The Work of Christ*, ed. R. David Nelson (Delhi, NY: American Lutheran Publicity Bureau, 2018), 9–37; Preus, *From Shadow to Promise*; Brian T. German, *Psalms of the Faithful: Luther's Early Reading of the Psalter in Canonical Context* (Bellingham, WA: Lexham, 2017).

71. "The deliverance of Israel from Egypt found its validation, basis, and reason in what was fulfilled in Christ. So the calling of Christ out of Egypt has the primacy as archetype, though not historical priority. In other words, the type is derived from the archetype or antitype." John Murray, *Collected Writings of John Murray: Claims of Truth* (Carlisle, PA: Banner of Truth, 1976), 1:26.

this claim, as is the case with all exegesis, the church has always insisted that this claim coheres with and is "in accordance with" Israel's scriptures (1 Cor. 15:3–4). The church's christological teaching is not simply the result of imposing the christological goals of apostolic exegesis upon Israel's scriptures. Nor is it the result of force-feeding the inspired intentions of Old Testament authors with a diet of historical details peculiar to the New Testament era. However, once the inspired intentions of Old Testament authors lose their link with a larger providential account of biblical sense-making, it should come as no surprise that they are no longer able to link up with the future on their own terms.

Here again we find an attempt to construct an account of the Old Testament's christological sense in which the christological intention of its inspired words is now a bastard child, exiled from the providential framework in which it once found a home. The intended words of Old Testament authors are little more than broken syllables, because the providential and figural alphabet by which they did their sense-making has been scrambled by a historicized account of authorial intention. As far as the relation of the apostolic church to Israel's scriptures is concerned, christotelism gets matters all wrong. Following the lead of the apostle Paul in 1 Corinthians 15:3–4, Hans von Campenhausen rightly argues, "It is quite wrong to say that the Old Testament had no authority in its own right for the first Christians, and that it was taken over purely because people saw that it 'treated of Christ' or pointed toward him. . . . The situation was in fact quite the reverse. Christ is certainly vindicated to unbelievers out of the Scripture; but the converse necessity, to justify the Scriptures on the authority of Christ, is as yet nowhere even envisaged."[72]

Wirkungsgeschichte *and the New Testament's Use of the Old Testament*

Like the interpretive model provided by *sensus plenior*, christotelism also failed to find a home for the Old Testament's christological sense on the level of its original sense and voice. This fostered a defective Christology in Old Testament interpretation that identified its christological witness with the historical goal of Christ's incarnation, while at the same time undercutting his identity as the eternal Archē by which all of time is structured. The issues these models raise for the nature of the Old Testament's witness to Christ are not often a matter of concern for evangelical modernism, but this only demonstrates the pervasive reality of the loss of Old Testament consciousness in the modern church—a loss that goes hand in hand with the eclipse

---

72. Hans von Campenhausen, *The Formation of the Christian Bible,* trans. J. A. Baker (Philadelphia: Fortress, 1972), 63–64.

of providence and figure in biblical poetics. How troubled should one be by these models for understanding the character of the Old Testament's literal sense? While a surface reading of *sensus plenior* and christotelism might suggest they are merely registering the fact that the access the Old Testament provides to Christ is differently instrumental than that of the New Testament, this is decidedly not the case. The clear implication of both these accounts is that there is no access to the Old Testament's christological sense on the level of the Old Testament original sense per se. Once this premise is firmly in place, it necessarily has a ripple effect on our understanding of the New Testament and its role vis-à-vis the Old Testament.[73] The role of the New Testament's witness becomes that of correcting and supplementing a deficiency in the Old Testament's original sense. In other words, the Old Testament is not only differently instrumental in its rendering of Christ but also instrumentally deficient.

The common premise at work in both *sensus plenior* and christotelism is that the Old Testament's christological sense is the function of a later historical or material *effect* lying beyond the Old Testament's own horizon. In this regard both approaches are species of a larger genus for construing biblical sense-making and are variously styled effective history, reception history, the history of interpretation, or, in German, *Wirkungsgeschichte*. In contrast to the concern with original intention and original historical context in eighteenth- and nineteenth-century forms of historicism, reception history focuses on the effects of biblical texts upon their readers through time. It offers a corrective to historicism's focus upon origins by reminding us that history is not simply origins but also effects. In its milder versions it is simply the recognition that rather than engaging in speculative reconstructions, a more fruitful way to access the meaning of Scripture's literal sense is to study the various ways in which it has been received and interpreted by reading communities through time, for a text's meaning is disclosed through its *uses* as well as its *origins*. In its stronger forms the theory amounts to the claim that the meaning of biblical texts is *constituted* by their effective history. On this approach the original meaning of Scripture's literal sense came to be identified with its effects upon future readers, creating a whole new set of problems for the hermeneutical fortunes of the Old Testament's christological sense.

---

73. See Christopher R. Seitz, "Old Testament or Hebrew Bible? Some Theological Considerations," in *Word without End: The Old Testament as Abiding Theological Witness* (Grand Rapids: Eerdmans, 1998), 61–74; cf. also Eugene Fisher, "Hebrew Bible or Old Testament: A Response to Christopher Seitz," *ProEccl* 6, no. 2 (1997): 133–36; Christopher R. Seitz, "On Not Changing 'Old Testament' to 'Hebrew Bible': A Response to Eugene Fisher," *ProEccl* 6, no. 2 (1997): 136–40.

One way to account for the rise of *Wirkungsgeschichte* as an interpretive model in biblical studies is to view it as the natural outcome of models like *sensus plenior* and christotelism. Access to the Old Testament's christological sense was deferred to historical contexts beyond its own horizon because of the inability of these models to locate the Old Testament's christological witness in its original sense, especially once providence ceased to provide the historical and material means for uniting the Bible's literal and theological senses. Original authorial intention of the sort envisaged by *sensus plenior* and christotelism could not carry this freight apart from coming to terms with the hermeneutical significance of providential affiliation in Scripture, as well as the figural ordering of time inherent to that. In the case of *sensus plenior*, the best it could do was to provide a formal link, while christotelism does not even make it that far. Both approaches would now have to look to the future for the hope of finding a material means by which to reunite the Old Testament with its christological witness, and the New Testament was assumed to be the obvious candidate for the job. In a culture of biblical reading where these hermeneutical assumptions hold sway, it is not difficult to understand why the New Testament's use of the Old emerges as the interpretive category of choice for negotiating the christological witness of Israel's scriptures.

However, in our day the parent-child relation between reception history and the New Testament's use of the Old has a number of troubling implications for understanding the Old Testament's christological witness. In strong versions of reception history, the objective reality of biblical texts is at risk. This has implications for how we understand the way in which the Bible, especially the Old Testament, accomplishes its objective work upon us. When the meaning of biblical texts is identified too closely with their reception, their meanings are inserted into the history of their effects, and their objective reality is either blurred or undercut entirely. Biblical texts are no longer encountered as objective realities pressing in upon us, because the terms of their reception are now fully determined by the history of their interpretation. In the case of Israel's scriptures, this compromises the Old Testament's ability to exert a specific theological pressure upon the apostles that is not capable of being folded into the hermeneutical traditions at work in their contemporary environment. While the Old Testament is capable of speaking in and through those traditions, its inseparable relation with the triune LORD who speaks within it also enables it to "speak over the head" of its effective history. Thus while the argument can be made that the interpretations of biblical texts *constitute* the historical reality of their being, their relation to the triune LORD means that they are never merely historical realities but also the material means for the communication of abiding theological realities.

For this reason the Old Testament's theological sense can never be coextensive or directly identifiable with the history of its interpretation, still less a particular historical era or moment in its reception history. The meaning of Old Testament texts shares in that history but cannot be identified with it in a manner that is wholly unequivocal.

The interpretive model offered by strong versions of *Wirkungsgeschichte* has helped foster a hermeneutical climate that privileges the New Testament's reception of the Old—an interpretive category that now defines the scope of the Old Testament's christological sense for not a few of its readers, both evangelical and mainline. Identifying the Old Testament's christological voice with its New Testament reception mutes that voice by absorbing it into the New Testament, such that the Old Testament becomes incapable of sounding its notes apart from the interpretive filters provided by the New Testament or, for that matter, late Second Temple Judaism. Here it is helpful to recall the words of warning issued by Brevard Childs:

> The two testaments have been linked as Old and New, but this designation does not mean that the integrity of each individual testament has been destroyed. The Old Testament bears its true witness as the Old which remains distinct from the New. It is promise, not fulfillment. Yet its voice continues to sound and it has not been stilled by the fulfillment of the promise. The significance of emphasizing the continuing canonical integrity of the Old Testament lies in resisting the Christian temptation to identify Biblical Theology with the New Testament's interpretation of the Old, as if the Old Testament's witness were limited to how it was once heard and appropriated by the early church.[74]

The thesis that the Old Testament's christological witness is authoritative only insofar as it is received by or correlated with the New Testament damages the Old Testament's theological integrity, silencing its voice by identifying it with the New Testament's reception of it. It also fails to do justice to the New Testament's own discrete voice by construing it as a material "effect" of the Old Testament. This also suggests a serious problem inherent in the employment of reception history as an interpretive model for relating the testaments. Given the assumptions undergirding this model, there is no compelling reason to shut down the ongoing effective history of the Old Testament by stopping with the New Testament. The enthusiastic disciples of this model for construing the two testaments are now on the horns of a destructive dilemma. Either the New Testament shuts down the Old Testament's effective history,

---

74. See Brevard S. Childs, *Biblical Theology of the Old and New Testaments: Theological Reflection on the Christian Bible* (Minneapolis: Fortress, 1992), 77–78.

in which case it no longer continues to sound its own notes alongside the New Testament, or the New Testament does not shut down Old Testament effective history, in which case the New Testament becomes just one phase among others in the ongoing reception history of Israel's scriptures. Stated differently, the Old Testament is merely the prolegomena to the New (option 1), or the New Testament is simply the aftermath of the Old (option 2). How does one move from the dichotomy of these two choices to an account of the two testaments as two unique witnesses disclosing the triune God speaking in Christ by the Spirit on their own terms?

As an interpretive model for uniting the two testaments, reception history does not work with a concept of Old Testament as canon. It therefore has no way to clearly distinguish the Old Testament canon from the New or, for that matter, the New Testament from the history of the post-apostolic church. Although thinkers like Lessing and countless others after him have argued the authority of the New Testament originated in the apostolic church, even an otherwise unfriendly critic of the Old Testament like Harnack recognized that the source of the New Testament's authority was actually older than the church and originated with the Old Testament. The New Testament was recognized as canon on analogy with the prior canonical authority of the scriptures of Israel. As that which was "in accordance with" those scriptures (1 Cor. 15:3–4), the authority of the New Testament achieved canonical status "because it followed and was paired with the authoritative scriptures of Israel, which already possessed this status."[75] In this way Israel's scriptures came to be called the Old Testament, and both testaments were set apart from the ecclesial tradition that followed the post-biblical era.[76] Reception history has no internal theological mechanism for reckoning with the

75. Commenting on Lessing's view, Harnack notes that Lessing "perceived that the New Testament as a book and as the recognized fundamental document of the Christian religion originated in the *Church*. But Lessing did not recognize that the Book from the moment of its origin freed itself from all conditions of its birth, and at once claimed to be an *entirely independent and unconditioned authority*. This was indeed only possible because the book at once took its place beside the Old Testament, which occupied a position of absolute and unquestionable independence because it was more ancient than the Church." Adolph Harnack, *Bible Reading in the Early Church* (London: Williams and Norgate, 1912), 145, emphasis original. For sources and bibliography on the debate, see Christopher R. Seitz, *Elder Testament: Canon, Theology, Trinity* (Waco: Baylor University Press, 2018), 24n6; cf. also Stephen B. Chapman, *The Law and the Prophets: A Study in Old Testament Canon Formation*, FAT 27 (Tübingen: Mohr Siebeck, 2000).

76. The logic at work here is reversed by Craig Allert, who argues that the Old Testament attained the status of canon on analogy with the canonization of the New Testament, the latter of which was established by the church in the fourth century AD. See Craig Allert, *A High View of Scripture? The Authority of the Bible and the Formation of the New Testament Canon* (Grand Rapids: Baker Academic, 2007).

privileged status Israel's scriptures had for the apostolic church. Once reception history is adopted as a suitable model for relating the testaments, the theological rationale undergirding the distinction between the testaments collapses, because the scope of Scripture has been reconfigured in terms of a historical model for sense-making that either marginalizes or erases the theological reality crucial for the reality of canon-making. Much like the problems inherent in an older model for relating the testaments known as tradition history,[77] the construction of meaning in reception history keeps motoring on into the future as one question gives way to an answer, which then becomes the basis for another question, and so on as the church moves on into the great wide open.[78]

Advocates of this reception history model construe the New Testament as the ultimate or consummate phase of the Old Testament's reception history because they wish to invoke the New Testament as a material control on the Old Testament's meaning. Yet once again an irony emerges in the wake of this program for retooling the Old Testament's literal sense; for without a theological concept of the Old Testament as canon to frame and identify the emergent character of the New Testament alongside Israel's scriptures, there is no reason to assign the New Testament this role. On the other hand, once the New Testament's witness is framed in terms of canon vis-à-vis the Old Testament, it loses its identity as the consummate phase of Old Testament effective history and properly takes its place as an accorded witness alongside the original witness of the Old.[79] It is the character of the New Testament as an accorded witness that establishes its distinctive canonical status *alongside* the Old Testament, rather than simply *after* it. Rather than the New Testament functioning as a material control on the Old Testament's meaning, its canonical form and function consists in providing a material control on the meaning of the particular historical economy associated with it—namely, the *new* historical economy defined by the advent of the Word made flesh.[80]

Recognizing this allows us to speak of the testaments in terms of *two* unique witnesses to the one triune God speaking in Christ by the Spirit, rendered through *two* historically different economies. The New Testament is not somehow "closer" than the Old Testament to the theological reality it renders, since the two testaments speak of one theological subject matter, rather than two.

---

77. See the incisive discussion of von Rad in Seitz, *Prophecy and Hermeneutics*, 155–82.

78. For a discussion of the way in which this hermeneutic works itself out in the contemporary controversy over traditional marriage and related ethical issues, see Seitz, *Character of Christian Scripture*, 173–90.

79. See the remarks in Seitz, *Character of Christian Scripture*, 94n1.

80. Cf. Childs, *Biblical Theology of the Old and New Testaments*, 76.

While each testament renders this subject matter in terms of its own distinctive voice and context, the fact that they are united by one reality positions both testaments as equidistant and equi-instrumental witnesses, in contrast to the "one-after-another" logic driving models based upon *sensus plenior*, christotelism, and reception history. In sum, the New Testament is neither the reification of the Old nor simply its effect or aftermath—still less a Second Temple text with a DNA that primarily derives from its contemporary historical milieu. Its genre is perhaps best described in terms of *a transformed Old Testament* that receives its place alongside the Old on analogy and in accordance with the Old Testament's antecedent authority (1 Cor. 15:3–4).

Wirkungsgeschichte *and Second Temple Judaism*

Reception history classifies the Old Testament's literal sense as a species whose meaning properly belongs to the category of effects rather than origins. Stripped bare by the removal of their providential dress, the naked "original" intentions of biblical authors proved insufficient for the task of reconnecting the Old Testament's original sense with its christological sense, because the authors' ability to speak more than they knew depended on their relation to a larger providential framework and background. Some mechanism other than original intention and context had to be found in order to save the Old Testament's christological sense. An account of meaning *as* effect stepped in to fill the vacuum but did so at the price of fully eschatologizing that sense. The rise of *Wirkungsgeschichte* as an interpretive model and the eclipse of providence are thus bound up with one another.

The influence of reception history as an interpretive model also helps account for recent efforts to construct the Old Testament's christological sense on the basis of the hermeneutical traditions native to the Second Temple period. In addition to the New Testament's use of the Old, the interpretive traditions and methods of this era are also bound up with the Old Testament's effective history. The operative assumption of not a few biblical theologies in our day is that the comparative hermeneutical context provided by this historical era is the key to integrating both testaments. Viewed from this angle, hermeneutical interest in the Second Temple period reflects the most recent appropriation of comparative religion as a method for negotiating the meaning of Scripture's literal sense, biblical studies having now moved on from its earlier love affair with the archaeology of early Palestine. The point has already been made that the integration point for both testaments is not a concept or theme but the eternal person and historical work of Jesus Christ, triunely configured. At the end of the day, locating the unity of the testaments in the interpretive traditions and methods of a particular historical era partakes of the same shortcomings that arise when Scripture's proper historical center is displaced by a master interpretive category.[81]

In approaching this issue the usual and somewhat obvious disclaimers apply: Paul and the apostolic community were historically situated within this milieu, were familiar with and/or trained in its methods, utilized its literary conventions, and so forth. All these matters may be taken as historical givens, more or less. The question that needs to be addressed at this juncture is whether the apostles' relationship to this external milieu *explains* their reading of Israel's scriptures. Because this historical era belongs to the Old Testament's effective history, this approach rightly recognizes that we may learn much about the Old Testament through the application of comparative methods. However, it struggles to avoid collapsing the meaning of the Old Testament's literal sense into its received sense. While the literal sense requires both text *and* reception, the received sense does not. Strong versions of reception history exercise a reductive pressure on the distinction between Scripture's literal sense and received sense that either weakens that distinction or collapses it altogether. The result is a reading of the Old Testament that *identifies* its literal sense with readings of Israel's scriptures performed by religious communities during the Second Temple period or with what others have variously styled the traditioned sense, received sense, or ecclesial sense. Although the community of faith remains the proper sphere in which to read the Old Testament, its literal sense is not simply identical with its traditioned sense. To argue otherwise not only inserts the Old Testament's literal sense into its effective history but also undercuts its ability to do its objective work through the literal sense.

---

81. It is precisely for this reason that its unity cannot ultimately be identified with a concept, theme, or master category. D. Stephen Long notes,

> Ancient Christian theologians expressly forbade thinking or speaking of God in these terms. They said "God cannot be placed within any category" using a famous Latin expression, *Deus non est genere.* This entails a radical idea: God cannot be placed in any category larger than God in order to understand God. If we define God in a category that is more encompassing than what we mean by "God", then that larger category would truly be what we mean by "God" and our use of the term "God" would be subordinate to that larger category. This is why theology begins with the claim that God is not a genus or that God is not a category. We know this only because of the revelation given to Moses when God tells him that God's proper name is "I am". God alone is the one who truly is; God cannot be contained within any conceptual framework that we devise for ourselves, even though we must use our conceptual systems in order to speak of God. (D. Stephen Long, *Theology and Culture: A Guide to the Discussion* [Eugene, OR: Cascade, 2008], 1–2)

Cf. also Katherine Sonderegger's discussion of Thomas Aquinas on this point in her *Systematic Theology,* vol. 1, *The Doctrine of God* (Minneapolis: Fortress, 2015), 30–35.

Much can be learned from studying the hermeneutical methods on hand in Paul's day, including those at work in Qumran.[82] But we also need to recognize that these methods can take us only part of the way when it comes to providing a motive for the apostolic exegesis of Israel's scriptures. The proper lineage of apostolic exegesis is now obscured, because its proper sphere of operation has been transposed from the frame of reference figurally disclosed in Israel's scriptures to the hermeneutical environment of the Second Temple period. The "original" or genealogical context for the Old Testament's literal sense is the inner life of the triune God. Viewed from this perspective, the difficulty with modern strategies for construing the Old Testament's christological sense is not that they ignored the importance of original context but that they were not original enough. Accepting this does not mean we are not free to learn from the methods and results of comparative religion. But it does subordinate the project of theological construction through correlation with Second Temple Judaism to the "comparative context" provided by the Old Testament's own witness, which "got there first."

82. Francis Watson, *Paul and the Hermeneutics of Faith* (London: T&T Clark, 2004); Richard Bauckham, *Jesus and the God of Israel: God Crucified and Other Studies on the New Testament's Christology of Divine Identity* (Grand Rapids: Eerdmans, 2008), 1–17.

5

Epilogue

J. P. Gabler's 1787 address is not the only eighteenth-century manifesto on biblical interpretation underwriting the use of Scripture's historical sense as the independent control on its meaning.[1] But there can be no doubt that it serves to mark the beginning of an age in biblical interpretation when exegesis guided by the church's creeds and confessions came under critical attack. After Gabler, the profiles of two competing visions for exegetical reason began to emerge in sharp relief, one rooted in confessional exegesis and the other in scientific exegesis. Confessional exegesis takes its bearings from the theological framework or rule of faith that finds its most well-known expression in the Nicene Creed, while scientific exegesis works with a frame of reference rooted in modernity's use of historical reconstruction as a critical and objective control upon Scripture. Of course, stating the contrast in these terms is a bit schematized and misleading, since both approaches to exegesis appeal to particular accounts of history, and both operate on the basis of a set of theological assumptions, as we have already argued. Bearing these qualifications in mind, it is helpful to think of these two frames of reference as contrasting rules of faith for relating Scripture's literal sense to the theological reality of which it speaks. These two rules or frames of reference for appropriating the meaning of Scripture's literal sense underwrite the basic differences between confessional exegesis and scientific exegesis or what we will call Nicene reason and scientific reason. Alternatively, we may also speak of these two approaches in terms of ecclesial reason and critical reason or in terms of the Nicene project and the *Wissenschaft* project.

1. See Christopher R. Seitz, *Prophecy and Hermeneutics: Toward a New Introduction to the Prophets* (Grand Rapids: Baker Academic, 2007), 34: "Gabler was indebted to a history of ideas and to far greater figures ahead of him in that history (Spinoza, Simon, Ernesti, Semler, Eichhorn), so in many ways his Altdorf address has achieved a proportion that is artificial. But it is a convenient marker, and the content of the address classifies in a compact way some of the reigning assumptions of the period."

The Nicene Project and Figural Reading

The excellence of catholicity in Nicene reason is found in its universal scope. Nicene reason offered its own set of objective controls upon biblical meaning by which to critically assess biblical interpretation and adjudicate its claims to meaning. These objective norms or controls upon biblical meaning were generated by means of exegetically authorized theological creeds and confessions. Insofar as the claims of critical reason and objectivity operated within the Nicene project, they functioned within the parameters established and delimited by these confessions. On this approach objectivity was possible just insofar as ecclesial reason in the community of faith submits its thoughts to the God of Israel's triune self-disclosure in the two-testament canon of Scripture. Stated in classically Augustinian terms, objective thinking is thinking God's thoughts *after* him—that is, *post verbum Dei*. Canonically contextualized and biblically interpreted, the reality of God's self-disclosure in history thus offers the possibility of objective meaning and a truly critical perspective, though only insofar as we order our thoughts in obedience to Scripture. Human reason and the methods it proposes occupy a *post hoc* role in relation to faith, and they gain access to a critical perspective only through faith in the Word of God mediated in Scripture and sacrament. This Augustinian approach to objectivity and critical reason expresses itself in the Anselmian motto *credo ut intelligam*, "I believe so that I may understand," which famously restated Augustine's interpretive gloss on Isaiah 7:9.[2] A similar understanding of the relation between faith and reason is also enshrined in Anselm's account of knowledge as *fides quaerens intellectum* (faith seeking understanding). This Nicene project should not be confused with modern forms of epistemological foundationalism, in which the order of being gives way to the order of knowing and epistemology legislates ontology. Rather, the canon of Scripture remains fully located within the saving economy of God, thereby precluding the possibility of "the dogmatic mislocation" of the canon.[3] The proper location for the doctrine of Scripture is the doctrine of God, and the proper sphere for reading Scripture is the church.

The quest for objectivity that marked the age of Enlightenment has often been interpreted as the emancipation of reason from externally imposed

---

2. *Crede, ut intelligas*: Believe(!), so that you may understand. Augustine's Latin rendering is derived from the Septuagint translation of Isa. 7:9 and is frequently cited in his writings. See, for example, *On Christian Doctrine*, bk. 2, chap. 12, sec. 17.

3. John Webster, "The Dogmatic Location of the Canon," in *Word and Church: Essays in Christian Dogmatics* (London: Bloomsbury T&T Clark, 2016), 9–46.

authorities.[4] Another way to read this is to view it as a secularized form of Augustinianism that restates the Nicene concern for catholicity in modern form, a reading that has been articulated by more than one historiographer of the Enlightenment in our day.[5] The *Wissenschaft* project of the Enlightenment emancipated critical reason and objectivity from the frame of reference provided by Nicene reason. This relocated the norms of objectivity provided for biblical interpretation by ecclesial reason in a new form of historical reason. It would be not the catholicity of Nicene reason but the catholicity of historical reason Gabler and many after him would place their hope in to reestablish catholic consensus in the divided church of post-Reformation modernity. Noteworthy, however, is the fact that this project for retooling biblical interpretation continued the Nicene project's concern to generate and maintain the existence of catholic consensus by establishing objective norms for adjudicating the truth or falsehood of exegetical claims. It simply transposed those Nicene values into another organizing framework for understanding their meaning and function. Viewed in this light, the *Wissenschaft* project for reading Scripture emerges as a successor discipline to the Nicene project, operating with its own sets of theological assumptions, confessions, and objective controls on Scripture's literal sense.

In fact, the scientific concern for objectivity in Gabler's version of historical reason is already anticipated in Nicene reason in its concern to preserve figural exegesis as a valid mode of biblical interpretation. As a form of *other*-speaking, figural exegesis privileges Scripture's theological frame of reference when constructing the objective norms and confessions by which biblical interpretation is governed. It preserves a referential mode of knowing that highlights the intrinsic character of the relation between Scripture

4. The classic statement of this view remains Kant's eighteenth-century essay "Was ist Aufklärung?" For an English translation, see *Kant: Selections*, ed. Lewis White Beck (New York: MacMillan, 1988), 461–67.

5. Carl Becker, *The Heavenly City of the Eighteenth-Century Philosophers* (New Haven: Yale University Press, 1964). To take but one example, consider Descartes's famous dictum "I think, therefore I am" (*cogito ergo sum*). The phrase bears a striking resemblance to Augustine's refutation of skeptics in his *Civitas Dei*, bk. 11, chap. 26, in which he argues against skeptical attempts to undercut existential knowledge claims by pointing out that "if I am deceived, I still am" (*si fallor, sum*). The main difference between these two arguments, which was not lost on Descartes himself, is that Augustine's statement derives its force from a frame of reference provided by Nicene reason, while the statement of Descartes operates within the context of the new scientific reason of his day. For a discussion of Augustine's arguments against the skeptics of the Third Academy, see Ronald Nash, *The Light of the Mind: St. Augustine's Theory of Knowledge* (Lexington: University Press of Kentucky, 1969), 12–23; cf. the additional remarks in Francis Copleston, *A History of Philosophy: Descartes to Leibniz* (Westminster, MD: Newman, 1961), 90–91.

and the triune LORD upon whom Scripture's meaning depends, reminding us that biblical language does not render its sense as a self-contained or self-authenticating reality but requires a triune and eternal "other" in order to do its sense-making. Viewed in this light, the sharp contrast typically drawn between confessional and scientific exegesis is misleading. The question for biblical interpretation—indeed, any form of interpretation—is not whether we can avoid appealing to objective frames of reference, theological rules for reading Scripture, or even the "covering laws" of history preferred by scientific interpretation.[6] Rather, the question is which frame of reference does the best job of accounting for the subject matter testified to in Scripture.[7]

The other-speaking basic to the quest for objectivity in biblical exegesis requires the referential logic of figural reading to function. But without a theological frame of reference in which to situate that logic, the language of the Old Testament is inevitably taken over by the logic of deferral.[8] Old Testament words without ontological tethers reaching beyond the flux of history become signs "whose meaning cannot be fixed but is continually deferred, both calling for and resisting interpretation." As the "sign of a deferred or absent meaning,"[9] their basic nature is apophatic rather than epiphanic. The reader of Scripture poses a question to the Old Testament: "What are you talking about?" The Old Testament answers: "I'm not talking about myself

6. Though secular scholars sharply distinguish scientific methods from figural exegesis, when studying either nature or history, they nevertheless work with a referential logic for organizing empirical data akin to the instincts at work in figural reading and the rule of faith. As O'Keefe and Reno state, "Any large-scale interpretive project, whether of diverse fossil data or diverse scriptural material, requires an initial, rule-governed approach by which the details might be brought into their proper order. . . . Mistaken assumptions and ill-conceived rules lead us into dead-ends and force us to manhandle the data to make it fit" (124). Cf. also their earlier remark that "historians need to presume an economy of causality and influence that allows them to connect events and organize the data into some meaningful whole" (112). John J. O'Keefe and R. R. Reno, Sanctified Vision: An Introduction to Early Christian Interpretation of the Bible (Baltimore: Johns Hopkins University Press, 2005).

7. A critique of exegesis in terms of subject matter (Sachkritik) is one in which Scripture's subject matter serves as a critical norm for judging the adequacy of exegesis. This form of Sachkritik is to be clearly distinguished from "a form of critical reductionism which sets witness against res in radical antagonism, as if word and spirit were natural enemies" (Brevard S. Childs, Biblical Theology of the Old and New Testaments: Theological Reflection on the Christian Bible [Minneapolis: Fortress, 1993], 85; cf. his closing comments on p. 89). Inasmuch as the purpose of the rule of faith is to illumine Scripture's subject matter, the latter serves as a critical norm for the former.

8. See Paul de Man, "Semiology and Rhetoric," Diacritics 3, no. 1 (1973): 27–33, reprinted in The Norton Anthology of Theory and Criticism, ed. Vincent B. Leitch, William B. Cain, Laurie Finke, and Barbara Johnson (New York: Norton, 2001), 1515–26.

9. Rita Copeland and Peter T. Struck, "Introduction," in The Cambridge Companion to Allegory, ed. Rita Copeland and Peter T. Struck (Cambridge: Cambridge University Press, 2010), 10.

but about something over there." The reader then stands "over there" and repeats the question, only to find the Old Testament answering in the same way: "I'm not talking about myself but about something out there, over there but not here." And so on, *ad infinitum*. Deferral is endless, much like the sign in a pub that reads "Free drinks tomorrow."

While referential modes of knowing also remain crucial for the logic of figural reading, their objective or scientific potential is not rooted in modern constructions of history but bound up with providence and the rule of faith by which Scripture is properly related to its theological subject matter. Both the objective potential and the reach of Scripture's literal sense are the hermeneutical consequence of the Bible's scope, because the figural logic of *verba-res* reaches beyond communities and historical traditions to the triune God who speaks in Christ by the Spirit. By excluding theological frames of reference from scientific exegesis proper, the *Wissenschaft* project places a burden upon "history" it ultimately cannot bear. In place of Scripture's theological ontology, an ontology of pride arose that replaced the triune God with a historically reconstructed ideal as the basis for objectivity. Whether this alternative or the countless others advanced in its wake can carry the christological burden of Old Testament history remains doubtful. From the point of view of Scripture's own witness, such a project is impossible and therefore doomed to failure. However, what it means to speak of "failure" varies according to the different standards used to assess it, and for some the loss of Old Testament consciousness and figural imagination remains "a world well lost." In the meantime, the Nicene project's affirmation of the Old Testament's universal scope and Christian voice still holds promise, recognizing that Scripture's universal reach is founded upon, indeed made possible by the theological reach native to the Old Testament's witness to creation, providence, and Jesus Christ, the eternal Word and Archē of creation who became flesh in time.

Bibliography

Abma, R. *Bonds of Love: Methodic Studies of Prophetic Texts with Marriage Imagery (Isaiah 50:1–3 and 54:1–10, Hosea 1–3, Jeremiah 2–3)*. Assen, Netherlands: Van Gorcum, 1999.

Adamson, Sylvia, Gavin Alexander, and Katrin Ettenhuber, eds. *Renaissance Figures of Speech*. Cambridge: Cambridge University Press, 2007.

Alderman, Brian J., and Brent A. Strawn. "A Note on Peshitta Job 28:23." *CBQ* 129, no. 3 (2010): 449–56.

Allert, Craig. *A High View of Scripture? The Authority of the Bible and the Formation of the New Testament Canon*. Grand Rapids: Baker Academic, 2007.

Ameriks, Karl, ed. *The Cambridge Companion to German Idealism*. Cambridge: Cambridge University Press, 2000.

Andersen, Ragnar. "The Elihu Speeches: Their Place and Sense in the Book of Job." *TynBul* 66, no. 1 (2015): 75–94.

Aquinas, Thomas. *Commentary on the Gospel of Saint Matthew*. Translated by Paul M. Kimball. Camillus, NY: Dolorosa Press, 2012.

———. *The Literal Exposition of Job: A Scriptural Commentary Concerning Providence*. Translated by Anthony Damico. Oxford: Oxford University Press, 1989.

———. *The Power of God*. Translated by Richard J. Regan. Oxford: Oxford University Press, 2012.

———. *Summa Contra Gentiles*. Translated by Anton C. Pegis, James F. Anderson, Vernon J. Bourke, and Charles J. O'Neil. 4 vols. Notre Dame, IN: University of Notre Dame Press, 1975.

_____. *Summa Theologiae*. Translated by the Fathers of the English Dominican Province. 5 vols. Westminster, MD: Christian Classics, 1981.

Auerbach, Erich. *Mimesis: The Representation of Reality in Western Literature*. Princeton: Princeton University Press, 1953.

Augustine. *"De doctrina Christiana": A Classic of Western Spirituality*. Edited by Duane Arnold and Pamela Bright. Notre Dame, IN: University of Notre Dame Press, 1995.

———. *The Confessions*. Translated by Henry Chadwick. Oxford: Oxford University Press, 1991.

———. "Letter 93: Augustine to Vincent." In *The Works of St. Augustine: A Translation for the 21st Century, Letters 1–99*, ed. John E. Rotelle, 376–408. Translation and notes by Roland Teske, S.J. Hyde Park, NY: New City Press, 2001.

———. *On Christian Doctrine*. Translated by D. W. Robertson Jr. New York: MacMillan, 1958.

Barth, Karl. *Church Dogmatics* IV/3.1. Translated and edited by Geoffrey W. Bromiley and Thomas F. Torrance. Edinburgh: T&T Clark, 1956.

Barton, John. *The Nature of Biblical Criticism*. Louisville: Westminster John Knox, 2007.

Bates, Matthew. *The Birth of the Trinity: Jesus, God, and Spirit in New Testament and Early Christian Interpretation of the Old Testament*. Oxford: Oxford University Press, 2015.

Bauckham, Richard. *Jesus and the God of Israel: God Crucified and Other Studies on the New Testament's Christology of Divine Identity*. Grand Rapids: Eerdmans, 2008.

Beauchamp, Paul. *L'un et l'autre Testament Tome 2: Accomplir les Écritures*. Paris: Seuil, 1990.

Becker, Carl. *The Heavenly City of the Eighteenth-Century Philosophers*. New Haven: Yale University Press, 1964.

Beiser, Frederick. "The Enlightenment and Idealism." In *The Cambridge Companion to German Idealism*, ed. Karl Ameriks, 18–36. Cambridge: Cambridge University Press, 2000.

Berkeley, George. *A Treatise Concerning the Principles of Human Knowledge*. Edited by Kenneth Winkler. Indianapolis: Hackett, 1982.

Beuken, Willem. "*Mišpaṭ*: The First Servant Song and Its Context." *VT* 22 (1972): 1–30.

Blowers, Paul M. *The Drama of the Divine Economy: Creator and Creation in Early Christian Theology and Piety*. Oxford: Oxford University Press, 2012.

———. "The *Regula Fidei* and the Narrative Character of Early Christian Faith." *ProEccl* 6 (1997): 199–228.

Böhm, Thomas. "Allegory and History." In *Handbook of Patristic Exegesis*, ed. Charles Kannengiesser, 1:213–26. Leiden: Brill, 2004.

Brooks, Cleanth. *The Well Wrought Urn: Studies in the Structure of Poetry*. New York: Harcourt, Brace, 1947.

Brown, Ray. *The* Sensus Plenior *of Sacred Scripture*. Baltimore: St. Mary's University Press, 1955.

Brown, William P. *Seeing the Psalms: A Theology of Metaphor*. Louisville: Westminster John Knox, 2002.

Bruns, Gerald. *Hermeneutics: Ancient and Modern*. New Haven: Yale University Press, 1992.

———. "On the Weakness of Language in the Human Sciences." In *The Rhetoric of the Human Sciences: Language and Argument in Scholarship and Public Affairs*, ed. John S. Nelson, Allan Megill, and Donald N. McCloskey, 239–62. Madison: University of Wisconsin Press, 1987.

Bucur, Bogdan. "Justyn Martyr's Exegesis of Biblical Theophanies." *TS* 75, no. 1 (2014): 34–51.

Burney, C. F. "Christ as the ΑΡΧΗ of Creation." *JTS* 27 (1926): 160–77.

Burrows, Mark. "Jean Gerson on the 'Traditioned Sense' of Scripture as an Argument for an Ecclesial Hermeneutic." In *Biblical Hermeneutics in Historical Perspective: Studies in Honor of Karlfried Froehlich on His Sixtieth Birthday*, ed. Mark Burrows and P. Rorem, 152–72. Grand Rapids: Eerdmans, 1991.

Butterfield, Herbert. *The Whig Interpretation of History*. New York: Norton, 1965.

Calvin, John. *Institutes of the Christian Religion*. Edited by John T. McNeill. 2 vols. Philadelphia: Westminster, 1960.

Cameron, Michael. *Christ Meets Me Everywhere: Augustine's Early Figurative Exegesis*. Oxford: Oxford University Press, 2012.

Campenhausen, Hans von. *The Formation of the Christian Bible*. Translated by J. A. Baker. Philadelphia: Fortress, 1972.

Cazelles, Henri. "*Aḥiqar, Ummân*, and *Amun* and Biblical Wisdom Texts." In *Solving Riddles and Untying Knots: Biblical, Epigraphic, and Semitic Studies in Honor of Jonas C. Greenfield*, ed. Ziony Zevit, Seymour Gitin, and Michael Sokoloff, 45–56. Winona Lake, IN: Eisenbrauns, 1995.

Chapman, Stephen B. *The Law and the Prophets: A Study in Old Testament Canon Formation*. FAT 27. Tübingen: Mohr Siebeck, 2000.

———. "Reading the Bible as Witness: Divine Retribution in the Old Testament." *PRSt* 31, no. 2 (2004): 171–90.

Childs, Brevard S. "Allegory and Typology within Biblical Interpretation." In *The Bible as Christian Scripture: The Work of Brevard S. Childs*, ed. Christopher R. Seitz and Robert C. Kashow, 299–310. Atlanta: Society of Biblical Literature, 2013.

———. *Biblical Theology of the Old and New Testaments: Theological Reflection on the Christian Bible*. Minneapolis: Fortress, 1993.

———. *The Church's Guide for Reading Paul: The Canonical Shaping of the Pauline Corpus*. Grand Rapids: Eerdmans, 2008.

———. "Critique of Recent Intertextual Canonical Interpretation." *ZAW* 115 (2003): 173–84.

———. "Does the Old Testament Witness to Jesus Christ?" In *Evangelium, Schrift-auslegung, Kirche: Festschrift für Peter Stuhlmacher zum 65. Geburtstag*, ed. J. Ådna, S. Hafemann, and O. Hofius, 57–64. Göttingen: Vandenhoeck & Ruprecht, 1997.

———. "Excursus III: The Canonical Approach and the 'New Yale Theology.'" In *New Testament as Canon: An Introduction*, 541–46. Philadelphia: Fortress, 1985.

———. *Introduction to the Old Testament as Scripture*. Philadelphia: Fortress, 1979.

———. "The *Sensus Literalis* of Scripture: An Ancient and Modern Problem." In *Beiträge zur alttestamentlichen Theologie: Festschrift für Walther Zimmerli Zum 70. Geburtstag*, ed. Herbert Donner, Robert Hanhart, and Rudolf Smend, 80–93. Göttingen: Vandenhoeck & Ruprecht, 1977.

Clifford, Richard J. *Proverbs*. Louisville: Westminster John Knox, 2016.

Collett, Don. "The Christomorphic Shaping of Time in Radner's *Time and the Word*." *ProEccl* 27, no. 3 (2018): 276–88.

———. "Christ's Work in the Psalms: Luther on Psalm 8 and Scripture's Literal Sense." In *Who Is Jesus Christ for Us Today?—Part II: The Work of Christ*, ed. R. David Nelson, 9–37. Delhi, NY: American Lutheran Publicity Bureau, 2018.

———. "The Defenestration of Prague and the Hermeneutics of 'Story': A Response to Peter Leithart." *Reformed Faith & Practice* 3, no. 2 (2018): 32–38.

———. "A Place to Stand: Proverbs 8 and the Construction of Ecclesial Space." *SJT* 70, no. 2 (2017): 166–83.

———. "Reading Forward: The Old Testament and Retrospective Stance." *ProEccl* 24, no. 3 (2015): 178–96.

———. "Review Essay of Daniel R. Driver's *Brevard Childs, Biblical Theologian for the Church's One Bible*." *ProEccl* 23, no. 1 (2014): 99–112.

———. "A Tale of Two Testaments: Childs, Old Testament Torah, and *Heilsge-schichte*." In *The Bible as Christian Scripture: The Work of Brevard S. Childs*, ed. Christopher R. Seitz and Robert C. Kashow, 185–219. Atlanta: Society of Biblical Literature, 2013.

Collins, C. John. "Discourse Analysis and the Interpretation of Genesis 2:4–7." *WTJ* 61, no. 2 (1999): 269–76.

Copeland, Rita, and Peter T. Struck. "Introduction." In *The Cambridge Companion to Allegory*, ed. Rita Copeland and Peter T. Struck, 1–12. Cambridge: Cambridge University Press, 2010.

Copleston, Francis. *A History of Philosophy: Descartes to Leibniz*. Westminster, MD: Newman, 1961.

Davis, Ellen. "'And Pharaoh Will Change His Mind . . .' (Ezekiel 32:31): Dismantling Mythical Discourse." In *Theological Exegesis: Essays in Honor of Brevard S. Childs*, ed. Christopher R. Seitz and Kathryn E. Greene-McCreight, 224–39. Grand Rapids: Eerdmans, 1998.

Dawson, John David. "Against the Divine Ventriloquist: Coleridge and De Man on Symbol, Allegory, and Scripture." *JLT* 4, no. 3 (1990): 293–310.

———. *Christian Figural Reading and the Fashioning of Identity*. Berkeley: University of California Press, 2002.

Dell, Katherine. *The Book of Job as Skeptical Literature*. BZAW 197. Berlin: de Gruyter, 1991.

Descartes, René. "Meditations on First Philosophy." In *Philosophy of the 16th and 17th Centuries*, ed. Richard Popkin, 121–80. New York: Free Press, 1966.

Dhorme, Édouard. *A Commentary on the Book of Job*. Translated by Harold Knight. Nashville: Nelson, 1984.

Driver, Daniel R. *Brevard Childs, Biblical Theologian for the Church's One Bible*. Tübingen: Mohr Siebeck, 2010.

Ebeling, Gerhard. "The Beginnings of Luther's Hermeneutics." *LQ* 7, no. 2 (1993): 129–58.

———. "The Beginnings of Luther's Hermeneutics." *LQ* 7, no. 3 (1993): 315–38.

———. "The Beginnings of Luther's Hermeneutics." *LQ* 7, no. 4 (1993): 451–68.

Eichrodt, Walther. "In the Beginning: A Contribution to the Interpretation of the First Word of the Bible." In *Creation in the Old Testament*, ed. Bernhard Anderson, 65–73. Philadelphia: Fortress, 1985.

Elliger, Karl, and Wilhelm Rudolph, eds. *Biblia Hebraica Stuttgartensia*. Stuttgart: Deutsche Bibelgesellschaft, 1977.

Enns, Peter. "Fuller Meaning, Single Goal: A Christotelic Approach to the New Testament Use of the Old in Its First-Century Interpretive Environment." In *Three Views on the New Testament Use of the Old Testament*, ed. Kenneth Berding and Jonathan Lunde, 167–217. Grand Rapids: Zondervan, 2008.

———. *Inspiration and Incarnation: Evangelicals and the Problem of the Old Testament*. Grand Rapids: Baker Academic, 2005.

Enns, Peter, and Dan McCartney. "Matthew and Hosea: A Response to John Sailhamer." *WTJ* 63 (2001): 97–105.

Fergusson, David. *Creation*. Grand Rapids: Eerdmans, 2014.

Fiedrowicz, Michael. "General Introduction." In *Expositions of Psalms 1–32*. Works of Saint Augustine III/15, pp. 50–60. Translated by Maria Boulding, O.S.B. Hyde Park, NY: New City Press, 2000.

Fishbane, Michael. "The Teacher and the Hermeneutical Task: A Reinterpretation of Medieval Exegesis." *JAAR* 43, no. 4 (1975): 709–21.

Fisher, Eugene. "Hebrew Bible or Old Testament: A Response to Christopher Seitz." *ProEccl* 6, no. 2 (1997): 133–36.

Floyd, Mike. "The מַשָּׂא (*Maśśāʾ*) as a Type of Prophetic Book." *JBL* 121, no. 3 (2002): 401–22.

Fowl, Stephen E. *Theological Interpretation of Scripture*. Eugene, OR: Cascade, 2009.

Fox, Christopher. *Locke and the Scriblerians: Identity and Consciousness in Early Eighteenth-Century Britain*. Berkeley: University of California Press, 1988.

Fox, Michael. "'*AMON* Again." *JBL* 115 (1996): 699–702.

Freedman, Harry, trans. *Midrash Rabbah: Genesis*. London: Soncino, 1951.

Freeman, Louise Gilbert. "The Metamorphosis of Malbecco: Allegorical Violence and Ovidian Change." *Studies in Philology* 97, no. 3 (2000): 308–30.

Frei, Hans. *The Eclipse of Biblical Narrative: A Study in Eighteenth and Nineteenth Century Hermeneutics*. New Haven: Yale University Press, 1974.

———. "The 'Literal Reading' of Biblical Narrative in the Christian Tradition: Does It Stretch or Break?" In *The Bible and the Narrative Tradition*, ed. F. McConnell, 36–77. Oxford: Oxford University Press, 1986.

Fretheim, Terence E. *The Pentateuch*. Nashville: Abingdon, 1989.

Futato, Mark D. "Because It Had Rained: A Study of Gen 2:5–7 with Implications for Gen 2:4–25 and Gen 1:1–2:3." *WTJ* 60 (1998): 1–21.

Gadamer, Hans-Georg. *Dialogue and Dialectic: Eight Hermeneutical Studies on Plato*. Translated by P. Christopher Smith. New Haven: Yale University Press, 1980.

———. *Truth and Method*. 2nd rev. ed. Translated by J. Weinsheimer and D. Marshall. London: Continuum, 2006.

German, Brian T. *Psalms of the Faithful: Luther's Early Reading of the Psalter in Canonical Context*. Bellingham, WA: Lexham, 2017.

Greene-McCreight, Kathryn E. *How Augustine, Calvin, and Barth Read the "Plain Sense" of Genesis 1–3*. New York: Peter Lang, 1999.

———. "Literal Sense." In *Dictionary for Theological Interpretation of the Bible*, ed. Kevin Vanhoozer, Craig Bartholomew, Daniel Treier, and N. T. Wright, 455–56. Grand Rapids: Baker Academic, 2005.

Greenfield, Jonas C. "The Seven Pillars of Wisdom (Prov. 9:1)—A Mistranslation." *JQR* 76, no. 1 (1985): 13–20.

Gunton, Colin. *The Triune Creator: A Historical and Systematic Study*. Edinburgh: Edinburgh University Press, 1998.

Habel, Norman. *The Book of Job: A Commentary*. OTL. Philadelphia: Westminster, 1985.

Hankins, Davis. "Wisdom as an Immanent Event in Job 28, Not a Transcendent Ideal." *VT* 63, no. 2 (2013): 210–35.

Harnack, Adolph. *Bible Reading in the Early Church*. London: Williams and Norgate, 1912.

Hays, Richard. *Echoes of Scripture in the Letters of Paul*. New Haven: Yale University Press, 1993.

———. *First Corinthians*. IBC. Louisville: Westminster John Knox, 1997.

Heidegger, Martin. *Poetry, Language, Thought*. Translated by Albert Hofstadter. New York: Harper & Row, 1971.

Helm, Paul. *Calvin at the Centre*. Oxford: Oxford University Press, 2010.

———. *John Calvin's Ideas*. Oxford: Oxford University Press, 2004.

Helmer, Christine. "Luther's Trinitarian Hermeneutic and the Old Testament." *MT* 18, no. 1 (2002): 49–83.

Hilary of Poitiers. *On the Trinity*. NPNF², vol. 9. Translated by E. W. Watson and L. Pullan. Edited by Philip Schaff and Henry Wace. Buffalo, NY: Christian Literature Publishing Co., 1899.

Hirsch, E. D., Jr. *Validity in Interpretation*. New Haven: Yale University Press, 1967.

Howell, Brian C. *In the Eyes of God: A Metaphorical Approach to Biblical Anthropomorphic Language*. Cambridge: James Clark, 2014.

Hübner, Hans. *Biblische Theologie des Neuen Testaments*. 3 vols. Göttingen: Vandenhoek & Ruprecht, 1990–95.

Hugh of St. Victor. *"The Didascalicon" of Hugh of St. Victor: A Medieval Guide to the Arts*. Translated by Jeremy Taylor. New York: Columbia University Press, 1961.

Hwang, Jin K. "Jewish Pilgrim Festivals and Calendar in Paul's Ministry with the Gentile Churches." *TynBul* 64, no. 1 (2014): 89–107.

Illich, Ivan. *In the Vineyard of the Text: A Commentary to Hugh's "Didascalicon."* Chicago: University of Chicago Press, 1993.

Irvine, Martin. *The Making of Textual Culture: "Grammatica" and Literary Theory 350–1100*. Cambridge: Cambridge University Press, 1994.

Ivanski, Dariusz. *The Dynamics of Job's Intercession*. Rome: Pontifical Biblical Institute, 2006.

Janzen, J. Gerald. *Job*. IBC. Atlanta: John Knox, 1985.

Johnson, Steven. *Where Good Ideas Come From: The Natural History of Innovation*. New York: Riverhead, 2010.

Jones, Scott C. "Job 28 and Modern Theories of Knowledge." *Theology Today* 69, no. 4 (2013): 486–95.

Jowett, Benjamin. "On the Interpretation of Scripture." In *Essays and Reviews*, 330–433. London: Parker & Sons, 1860.

Kant, Immanuel. *Critique of Judgment*. Translated by Werner S. Pluhar. Indianapolis: Hackett, 1987.

———. *Critique of Pure Reason*. Translated by Norman K. Smith. London: Macmillan, 1958.

———. *Kant: Selections*. Edited by Lewis White Beck. New York: MacMillan, 1988.

Kline, Meredith G. "Because It Had Not Rained." *WTJ* 20, no. 2 (1958): 146–57.

Knierim, Rolf P. *The Task of Old Testament Theology: Method and Cases*. Grand Rapids: Eerdmans, 1995.

Kolbet, Paul R. "Athanasius, the Psalms, and the Reformation of Self." In *The Harp of Prophecy: Early Christian Interpretation of the Psalms*, ed. Brian E.

Daley, S.J., and Paul R. Kolbet, 75–96. Notre Dame, IN: University of Notre Dame Press, 2015.

———. *Augustine and the Cure of Souls: Revising a Classical Ideal.* Notre Dame, IN: University of Notre Dame Press, 2010.

Kripke, Saul. *Naming and Necessity.* London: Blackwell, 1980.

Lachterman, David. *The Ethics of Geometry: A Genealogy of Modernity.* New York: Routledge, 1989.

Leithart, Peter J. *Deep Exegesis: The Mystery of Reading Scripture.* Waco: Baylor University Press, 2009.

———. *1 & 2 Kings.* BTC. Grand Rapids: Brazos, 2006.

Lenzi, Alan. "Proverbs 8:22–31: Three Perspectives on Its Composition." *JBL* 125, no. 4 (2006): 687–714.

Lewis, C. S. *The Allegory of Love: A Study in Medieval Tradition.* Oxford: Clarendon, 1936; repr., Cambridge: Cambridge University Press, 2013.

Lindbeck, George. "The Church." In *The Church in a Postliberal Age*, ed. James J. Buckley, 145–65. Grand Rapids: Eerdmans, 2003.

———. *The Nature of Doctrine: Religion and Theology in a Postliberal Age.* Louisville: Westminster John Knox, 1984.

———. "The Story-Shaped Church: Critical Exegesis and Theological Interpretation." In *Scriptural Authority and Narrative Interpretation*, ed. Garrett Green, 161–78. Philadelphia: Fortress, 1987.

Lo, Alison. *Job 28 as Rhetoric: An Analysis of Job 28 in the Context of Job 22–31.* Brill: Leiden, 2003.

Locke, John. *An Essay Concerning Human Understanding.* Edited by R. Woolhouse. London: Penguin, 1997.

Loewe, Ralph. "The 'Plain Meaning' of Scripture in Early Jewish Exegesis." In *Papers of the Institute of Jewish Studies London I*, ed. J. G. Weiss, 140–85. Jerusalem: Magnes, 1964.

Long, D. Stephen. *Theology and Culture: A Guide to the Discussion.* Eugene, OR: Cascade, 2008.

Longman, Tremper, III. *How to Read Proverbs.* Downers Grove, IL: InterVarsity, 2002.

———. *Job.* BCOTWP. Grand Rapids: Baker Academic, 2012.

———. *Proverbs.* BCOTWP. Grand Rapids: Baker Academic, 2006.

Louth, Andrew. *Discerning the Mystery: An Essay on the Nature of Theology.* Oxford: Clarendon, 2003.

Lubac, Henri de. *History and Spirit: The Understanding of Scripture according to Origen.* Translated by Anne E. Nash. San Francisco: Ignatius, 2007.

———. *Medieval Exegesis: The Four Senses of Scripture.* Translated by Mark Sebanc and E. M. Macierowski. 3 vols. Grand Rapids: Eerdmans, 1998.

———. *Surnaturel*. In *Augustinianism and Modern Theology*. Translated by Lancelot Sheppard. New York: Crossroad, 2000.

Luther, Martin. *Answer to the Hyperchristian, Hyperspiritual, and Hyperlearned Book by Goat Emser in Leipzig—Including Some Thoughts Regarding His Companion, the Fool Murner*. In *Luther's Works*. Vol. 39, *Church and Ministry I*, 139–224. Translated by Eric and Ruth Gritsch. Philadelphia: Fortress, 1970.

Luxon, Thomas H. *Literal Figures: Puritan Allegory and the Reformation Crisis in Representation*. Chicago: University of Chicago Press, 1995.

Man, Paul de. "The Return to Philology." In *The Resistance to Theory*, 21–26. Minneapolis: University of Minnesota Press, 1986.

———. "Semiology and Rhetoric." *Diacritics* 3, no. 1 (1973): 27–33. Reprinted in *The Norton Anthology of Theory and Criticism*, ed. Vincent B. Leitch, William B. Cain, Laurie Finke, and Barbara Johnson, 1515–26. New York: Norton, 2001.

Marsh, William M. *Martin Luther on Reading the Bible as Christian Scripture: The Messiah in Luther's Biblical Hermeneutic and Theology*. PTMS. Eugene, OR: Pickwick, 2017.

Martens, Peter. "Revisiting the Allegory/Typology Distinction: The Case of Origen." *JECS* 16, no. 3 (2008): 283–317.

McGinn, Colin. *The Making of a Philosopher*. New York: Harper Perennial, 2003.

Minnis, Alastair. *Medieval Theory of Authorship: Scholastic Literary Attitudes in the Later Middle Ages*. 2nd ed. Philadelphia: University of Pennsylvania Press, 2010.

Minnis, Alastair, and A. B. Scott. *Medieval Literary Theory and Criticism, c. 1100–1375: The Commentary Tradition*. Oxford: Clarendon, 1988.

Moo, Douglas J. "The Problem of *Sensus Plenior*." In *Hermeneutics, Authority, and Canon*, ed. D. A. Carson and John D. Woodbridge, 175–211. Grand Rapids: Zondervan Academic, 1986.

Morales, L. Michael. *Who Shall Ascend the Mountain of the Lord? A Biblical Theology of the Book of Leviticus*. Downers Grove, IL: InterVarsity, 2015.

Muller, Richard A. "Biblical Interpretation in the Era of the Reformation: The View from the Middle Ages." In Muller and Thompson, *Biblical Interpretation in the Era of the Reformation*, 3–22.

———. "The Hermeneutic of Promise and Fulfillment in Calvin's Exegesis of the Old Testament Prophecies of the Kingdom." In *The Bible in the Sixteenth Century*, ed. David Steinmetz, 68–82. Durham, NC: Duke University Press, 1990.

———. *Post-Reformation Reformed Dogmatics: The Rise and Development of Reformed Orthodoxy, ca. 1520 to ca. 1725*. Vol. 2. 2nd ed. Grand Rapids: Baker Academic, 2003.

———. "Reflections on Persistent Whiggism and Its Antidotes in the Study of Sixteenth-and-Seventeenth-Century Intellectual History." In *Seeing Things Their Way: Intellectual History and the Return of Religion*, ed. Alister Chapman, John

Coffey, and Brad S. Gregory, 134–53. Notre Dame, IN: University of Notre Dame Press, 2009.

Muller, Richard A., and John L. Thompson, eds. *Biblical Interpretation in the Era of the Reformation: Essays Presented to David C. Steinmetz in Honor of His Sixtieth Birthday*. Grand Rapids: Eerdmans, 1996.

Murphy, Francesca. *God Is Not a Story: Realism Revisited*. Oxford: Oxford University Press, 2007.

Murphy, Roland. *Proverbs*. WBC 22. Nashville: Nelson, 1998.

Murray, John. *Collected Writings of John Murray*. Vol. 1, *Claims of Truth*. Carlisle, PA: Banner of Truth, 1976.

Nadler, Steven. "Malebranche on Causation." In *The Cambridge Companion to Malebranche*, ed. Steven Nadler, 112–38. Cambridge: Cambridge University Press, 2000.

Nash, Ronald. *The Light of the Mind: St. Augustine's Theory of Knowledge*. Lexington: University Press of Kentucky, 1969.

Newsom, Carol A. *The Book of Job: A Contest of Moral Imaginations*. Oxford: Oxford University Press, 2003.

———. "Dialogue and Allegorical Hermeneutics." In *Job 28: Cognition in Context*, ed. Ellen van Wolde, 299–305. BIS 64. Leiden: Brill, 2003.

Oberman, Heiko. *The Harvest of Medieval Theology: Gabriel Biel and Late Medieval Nominalism*. Durham: Labyrinth, 1983.

Ocker, Christopher. *Biblical Poetics before Humanism and Reformation*. Cambridge: Cambridge University Press, 2002.

Oeming, Manfred. "Ihr habt nich recht von mir geredet wie mein Knecht Hiob." *Evangelicalische Theologie* 60 (2000): 103–16.

O'Keefe, John J., and R. R. Reno. *Sanctified Vision: An Introduction to Early Christian Interpretation of the Bible*. Baltimore: Johns Hopkins University Press, 2005.

Olson, Dennis T. *The Death of the Old and the Birth of the New: The Framework of the Book of Numbers and the Pentateuch*. Chico, CA: Scholars Press, 1985.

Ormiston, Gayle, and Alan Schrift, eds. *The Hermeneutic Tradition: From Ast to Ricoeur*. Albany, NY: SUNY Press, 1990.

Pak, G. Sujin. *The Judaizing Calvin: Sixteenth-Century Debates over the Messianic Psalms*. Oxford: Oxford University Press, 2010.

Patrick, Dale. "Job's Address of God." *ZAW* 91 (1979): 268–82.

Pelikan, Jaroslav. *The Christian Tradition: A History of the Development of Doctrine*. Vol. 1, *The Emergence of the Catholic Tradition, 100–600*. Chicago: University of Chicago Press, 1975.

Preus, James S. *From Shadow to Promise: Old Testament Interpretation from Augustine to the Young Luther*. Cambridge, MA: Harvard University Press, 1969.

Rad, Gerhard von. *Genesis: A Commentary*. OTL. Philadelphia: Westminster, 1972.

Radner, Ephraim. *The End of the Church: A Pneumatology of Christian Division in the West.* Grand Rapids: Eerdmans, 1998.

———. *Hope among the Fragments: The Broken Church and Its Engagement of Scripture.* Grand Rapids: Brazos, 2004.

———. *Time and the Word: Figural Reading of the Christian Scriptures.* Grand Rapids: Eerdmans, 2016.

Reno, R. R. *In the Ruins of the Church: Sustaining Faith in an Age of Diminished Christianity.* Grand Rapids: Brazos, 2002.

Robinson, Robert Bruce. *Roman Catholic Exegesis since "Divino Afflante Spiritu": Hermeneutical Implications.* Atlanta: Scholars Press, 1988.

Rogers, Eugene, Jr. "How the Virtues of the Interpreter Presuppose and Perfect Hermeneutics: The Case of Thomas Aquinas." *JR* 76 (1996): 64–81.

Sandys-Wunsch, J., and L. Eldredge. "J. P. Gabler and the Distinction between Biblical and Dogmatic Theology: Translation, Commentary, and Discussion of His Originality." *SJT* 33, no. 2 (1980): 133–58.

Schaff, Philip. "Calvin as a Commentator." *Presbyterian and Reformed Review* 3, no. 11 (1892): 462–69.

Schifferdecker, Katherine. *Out of the Whirlwind: Creation Theology in Job.* Cambridge, MA: Harvard University Press, 2008.

Schleiermacher, Friedrich. "The Hermeneutics: Outline of the 1819 Lectures." In Ormiston and Schrift, *Hermeneutic Tradition,* 85–100.

Scholnick, Sylvia. "The Meaning of *Mišpaṭ* in the Book of Job." *JBL* 101 (1982): 521–29.

Schreiner, Susan. *Where Shall Wisdom Be Found? Calvin's Exegesis of Job from Medieval and Modern Perspectives.* Chicago: University of Chicago Press, 1994.

Schwartz, Sarah. "Narrative *Toledot* Formulae in Genesis: The Case of Heaven and Earth, Noah, and Isaac." *JHS* 16, no. 8 (2016): 1–36.

Seitz, Christopher R. *The Character of Christian Scripture: The Significance of a Two-Testament Bible.* Grand Rapids: Baker Academic, 2011.

———. *Colossians.* BTC. Grand Rapids: Brazos, 2014.

———. *The Elder Testament: Canon, Theology, Trinity.* Waco: Baylor University Press, 2018.

———. *Figured Out: Typology and Providence in Christian Scripture.* Louisville: Westminster John Knox, 2001.

———. *The Goodly Fellowship of the Prophets: The Achievement of Association in Canon Formation.* Grand Rapids: Baker Academic, 2009.

———. "Isaiah 1–66: Making Sense of the Whole." In *Reading and Preaching the Book of Isaiah,* ed. Christopher R. Seitz, 105–26. Eugene, OR: Wipf & Stock, 2002.

———. "Job: Full-Structure, Movement, and Interpretation." *Int* 43, no. 1 (1989): 5–17.

———. "Old Testament or Hebrew Bible? Some Theological Considerations." In *Word without End: The Old Testament as Abiding Witness*, 61–74. Grand Rapids: Eerdmans, 1998.

———. "On Not Changing 'Old Testament' to 'Hebrew Bible': A Response to Eugene Fisher." *ProEccl* 6, no. 2 (1997): 136–40.

———. *Prophecy and Hermeneutics: Toward a New Introduction to the Prophets.* Grand Rapids: Baker Academic, 2007.

———. "Reader Competence and the Offense of Biblical Language: The Limitations of So-Called Inclusive Language." In *Word without End: The Old Testament as Abiding Theological Witness*, 292–99. Grand Rapids: Eerdmans, 1998.

———. "Reconciliation and the Plain Sense Witness of Scripture." In *The Redemption: An Interdisciplinary Symposium on Christ as Redeemer*, ed. Stephen T. Davis, Daniel Kendall, and Gerald O'Collins, 25–42. Oxford: Oxford University Press, 2004.

———. "Review of Richard Bauckham's *God Crucified: Monotheism and Christology in the New Testament*." *IJST* 2, no. 1 (2000): 112–16.

———. "Scriptural Author and Canonical Prophet: The Theological Implications of Literary Association in the Canon." In *Biblical Interpretation and Method: Essays in Honour of John Barton*, ed. Katherine Dell and Paul Joyce, 176–88. Oxford: Oxford University Press, 2013.

———. "The Trinity in the Old Testament." In *The Oxford Handbook on the Trinity*, ed. Gilles Emery and Matthew Levering, 28–40. Oxford: Oxford University Press, 2011.

Seow, Choon-Leong. "Elihu's Revelation." *Theology Today* 68, no. 3 (2011): 253–71.

Shields, Martin. "Was Elihu Right?" *Journal for the Evangelical Study of the Old Testament* 3, no. 2 (2014): 155–70.

Smith, Basil. "John Locke, Personal Identity, and Memento." In *The Philosophy of Neo-Noir*, ed. Mark T. Conard, 35–46. Lexington: University Press of Kentucky, 2009.

Smith, George Adam. *Modern Criticism and the Preaching of the Old Testament: Eight Lectures on the Lyman Beecher Foundation, Yale University.* New York: Armstrong & Son, 1911.

Sneed, Mark. "Is the 'Wisdom Tradition' a Tradition?" *CBQ* 73, no. 1 (2011): 53–71.

Sonderegger, Katherine. *Systematic Theology.* Vol. 1, *The Doctrine of God.* Minneapolis: Fortress, 2015.

Soskice, Janet. *Metaphor and Religious Language.* Oxford: Clarendon, 1985.

Soulen, Kendall. "YHWH the Triune God." *MT* 15, no. 1 (1999): 25–54.

Steiner, George. *Martin Heidegger.* Chicago: University of Chicago Press, 1989.

Sumner, Darren O. "The Twofold Life of the Word: Karl Barth's Critical Reception of the *Extra Calvinisticum*." *IJST* 15, no. 1 (2013): 42–57.

Tanner, Kathryn. "Scripture as Popular Text." *MT* 14, no. 2 (1998): 279–98.

———. "Theology and the Plain Sense." In *Scriptural Authority and Narrative Interpretation*, ed. Garrett Green, 59–78. Philadelphia: Fortress, 1987.

Teskey, Gordon. *Allegory and Violence*. Ithaca, NY: Cornell University Press, 1996.

Theophilus of Antioch. *Ad Autolycum*. Translated by Robert Grant. Oxford: Clarendon, 1970.

Thiselton, Anthony C. "'Behind' and 'In Front of' the Text: Language, Reference, and Indeterminacy." In *After Pentecost: Language and Biblical Interpretation*, ed. Craig Bartholomew, Colin Greene, and Karl Möller, 97–120. Scripture and Hermeneutics 2. Grand Rapids: Zondervan, 2001.

Tillyard, E. M. W. *The Elizabethan World Picture*. New York: Vintage Books, 1959.

Torjesen, Karen J. *Hermeneutical Procedure and Theological Method in Origen's Exegesis*. PTS 28. Berlin: de Gruyter, 1985.

Toulmin, Stephen. *Cosmopolis: The Hidden Agenda of Modernity*. Chicago: University of Chicago Press, 1990.

Tov, Emanuel. *Textual Criticism of the Hebrew Bible*. 2nd rev. ed. Minneapolis: Fortress, 2001.

Treier, Daniel J. *Introducing Theological Interpretation: Recovering a Christian Practice*. Grand Rapids: Baker Academic, 2008.

Turner, Denys. "Allegory in Late Christian Antiquity." In *The Cambridge Companion to Allegory*, ed. Rita Copeland and Peter T. Struck, 71–82. Cambridge: Cambridge University Press, 2010.

Vanhoozer, Kevin J. *Is There a Meaning in This Text? The Bible, the Reader, and the Morality of Literary Knowledge*. Grand Rapids: Zondervan, 1998.

Van Leeuwen, Ray C. "Cosmos, Temple, House: Building and Wisdom in Ancient Mesopotamia and Israel." In *From the Foundations to the Crenellations: Essays on Temple Building in the Ancient Near East and Hebrew Bible*, ed. Mark J. Boda and Jamie Novotny, 399–421. Munster: Ugarit-Verlag, 2010.

Vogels, Walter. "The Cultic and Civil Calendars of the Fourth Day of Creation (Genesis 1:14b)." *SJOT* 11, no. 2 (1988): 163–80.

Waltke, Bruce. *The Book of Proverbs: Chapters 1–15*. NICOT. Grand Rapids: Eerdmans, 2004.

Watson, Francis. "The Old Testament as Christian Scripture: A Response to Professor Seitz." *SJT* 52 (1999): 227–32.

———. *Paul and the Hermeneutics of Faith*. London: T&T Clark, 2004.

Webster, John. *Barth's Ethics of Reconciliation*. Cambridge: Cambridge University Press, 1995.

———. "The Dogmatic Location of the Canon." In *Word and Church: Essays in Christian Dogmatics*, 9–46. London: Bloomsbury T&T Clark, 2016.

———. "Theologies of Retrieval." In *The Oxford Handbook of Systematic Theology*, ed. John Webster, Kathryn Tanner, and Iain Torrance, 583–99. Oxford: Oxford University Press, 2007.

Weeks, Stuart. "The Context and Meaning of Proverbs 8:30a." *JBL* 125, no. 3 (2006): 433–42.

Westermann, Claus. *Genesis 1–11*. Translated by John J. Scullion, S.J. Continental Commentaries. Minneapolis: Augsburg, 1984.

White, Joel. "'He Was Raised on the Third Day according to the Scriptures' (1 Corinthians 15:4): A Typological Interpretation Based on the Cultic Calendar in Leviticus 23." *TynBul* 66, no. 1 (2015): 103–19.

Whybray, Norman. *Job*. Sheffield: Sheffield Phoenix, 2008.

Witt, William G. "Creation, Redemption, and Grace in the Theology of Jacob Arminius." PhD diss., University of Notre Dame, 1993.

Wolff, Hans Walter. *Hosea: A Commentary on the Book of the Prophet Hosea*. Translated by G. Stansell. Hermeneia. Philadelphia: Fortress, 1974.

Wolters, Al. "Job 32–37: Elihu as Mouthpiece of God." In *Reading and Hearing the Word of God from Text to Sermon: Essays in Honor of John H. Stek*, ed. Arie C. Leder, 107–23. Grand Rapids: Calvin Seminary and CRC Publications, 1998.

Woolhouse, R. S. *Descartes, Spinoza, and Leibniz: The Concept of Substance in Seventeenth Century Metaphysics*. New York: Routledge, 1993.

Wright, N. T. *The New Testament and the People of God*. Minneapolis: Fortress, 1992.

Yeago, David. "The New Testament and Nicene Dogma." *ProEccl* 3 (1994): 152–64.

Yee, Gale. "An Analysis of Prov 8:22–31 according to Style and Structure." *ZAW* 94, no. 1 (1982): 58–66.

Young, Frances. "Proverbs 8 in Interpretation (2): Wisdom Personified." In *Reading Texts, Seeking Wisdom*, ed. David Ford and Graham Stanton, 102–15. Grand Rapids: Eerdmans, 2004.

Zabán, Bálint Károly. *The Pillar Function of the Speeches of Wisdom: Proverbs 1:20–33, 8:1–36, and 9:1–6 in the Structural Framework of Proverbs 1–9*. BZAW 429. Berlin: de Gruyter, 2012.

Zehnder, Markus P. *Wegmetaphorik im Alten Testament: eine semantische Untersuchung der alttestamentlichen und altorientalischen Weg-Lexeme mit besonderer Berücksichtigung ihrer metaphorischen Verwendung*. BZAW 268. Berlin: de Gruyter, 1999.

Scripture and Ancient Writings Index

Psalms

Proverbs

Author Index

Abma, R., 104nn142–43, 105n144, 105n146
Alderman, Brian J., 79n58
Allert, Craig, 54n89, 156n76
Andersen, Ragnar, 79n59, 80n60, 80n61
Aquinas. *See* Thomas Aquinas
Auerbach, Erich, 46n64
Augustine, 26n3, 33n24, 40n45, 52n82, 52n83,
    108n152, 162n2

Barth, Karl, 68n17, 73n37, 83n73, 84n76
Barton, John, 27n5
Bates, Matthew, 148n63
Bauckham, Richard, 88n90
Beauchamp, Paul, 47n68
Becker, Carl, 163n5
Beiser, Frederick, 120n19
Berkeley, George, 149n64
Beuken, Willem, 85n80
Blowers, Paul, 10n1, 19n38, 49n73, 54n87
Böhm, Thomas, 43n59
Brooks, Cleanth, 49n73
Brower, Reuben, 50n77
Brown, Ray, 140n47
Brown, William P., 47n67, 63n6, 63n7
Bruns, Gerald, 36n32, 42n53, 42n54
Bucur, Bogdan, 88n90
Burney, C. F., 75n46, 88n88
Burrows, Mark, 32n22
Butterfield, Herbert, 121n21

Calvin, John, 18n35, 38n37, 46n63, 63n8, 80n61
Campenhausen, Hans von, 152, 152n72
Cazelles, Henri, 90n96

Chapman, Stephen B., 46n65, 156n75
Childs, Brevard S., 2n1, 2n4, 11n7, 12n13, 25n1,
    34n26, 37n34, 38n38, 44n60, 49n75, 50n78,
    86n83, 100n132, 115n6, 155n74, 157n80,
    164n7
Clifford, Richard J., 90n96
Collett, Don, 4n10, 19n38, 49n75, 68n17, 86n84,
    98n124, 145n53, 148n61, 149n66, 151n70
Collins, C. John, 11n6, 15n24
Copeland, Rita, 30n14, 31n18, 164n9
Copleston, Francis, 163n5

Davis, Ellen, 83n74
Dawson, John David, 34n29, 35n30, 48n71
Dell, Katherine, 70n23, 73n39
Descartes, René, 122n22, 125n28
Dhorme, Édouard, 76n48
Driver, Daniel R., 100n132

Ebeling, Gerhard, 34n28
Eichrodt, Walther, 12n13
Eldredge, L., 132n39, 133n41
Elliger, Karl, 82n67
Enns, Peter, 140n46, 146n54

Fergusson, David, 76n50
Fiedrowicz, Michael, 148n63
Fishbane, Michael, 32n23, 131n37
Fisher, Eugene, 153n73
Floyd, Mike, 52n80
Fowl, Stephen E., 27n7
Fox, Christopher, 123n25
Fox, Michael, 91n98

185

Subject Index